This book donated to the

Independence Public Library's
Aviation Shelf

by the Polk County
Oregon Pilot's Association

Above and Beyond

Pat Weiland kept his memoirs of World War II in this old Hong Kong chest.
He pulled them out to write this book.

Above and Beyond

CHARLES PATRICK WEILAND

Pacifica Press

Manufactured in the United States of America

ISBN 0-935553-22-3

Cover Painting by Charles Wissig, Orlando, Florida
Dustjacket by Carol Moody, Gladstone, Missouri

Library of Congress Cataloging-in-Publication Data:

Weiland, Charles Patrick
     Above and beyond / Charles Patrick Weiland
        p.   cm.
     ISBN 0-935553-22-3 (alk. paper)
     1. Weiland, Charles Patrick. 2. World War, 1939–1945—Aerial operations, American. 3. World War, 1939–1945—Personal narratives, American. 4. Fighter pilots—United States—Biography. 5. United States. Marine Corps—Biography. 6. Marines—United States—Biography. 7. World War, 1939–1945—Pacific Area.
I. Title.
D790.W113 1997
940.54'4973—dc21
                                                  97-3732
                                                      CIP

Table of Contents

Acknowledgments

To James F. "Jimbo" Ormond, whose intense interest in the proofreading and development of the book led to the first version titled *The Saga of VMF-452*. It was through Jimbo's efforts that we were able to pass copies of the original version to members of the squadron at a reunion at the Reno Air Races in September 1994. His help has been sincerely appreciated.

To Richard "Terry" Weiland, number one son, whose prowess in editing has helped shape this book. Once again, his loyalty to me has been demonstrated.

To Kathleen Laura "Kate" Samson, who has been most diligent and gracious in overseeing this book during the formative stages of publication and its final conclusion. For this I am most grateful.

To Col Robert L. "Bulgy" Bryson, whose input provided me invaluable aid in recalling long-forgotten events and techniques in those formative days of VMF-452.

To Col Herbert H. "Trigger" Long, a valued friend and contemporary of the early World War II days, who gave me vivid descriptions of "the way it was" as he saw it in combat.

To Col Jack "JB" Maas, the most friendly Marine I ever knew in the Corps. He was always eager to help, and the input he gave me was very much appreciated.

To Cdr Macgregor "Mac" Kilpatrick, an old pro right from the beginning of World War II, a Navy contemporary with me aboard the *USS Franklin,* and an essential element years later in reviving my memory of those old times.

To Margaret Holly, whose expertise in the editing and proofreading field greatly enhanced the readability of this book. Despite her full-time occupation editing and printing the *Beaufort Low Country* magazine, her devotion and interest in my project were always fruitful and satisfying. I thank her from the bottom of my heart.

x

I am also grateful to those stalwart members of VMF-452 who shared with me their experiences and recollections of those hectic but memorable days. They made this book possible.

And, of course, acknowledgment to my wife, Moran Seckinger (Salzburger) Weiland, whose wholehearted support overcame the test of patience.

To my littlest honey, Maria Kristina Haugen.

To my other son, John Arthur Weiland.

And to my other friends who lent encouragement and support.

Preface

The year was 1989 when, through the efforts of James F. "Jimbo" Ormond, Peter L. "Pete" Schaefer and Joseph R. "Joe" Warren, thirty addresses were obtained of former squadronmates of VMF-452. They also tabulated those officers deceased—a total of twenty. Eight squadron officers were unaccounted for. As a result of this research, a reunion was convened in Denver, Colorado, in 1990. Then, in October 1991, another reunion was held, aboard the carrier USS *Yorktown* at Charleston, South Carolina.

Many stories were swapped at these reunions. It suddenly occurred to me that a permanent record should be made of the trials, tribulations, and humorous events that took place during the tour of VMF-452. I decided to take on the task. The queries I made to my squadronmates and the responses received were overwhelming. Also, my own memories of long-forgotten events were revived by my letters to the folks, letters that had been saved by my mother all those years ago. Soon the bits and pieces dovetailed together, and the story evolved into *The Saga of VMF-452*. For the most part, the story was written in the first person, but in reality it was a consolidation of reminiscences by many members of VMF-452. Copies of this version of the book were distributed to the squadronmates at the reunion at the Reno Air Races in September 1994.

Eric Hammel came upon the scene shortly after my friend Col Bruce Porter, author of *Ace*, sent him my first version of the book. Eric, who owns a publishing company called Pacifica Press, took an interest in my project. He read it, analyzed it, then, in scorching terms, sent me back a treatise on everything wrong with it. The forest-and-trees syndrome had taken its toll. It was obvious to me now how I had abused chronological correctness and violated other various aspects of literary decorum. Also, there were many other hints and suggestions about issues that had to be addressed. So it became a cut-and-paste lesson throughout the whole manuscript. It took months to do and it was a complete rewrite, but I was faithful to Eric's tutoring.

Eric also had a copy of my first book, *Manuscript Found in a Battle*. It was about the first tactical squadron I was assigned to—VMO-251—and our involvement overseas in early 1942. Eric thought it propitious to include excerpts from that book in the new one. So now Guadalcanal had entered the picture, and the name of the book had to be changed. This was no problem. It was tagged *Above and Beyond*, a catchy title with implications both literal and figurative. I will be forever grateful to Eric Hammel for the generous advice and constructive criticism that eventually led to this book's publication.

I am sure there are conflicts in the story contained herein, but I have tried to be faithful to the facts. There may be a humble lack of literary style, but the essential point remains—it is a record of a fine group of Marines doing their duty in a quest to serve their country during World War II.

LtCol Charles Patrick Weiland
USMC (Ret)

PART I
The Air

N3N PRIMARY TRAINER

CHAPTER 1

Those Cherished Gold Wings

It was about 1930 when I flew that beautiful Lockheed Sirius low-winged monoplane. This was the same type that Wiley Post and Will Rogers had used on their ill-fated trip to circumnavigate the globe. They were killed when they crashed at Point Barrow, Alaska, on August 15, 1935. As I flew this plane from lofty heights, I looked down on the terrain: The tall weeds were trees, the grasses became jungle, and, out there on the horizon, that wonderful world lay just ahead. On occasion I would have to land my fine plane, then go out to round up the stray cows that I had been herding along the railroad tracks.

I had built this plane myself. The cowling was made of a tin can; the wings and fuselage were slats of wood glued and covered with distinctive wrapping paper. This model was only one of many I had built from scratch—like the Keystone Loening amphibian, the Curtiss Hawk, and the World War I Sopwith Experimental Number 5. This fantasy of flying and the yearning actually to do so was ever present; like Berndt Balchen and Admiral Byrd, I wanted to be one of those legendary pilots. The passion to fly was first and foremost in my life.

The Great Depression impacted the whole country in the 1930s. South Dakota, where I was born and raised, was no less devastated. But we were dealt a double whammy with an enduring drought that scorched the earth and ruined the crops year after year. The dust storms turned day into night. We called this time the "Dirty Thirties." The farmers—and almost everyone else for that matter— could not send their sons off to college. There was no money. I knew, however, that I could work my way through somehow, for I had the ambition and energy to lick the world at that point.

My father had two brothers, Frank and Art, who were doctors in Miami, Florida. Art was the kid in the family of eleven siblings raised on the homestead near Ashton, South Dakota. His much older brothers, John (my father) and Bill, took over the farm operations from their father, Julius. A friendship developed between John and Art that was more than just brotherly love. When I graduated from high school in 1936, it was out of deference to my father that my Uncle Art—now Doctor Arthur H. Weiland—saw fit to help me get a college education. So it was the University of Miami for me—going from the parched dry earth of the South Dakota plains to the sublime big city in Florida.

While going to the university, I was always air minded. My visits to Miami Municipal Airport, formerly Karl Voeker Field, were frequent. I got to know pilots like Howard Gimbel, of the department store chain. He would take me up in his new maroon, gull-winged Stinson Reliant. I was in ecstasy! Then I seized upon the opportunity to take advantage of the Civilian Pilot Training (CPT) program.

By 1939 the upheaval in Europe had increased world tension. Hitler was on the march, and Poland had already been overrun. Now France was deeply involved in the conflict. The United States, although isolated at the moment, was very much aware as was the rest of the world of the sudden cataclysmic events at hand. Certain visionaries in our government were already projecting options necessary in the event of our involvement. Out of one of these small facets of farsightedness came the CPT. The government knew that the United States might need a lot of pilots, so it put the colleges and universities to work, conscripting many of them throughout the country to participate in the program. It subsidized both the faculty and the flying schools.

It was sensed that this program would be an inducement for graduate pilots to join the U.S. military air forces. At the moment, however, there was absolutely no obligation on the part of the individual to do so. There was no cost to the participant, except perhaps the paper and pencils and a training manual, which was priced at 65 cents. The manual, put out by the Civil Aeronautics Administration under the Department of Commerce, was about 3/4 inch thick and was titled *Civil Pilot*. I noticed that the section about the controlled courses of flight training was the work of Capt Jack R. Cram, U. S. Marine Corps.

This program was initiated at the University of Miami in the fall of 1939. A total of twenty students filled the quota. The government contracted Embry-Riddle Flying School to do the training—ten students to be land-based, and ten students to be seaplane-based. Much of the ground school was held in the University of Miami classrooms at night. Expenses for the use of the classrooms and the salaries of the instructors were also picked up by the government.

My first flight under the CPT program was on December 7, 1939. I soloed in the brand-new J3-L Piper Cub on January 2, 1940 and received my private pilot's license, number 81296, on April 30, 1940.

In retrospect I have always felt that whoever those visionaries were in Washington, D.C., they also must have been clairvoyants. Once hostilities broke out involving the United States, most of those CPT private pilots did, indeed, join the military air forces. And the people who were looking ahead then were also probably the same people who initiated the nation-wide draft in 1940.

My Uncle Art had a fine reputation as an orthopedic surgeon. He had established the Coral Gables Clinic in 1926 and then much later founded the Miami Children's Variety Hospital. He always had it in the back of his mind to groom me for following in his footsteps. This would be a shoo-in for me, with a ready-made reputation, the clinic, and the instruments—all available for the asking.

My grooming included attending many medical events. On Sunday mornings, I would go with Uncle Art on his rounds to Saint Francis Hospital, Jackson Memorial, and sometimes the Fort Lauderdale Hospital. There were times when I would be included in the circle of antiseptic specialists who observed the operations he performed on patients. One was an overweight woman undergoing a sacroiliac operation. I watched layers of fat being cut through with the scalpel, the blood vessels being pinched off, the bone being chiseled, and then the professional wrap-up.

Many of these medical excursions were overshadowed by my thoughts of being elsewhere. Sometimes I would drop off my uncle at the hospital, saying, "Uncle Art, I'm going out to the airport to watch the airplanes, but I'll be back in time to pick you up." My desire to pursue the medical profession was, to say the least, halfhearted.

Then came the turning point in my life—the moment of truth when the decision had to be made. It happened in the backyard of my uncle's home on an early spring day in 1940. As we strolled along, I, at first, had no idea that I was being pinned down as to my future. To me, my uncle was God: I had never honored or admired a man so much in all my life. He could pull me out of the doldrums when I was down. His character exemplified everything that was good in life, and that which I should follow. How could I ever defy his wishes? It seemed there was a moral obligation to consider. It became obvious, however, that day out in the backyard, that my uncle had already resigned himself as to my preference. After an expletive or two, Uncle Art gave his full support for me to do the thing I always wanted to do: fly.

I still do not regret my decision. The business I eventually got into was not as lucrative as that of a surgeon, but when I look back on it all, mine was probably the most exciting and adventurous life a person could lead. And, best of all, I survived.

* * *

Leland Jamison was a friend of the family in Miami. He was Eastern Airlines's chief pilot and the author of stories published in *The Saturday Evening Post*. I had read these stories with rapture while still in South Dakota.

At that time the magazine had just come out with the first color rotogravures, and Jamison's stories contained illustrations of our American biplane fighters fending off aggressors who were attacking our carriers in the Caribbean.

One day I went down to Leland's office on Ponce de Leon Avenue in Coral Gables to discuss my future aviation career. The office was where he wrote his stories, and I was fascinated with his new electric typewriter. I had always heard of Kelly Field, Texas, where they trained Army Air Corps pilots, and this was where I'd set my sights on going. Leland, however, recommended the Marine Corps—a better outfit and one whose elimination flight training was at Opa Locka Naval Air Station, just north of Miami. He wrote the letter of recommendation I needed for application and sent it to the Marine Corps Reserve Aviation Unit at the Naval Reserve Aviation Base in Opa Locka.

* * *

It was a hot day in June 1940 when my instructor, Capt Ferry Reynolds, USMC, and I walked out to the N3N primary trainer for my first flight at Opa Locka. I climbed into the rear cockpit and he gave me some last-minute instructions. He adjusted the gosport, a student's earpiece connected to a voice tube running to the instructor's mouthpiece in the front cockpit. This would be the line of communication between instructor and student. He forgot to remind me to fasten my safety belt.

We taxied to the end of that short, 700-foot asphalt airstrip and poised for takeoff. Reynolds pushed the throttle forward, and the plane lurched ahead, gathering airspeed, and soon we were airborne in a gentle right turn. We flew just above the high mooring mast, which had been built to secure the dirigibles *Macon* and *Akron*. This was a familiarization flight, and, after reaching altitude, I was given the controls to make gentle turns to the left and right, as well as shallow dives and zooming climbs. My instructor had a booming voice at decibels that rang far above the roar of the engine. He didn't need a gosport; you could hear him a mile away. This harshness was an intimidation of sorts.

At one point my instructor took over control of the plane to demonstrate a small-field landing on an outlying cow pasture. In a hard left turn on final approach, he put the plane in a sideslip, and its descent was sudden. There was also a sudden separation between me and the seat. I was clawing leather, trying to stay in that airplane. Once the plane straightened out, gravity regained my seat for me as well as my composure. Because the instructor was sitting in the front cockpit, he didn't know all this was going on. I was too embarrassed at my forgetfulness to tell him, nor did I ever mention it to anyone else. That was the first and last time in my entire flying career that I would ever forget to fasten a safety belt.

When I checked into Opa Locka on June 15, 1940, I was appointed private first class in the Volunteer Marine Corps Reserves and designated a student aviation pilot. Transition from civilian life to a military lifestyle was fascinating. The discipline and regimen were ever present, yet things didn't seem quite up to the hardworking standard I had known in South Dakota. The Navy chief petty officers spent an awful lot of time drinking coffee—and they were getting paid a lot of money. I was very happy to receive $1.95 per day as pay for quarters and subsistence allowance.

Of course, the airplanes were the main attractions. They were mostly the Naval Aircraft Factory N3Ns built at the Philadelphia Navy Yard. But there were also the heavy Chance-Vought SBU dive-bombers. The Reserve pilots came out to fly these on weekends. They'd practice dive-bombing runs on the black-and-white circular target next to the runway, using miniature dummy bombs. There were also two flyable Grumman F1F-1s (Fifis) parked on the ramp. On one occasion Captain Reynolds took me up on a hop in a Fifi. It was a thrill big enough to write home about.

I successfully completed the course on July 12, 1940, and received orders to return to my home of record to await further orders for appointment as aviation cadet, U.S. Marine Corps Reserves. The letter from Washington, D.C., for the appointment was dated July 22 and was delivered in August. It was signed by Major General Commandant Thomas Holcomb. In September came the orders to report to Naval Air Station, Pensacola, to begin flight instruction. The assignment to Pensacola for cadet training was enough to foster a zest and exuberance that only a young kid could know.

Around the middle of September 1940, at the age of twenty-two, I climbed aboard the train at Aberdeen, South Dakota, and headed south. Midway through the trip, I met my soon-to-be-cadet cohorts, Stan Nicolay and Bill Batchelor from Washington State. They offered me a cigarette—my first ever. As I was now among peers of such high status, I naturally accepted.

At NAS Pensacola, the new class, 152-C, was promptly locked up for six weeks. This indoctrination into the training regimen and routine of a new cadet was grueling. Not being a very good student, I had to commit myself to many nighttime hours of classroom work, especially in celestial navigation. When primary flight training began, we were hauled from the brick cadet barracks to Corry Field in long, gray, trailerlike cattle cars. Once again we flew the N3N biplane trainers, but after the first of the year it was a mix of Stearman NS-1s and the new Stearman N2Ss.

After the first six weeks of monastic living, we were granted our first liberty. It was great to see the outside world again. A small group of us went into downtown Pensacola to case the joint. It was a splendid sight-seeing tour. After a couple of beers at one of the taverns, one of the old-time cadets in our party suggested that we walk down "Z Street." This cadet was probably only two weeks our senior, but he already knew his way around town. Zaragosa Street was Pensacola's red-light district. No red-blooded American boy could refuse this tour. I was wide-eyed at the madams standing on the front porches of those old houses, beckoning us in. Out of curiosity, we did step into the foyer of one house. Among the girls lounging about, I noticed a beautiful young blonde. I remember finding it impossible to believe that this fresh-faced beauty was a whore. We didn't tarry long and shortly returned to the base to meet curfew.

At the end of the primary training phase of the course, I received my first check hop. This test included small-field landing practice as well as dead-stick landings, during which the check pilot pulled back on the throttle and the student maneuvered the plane onto the grass field for a landing. The dead-stick landing part of the test was totally strange to me. I had not received intruction in this phase and so was caught unprepared. I flunked it. Being green and gullible, I felt trapped. This was a disaster! I would have one more chance, the next morning. If I flunked again, I would bust out of cadet training.

I was very distraught that night at the prospect of busting out, so in the barracks I huddled with some friends, including Howard K. "Bull" Marvin and Honore "Jack" Dalton, who were two or three weeks ahead of me in the program. They showed me on paper and in diagrams exactly what to do. The next morning I went up for the second check with some foreboding but lots of determination. At the end, we came back and landed at Corry Field. It seemed an interminable length of time before the check pilot gave me the thumbs-up signal. I discovered later that my instructor was a recently recalled airline pilot and had not been briefed on this aspect of instruction, thus my initial dismal failure.

Now I could move into the next phase, which was basic training in the big, heavy airplanes. The Chance-Vought O3U-1s and the SU-2 Corsair biplanes were formidable. Still, I took them in stride and flew them successfully. At the end of this training phase, the pilot would be given the eight-hour check and, if he passed, he was almost assured of getting his wings.

At this point in training, almost every cadet traipsed downtown to buy a new car. I was no exception. At Muldoon Motors I spied a beauty—a used 1940 Ford convertible with a black exterior and rich, tan leather seats. A lieutenant commander had owned it previously, but he had acquired a family and needed a station wagon. For about three days, I bargained with the dealer. The asking price was $750 and the odometer read 7,800 miles. I lay awake each night

Marine Cadet Pat Weiland, Class 152-C, at Pensacola, Florida. December 1940.
The airplane is a Naval Aircraft Factory N3N.

A Boeing F4B-4 Fighter.

A Grumman F3F-2 Fighter.

A Curtiss SBC-4 Helldiver Scout-bomber.

One of the *first* Corsairs, the Chance-Vought SW-1

A Grumman J2F-5 Duck amphibian utility plane.

A Brewster F2A-2 Buffalo Fighter.

wondering if I was making a good deal. Just before Washington's birthday in 1941, I took the plunge. (Incidentally, I kept this car until the end of World War II, then traded it in to a used-car dealer in Laguna Beach for $1,000. She turned right around and sold it to a second lieutenant for $1,300.) I couldn't believe it when my friend Stan Nicolay purchased a brand-new Buick four-door convertible for $1,600—a veritable fortune.

Around this time I became aware of a certain prestige that the Marine Corps uniform lent to a young pilot. The pay was nice, too. It was hard to believe that I was actually getting paid for doing the very thing I most wanted to do—fly. Among our forty cadets in Class 152-C, only four were Marine cadets. They were Stan Nicolay, Darrell "Slim" Irwin, Bill Batchelor, and me. During the evening meal, we proudly wore dress blues with the red stripe down the trousers.

Mustin Hall was the officers' club and the social center on the main base. It was a two-story, octagonal building not far from Chevalier Field. Sometimes, early on a Saturday evening, we were allowed to indulge in a couple of drinks there. Of course, three or four of us were in dress blues, sitting around sipping tall Tom Collinses. On one such occasion, I noticed Maj Oscar Brice with his wife and two or three other high-ranking officers sitting at a table beside us. Across the room were VAdm Albert Cushing Reed and his wife. I can now imagine how amusing it must have been for them, observing these young fledgling aviators acting (quietly, of course) like big-time pilots.

The instrument-flying phase of training was in Squadron 3, located at Chevalier Field on the main base. The student normally flew from the back cockpit. Inside the sliding canopy of the SNJ was the "hood," which the student operated. It was made of canvas and slid inside the canopy from back to front and completely denied the student any reference to the outside elements. There was absolutely no way to "sneak a peek" unless he popped it. This strange and complicated aspect of flying involved concentration on a multitude of instruments. There were the pitching, rolling, and yaw factors, which were the lateral, longitudinal, and vertical axes one had to control. This control, of course, was maintained by resorting to the two principal instruments of the day: the needle/ball and the airspeed indicator—the two instruments needed to maintain blind flying. This was coordinated with the altimeter and compass. The three-hour hops under the hood were grueling exercises.

I learned early on that unfamiliar forces were at work on me whenever under the hood. There were no familiar references, and I finally had to learn to distrust those false impressions. Relying on the instruments was paramount. To do so implicitly would soon eliminate those weird sensations that led to vertigo.

At this stage of the instrument art, the Sperry Gyroscope Company had just perfected its artificial horizon, soon to be installed on the instrument panels of all aircraft. This would enhance even more the confidence in blind flying.

We learned the procedures of flying the radio range, distinguishing the "A" quadrant signal from the "N" quadrant signal, and their convergence into a solid beam for a let-down to a field for landing. This was done by cranking in the correct radio frequency we called the "coffee grinder." The aircraft flown were usually the North American NJ-1s, which were mostly fabric covered and with nonretractable landing gear. The wheels sported streamlined "pants." Occasionally, we would fly the SNJ-2 with retractable gear.

VAdm Albert Cushing Reed was commandant of the Pensacola Naval Air Station. He is remembered as the first American pilot, along with his crew, to fly across the Atlantic, in the seaplane NC-4 in May 1919. His route took him to Spain via Newfoundland and the Azores. Admiral Reed issued my Instrument Flying Certificate prescribed for pilots of the U.S. Marine Corps. It was signed and dated April 16, 1941.

By March 4, I was transferred to the new Miami Naval Air Station at Opa Locka to finish cadet training. Here the planes were even bigger and faster. Our taskmasters included LCdr Howard P. "Bags" Bagdanovich and Lt Joseph "Jumpin' Joe" Clifton, both later to make admiral.

The first fighter airplane I ever flew was the Boeing F4B-4 biplane. I think that it was also probably the airplane that gave me the most fun. It may be a slight exaggeration, but when executing a snap roll it seemed to take three or four turns before it could be stopped. Then there were the Grumman F2F and F3F fighter biplanes in which we ransacked the blue, blazing the .30-caliber machine guns at tow targets and generally tearing up the sky. When lacing in and around the cumulus clouds above the Everglades in one of these machines, euphoria set in and, to quote a venerable pilot, "I touched the face of God."

On the bright, beautiful morning of April 11, 1941, in a Grumman F2F, I passed the fighter stunt check, which required doing two loops, four slow rolls, two snap rolls, and two spins in less than three and a half minutes.

Flying the Curtiss SBC-3 and SBC-4 Helldiver biplanes was another phase in the course of getting wings. It was the consensus of all that if the engine quit, these planes would drop like bricks. But at least two hops a day in these birds was the norm. Most flights consisted of two pilots going aloft together, with the pilot in the rear cockpit firing the .30-caliber machine guns at a tow target. Back on the ground, the pilots would switch places in the cockpits and take off again to do the same thing.

Finally came that long-anticipated day in May when I received those cherished gold wings and was commissioned second lieutenant, USMCR, retroactive to April 10, 1941. Admiral Chester W. Nimitz, chief of the U.S. Navy Bureau of Navigation, certified me as Naval Aviator number 7525 and signed the certificate May 5, 1941.

The next step in my career was a transfer from Miami to the Pensacola Naval Air Station as an instructor. When Ens Max Replogle, a friend and contemporary, received orders to remain at Miami as an instructor, I left my old University of Miami girlfriend in his hands. This may have been a mistake. He married her.

CHAPTER 2

A Really Hot Pilot

During my first month back at Pensacola, I was an instructor in aerobatics, flying the Stearman N2S. Then I moved across the street, so to speak, to become an instructor in instruments.

Ensign Jack Moeller, Lts Stanley R. Bailey, Darrell Irwin, and I rented an old house on East Jackson Street in Pensacola and commuted to work at Chevalier Field. In the meantime, Saufley Field was being built only a few miles to the northwest of Pensacola, and the whole of Instrument Squadron moved there in November.

The city fathers of Pensacola decided to clean up their city, and the first thing they did was to close down "Z Street." One November morning on our way to work, we passed many girls strung along the Mobile Highway, hoping to hitchhike to a more profitable and less hostile working environment.

While instructing in instruments, I built up my flying phenomenally. It was not unusual to fly two hops of three hours every day, including weekends. When a pilot had accumulated 100 hours before the end of the month, he got a couple of days off. If the month still hadn't ended, he could fly more hours. It wasn't unusual for me to build up 110 to 115 hours per month.

By January 1, 1942, I was a really hot pilot. That same day I was putting my student through the radio range procedures over Crestview, a small grass strip to the northeast of Pensacola. At the midway point during a three-hour instruction flight, it was routine to set down to critique the student's progress. This was usually on the grass strip at Crestview or at Folley Field, Alabama. On this particular day, I came in high over Crestview, making a split-S maneuver for a landing. I was dragging in and at one point kicked the left rudder for a correction. That kick caused an immediate stall, and I ended up hitting the ground well before the grass runway. The plane wheeled around, going backward. The flaps curled up under the wings as we went through a barbed-wire fence. The plane finally stopped on the runway, but I suffered a gash to my forehead. It eventually left a scar that I carry to this day.

I could plead no excuse before my higher-ups. It was definitely pilot error. It was probably due only to the exigencies of wartime conditions that I was immediately returned to flight status.

After weeks of this same routine, normal flying can get boring. So at times I would give the student a break in the air and take over the controls, then wring it out. I performed one particular maneuver—and have no idea what it would be called: I'd put the plane in a shallow dive, then pull out up in a wingover to the left, kick hard left rudder, and push the stick in the back left-hand corner. All hell would break loose. The plane would not only snap, it would also go end over end. At the possible point of an inverted spin, I would pull out. After this wringing out, it was wise to go back to normal instrument instruction.

A few months after having invented it, I tried this maneuver in an N3N I was ferrying back from the factory in Philadelphia. The flight was over Maryland, having hummed along for some time. I broke off from the rest of the formation and went into this wild maneuver. Unfortunately, the altitude was a little low for this sort of shenanigan, and when I pulled out I brushed the tree-tops. This was the last time I ever indulged in that sort of foolishness.

That trip to the Philadelphia Navy Yard was memorable for other reasons, too. The British aircraft carrier HMS *Furious* was in port for repair. Out of curiosity, I invited myself aboard. My impression of her was disappointing, for she was in deplorable condition. She just wasn't a clean ship—very unlike the kitchen-clean U.S. Navy ships I'd heard about.

Of the many ferry hops we undertook, the most choice was to fly new SNJ-3s from Dallas's Love Field back to Pensacola. A small group of us would be flown there in an R50-2 Lockheed transport for the pickup.

On one occasion I was flown there in a Boeing Model 247 twin-engine transport. This glorified commercial airliner was all the rage among airlines in the early thirties, especially United Airlines. It was the predecessor to the more sophisticated Douglas DC-2 and the DC-3.

It was always a RON (remain overnight) or longer, if the weather was bad. The Melrose Hotel in town was our headquarters. As soon as we arrived there, the assistant manager would get on the phone and call the gals. "Mazie, the Marines are in town. Can you make the party?" The Melrose offered the pent-house on the top floor for a carousing good time, complete with a bar and buffet—all on the house. Flying back to Pensacola the next day was kind of hazy, but it was all worth it.

One of the few Marine instructor pilots at Pensacola was a lieutenant by the name of Gregory Boyington. He was much older than most of our contemporaries, so he was aptly nicknamed "Pappy." During the summer months Pappy got really enthusiastic about an American volunteer group going to China to help patrol the Burma Road against the Japanese. He started conscripting volunteers for the company. Many of my Navy and Marine friends had already signed up. On August 7, 1941, my buddy 2dLt Darrell Irwin and I put in an application for this grand adventure. Was it providential for us when we were notified, much later, that the quota had already been filled?

* * *

The attack at Pearl Harbor created a flurry of activity. A handful of us Marines received orders to report to a Radar Fighter Director School in Norfolk, Virginia.

Probably the most memorable aspect of that sojourn on the Naval Operating Base at Norfolk was having the chance to satisfy my curiosity about aircraft carriers: I was able to go aboard the auxiliary carrier USS *Long Island* and the fleet carrier USS *Hornet.* I boarded the *Long Island* by myself on January 29. I sized her up and she scared me. She was the size of the proverbial postage stamp. I feared running out of runway before touchdown. Little did I know then that I would have my first carrier experience aboard her seven months later.

Two days later, aircraft off the carrier *Hornet* flew in from sea. You could hear the roaring above the overcast clouds, and then, one by one, they came in for a landing at Chambers Field. Many hours later, the *Hornet* put into port.

It was January 31 when Lts Darrell D. "Slim" Irwin, Howard K. "Bull" Marvin, Don "Jake" Jaeckels, and I went aboard to check out this behemoth. She was a new addition to the fleet, having been commissioned the October before—the eighth American aircraft carrier built.

Her fresh paint was gleaming. I was totally impressed. No sooner were we aboard than Ens Al Flemming, a Navy contemporary at Pensacola, ran up to greet us. Over hot chocolate down in the wardroom, Al tantalized us with stories of sea duty and shipboard activities. They had been out to sea for thirty days on a shakedown cruise. Al took it upon himself to become our tour guide. From the wardroom, we took a ladder up and out to the flight deck. From a midpoint opposite the island, I looked up at the bridge. Three officers were looking down at us. Al noticed my gaze. "That middle one is the captain of our ship."

"What's his name?" I asked.

"That's Capt Marc Mitscher" was his answer.

"Oh," I remember, was my uninterested reply.

We inspected the ship from superstructure to engine room. *Spic and span* were the words for her—beautifully built and, like a kitchen, clean as could be.

The engine room was particularly fascinating. A snarl of pipes crisscrossed in all directions. It must have taken a genius to figure out where everything went and why. Most remarkable was the fact that everything was coated with silver paint—not a black spot anywhere.

The landing deck was long enough to reassure me that perhaps even I could land a plane aboard without cracking up. It was a full 809 feet long with an 83-foot beam. The flight deck was well over 60 feet above the waterline. The hangar deck, just below the flight deck, ran the full length of the ship. I noticed the huge elevators that transported planes to and from the flight deck and the rubber-tired tractors that moved the planes about. The only planes that remained were those that had crashed while trying to land.

We watched two North American B-25 medium bombers being hoisted aboard the *Hornet*.

"What's going on here?" I queried.

Al Flemming's response was, "Oh, we're taking them out to sea to find out if they can take off from a short carrier deck."

I theorized that once they got out to sea quite some distance, the B-25s would take off for England, as some Army Air Corps pilots were with the bombers.

One morning sometime later, from our classroom, we saw the *Hornet* move slowly down Hampton Road and put out sea. We could see the bombers aboard. A few hours later, the *Hornet's* planes took off from the airfield to rendezvous with the carrier, somewhere off the coast.

Newspaper headlines blazed with reports of LtCol James H. "Jimmy" Doolittle's raid over Tokyo on April 18, 1942.

It was then that I knew what had been going on that day back in Norfolk.

* * *

The course was nearing its end when I met Josie Matthews from Roanoke Rapids, North Carolina. Our courtship gave new meaning to the term *whirlwind*. In order to beat the three-day waiting period in Norfolk, we were married at Elizabeth City, North Carolina, in a short ceremony at the Catholic church. My mother would never have accepted anything short of a Catholic wedding for her "little boy."

My next batch of orders directed me to report to the San Diego Naval Air Station on North Island. Upon arrival there I needed flight time. At the North Island Naval Air Station, I was able to find an available airplane, but it was one I had never flown before—a Grumman J2F biplane amphibian. Fortunately, I found an old-timer who agreed to check me out. His name was Navy Chief Petty Officer Word. We took off and he let me take over the controls immediately. I circled the field and made a couple of touch-and-go landings on the broad asphalt apron at North Island. It wasn't too many minutes later that Chief Word pronounced me checked out. We landed, taxied up to the line shack, and then shut down.

I went into Operations to file a flight plan to Yuma, Arizona, and return. I had just started the engine of the J2F when I saw six sailors running toward me. They opened the hatch to the bilge area and climbed right in. Apparently, they needed flight time too. Little did they realize that I'd never really flown this plane before! Lucky for them, and perhaps for me too, the flight was uneventful—and we all got in our flight time.

On April 22, 1942, I was assigned to Marine Observation Squadron (VMO-251), which was formed December 1, 1941. Its skipper was Maj John N. Hart, with organizers Majs Charles H. "Fog" Hayes and Elliot Bard, and Capts Ralph Yeaman, William "Soupie" Campbell, and Carl Longley. This nucleus grew into thirty officers and 250 enlisted men. Our primary mission was reconnaissance; the idea was to dash into enemy territory, take photographs, and dash out again. After much controversy, we acquired sixteen Grumman F4F-3 Wildcats of the most ancient vintage. Cameras were installed in the belly of each plane, but, as it turned out, we became a full-fledged fighter unit and never had the opportunity to use the planes for photography.

Never again was there a problem obtaining flight time. I immediately checked out in the Wildcat. My first attempt to fly it was one of much chagrin and embarrassment. At the North Island Naval Air Station, I taxied the plane to the point of takeoff on the wide asphalt apron. No sooner had the plane gathered speed when it began a ground loop to the left. When the left wingtip scraped the asphalt, I cut the engine. Later, Captain Yeaman gave me sage advice: "Keep your eyes glued to a point on the horizon. Once the nose tends to move away from that point, correct immediately." It worked. The scraped wingtip would be the first and only time ever, in twelve hundred hours flying time, that I would ever dent a Wildcat.

With those narrow landing gears, that airplane was a bear. It had a few other quirks that one had to get used to. For one thing, the landing gear didn't automatically retract. On takeoff, a pilot had to crank the gear up twenty-nine turns and lock it in place. The wheels and gear compressed themselves into the belly of the fuselage just under the leading edge of the wing. Then, prior to landing, he had to wind it down again—twenty-nine turns—and lock it in place. I had been accustomed to this procedure previously, however, having flown the biplane fighters F1F-1, F2F, and the F3F.

The crank was located in the cockpit next to the pilot's right leg. There were several occasions on record when, in a vertical dive and pulling out with hard G's, the landing gear popped out with the crank spinning, disintegrating the airplane. This had happened to one of my Pensacola cadet classmates of 152-C. Right after Pearl Harbor, he was transferred to Hawaii. During a dive-bombing run and pull-out, the plane exploded and he was killed.

This malfunction happened to me on a couple of occasions, but I was able to move my leg over to suppress the whirling handle. It beat my calf to a pulp, but there really was no other alternative.

At that time I also checked out in the Brewster F2A Buffalo. This plane had a wider landing gear than the Wildcat and was much easier to land and take off. In the air it was very maneuverable. But the Buffalo just didn't have the armor or armament that the Wildcat did. This inadequacy was proven in the heat of battle at Wake Island and Midway. The Marine pilots who participated in those battles were very dismayed at its performance. It was definitely inadequate against the superior Japanese Zero.

Things were accelerating! I was notified of my commission as first lieutenant, and on May 28, 1942, I was sworn in by BriGen Ross E. Rowell.

The fourth day of June caught our attention as we heard sketchy reports about the Battle of Midway, the consequence of which would be far-reaching.

PART II
The Island

GRUMMAN F4F WILDCAT

CHAPTER 3

The Hot Zone

The day of June 17, 1942, marked our boarding the good ship *Heywood,* named after the first major general commandant of the Marine Corps. At one time she had been a freighter-passenger vessel, before the Navy converted her into a troop transport. Now our dismantled Grumman Wildcats with wings and propellers in individual crates were lowered into her hold. The 1st Marine Raiders and the 2d Battalion, 2d Marine Regiment, also went aboard and descended to the thickly congested quarters in the hold below. At 1015 the next morning, the ship moved away from the North Island docks and down the bay toward Point Loma.

Those of us who had never been to sea before thrilled to the churning masses of vivid blue and rolling seas. But soon seasickness or the monotony of it all soon overcame any thrill. Along with the pitching, rolling motion of the ship were the engine vibrations, tremors, and creaking noises, which also grew progressively more irksome with each turn of the propeller.

For the first few days out, the skies were cool, sunny, and clear. Regular 0900 morning inspections and middle-afternoon lectures punctuated the days and helped enliven them. But, for the most part, we spent our days in our bunks, either reading or sleeping.

Our ship clipped along at 15 knots, which was far in excess of normal convoy speed. The base course of 210 T hinted of the Samoan Islands, but our destination was still shrouded in secrecy. So we zigzagged to avoid enemy subs and accepted this life at sea. The food was fair, with milk for breakfast, but a caution was issued not to waste fresh water for fear of a shortage. A daily bulletin for all hands, called *The Heywood Press,* enlightened us with the latest news flashes, so we fared rather well.

An albatross hovered about and reminded me of a favorite quotation: "It is an ancient Mariner and he stoppeth one of three. By thy long gray beard and glittering eye, now where fore stopp'st thou me?"

The Tropic of Cancer was crossed, and with that came hot, scorching winds. Green uniforms were tossed aside for khaki. Day by day we plowed through the glittering blue at 300 miles per day. Our wake left churning, varicolored greens and whirlpools of milky white foam. But Samuel Taylor Coleridge's *The Rime of the Ancient Mariner,* was still stuck in my head: "Water, water, everywhere."

At the end of a long day, darkness would settle fast over the sea, and blackout precautions would take effect. With portholes and doors secured, the staterooms became hotboxes and the odor from the galley an unendurable stench.

At dusk, to escape the suffocating heat belowdecks to the flying bridge above was perhaps one of the most pleasant interludes of the whole voyage. There one could be relaxed and refreshed, breathe the clean sea air, and feel the cool breezes ripple across one's cheek. The sight of different cloud types at sunset could be enthralling, the colors ranging from orange to pink to crimson.

From the flying bridge, one had a dominating view of the deck forward. Very little of the deck could be seen, though, as it was crowded with Higgins boats lying athwartships, which were as long as the ship was wide. The enlisted men filled in the gaps and, amid the hissing roar of the waves that scurried alongside as our ship plowed ahead, one could hear the men's faint laughter.

The bow of the ship would raise and lower itself slowly and majestically past the horizon. The night would move in on the only trace of sunset left, which was the color of old rose and tinted the bottom of the clouds that rippled high in the sky. In a still higher portion of the heavens, an almost full moon would pour its brilliant radiance through cloud masses and spill it onto the sea. Smaller wisps of clouds would scurry by like scared jackrabbits. Then lower, darker clouds would heave into view, and the moon would pass behind them, transforming itself into a pale silver disk before its total disappearance. A few seconds later, it would rush out with more vigorous brilliance than ever, and the stars would twinkle through empty patches in the sky.

Voices could occasionally be heard above the roar of the waves, but most of the men were wrapped in silent thoughts of their own. They would face a cool, stiff breeze from the direction of the bow and see the stack, cranes, pulleys, ropes, and lines silhouetted against the moonlit horizon. This was the unforgettable charm of the Pacific. Somehow I could not associate a world in turmoil with this soothing, pleasant solitude. This was the peaceful side of war. And our ship plowed on.

* * *

There is a custom known to men the world over that he who ventures far upon the Seven Seas is subject to a ritual on his first crossing of the Equator. This ceremony surrounds a tradition of Neptune, the Roman god of the sea. One not previously admitted into this league is very aptly named a "polliwog" who, in metamorphosis at the crossing, becomes a qualified "shellback" for all time to come. Despite a war, such an event as this ancient custom could not be ignored. So three days of intense ceremony began. It started on June 25, our seventh day out of port, and by the twenty-eighth the victims were full-fledged shellbacks.

The sunrise on our twelfth day out was an event of remarkable interest. In the opposite quadrant, a faint blue hump, partially dissolved on the horizon, was revealed. A few minutes later three humps with irregular profiles were discerned rearing themselves into the sky. It was our first sight of land since the beginning of our voyage.

This turned out to be the island of Manua, the most eastern of the Samoan group. We passed about 15 miles to Manua's starboard. Sixty miles farther west lay the island of Tutuila, a U.S. possession. After the 0900 muster, Tutuila could be seen dead ahead. Immense and dominating, it rose out of the ocean like a pedestal.

The entire troop and ship's personnel were on deck, gazing anxiously at good old terra firma and waiting for some signs of life. I couldn't have been more impressed if we were discovering it for the first time.

Naturally concealed Pago Pago lay at the end, looking very much civilized with Marine jeeps, military trucks, various construction jobs, and radio antennae scattered all around the harbor. The city was hardly worth mentioning, save its curious people, dwellings, and habits. It was now more or less a Marine post, however, which was humming with activity. Silver barrage balloons lay snuggled in the trees at strategic points, and two destroyers, some cargo ships, and other smaller vessels were anchored in the harbor. At 1156 the *Heywood* dropped its anchor.

It was a clear day and the scenic beauty of the island was beyond description. Almost immediately from the shoreline, the sheer hills rose upward for hundreds of feet. Word had it that this harbor was a volcanic crater with its depth unknown. So, from a geological standpoint, it was understandable why these sky-piercing mountains rose so steeply and entirely around the harbor. Along the sandy beach, the palm trees stood tall and crowded. They extended back and became sparse as the terrain began its rapid upward slope. This gave way to other tropical vegetation in the form of trees, dense vines, and hundreds of other botanical species that thickly shrouded the hills.

The officers were allowed to go ashore late in the afternoon. We tasted good San Francisco beer at the Ship's Service Store, which was nothing more than a shack, and observed a group of very diverse personalities. There were old salts of the sea—both Navy and Marine—but what struck me with particular interest were the islander enlisted sailors.

These Polynesians had oily, dark, wavy hair and deep brown skin. Their dress was the uniform of the day: white cap, blue shirt, and trousers. They were deficient in one thing, however: shoes. Not one islander wore shoes or socks. Having gone without them all their lives, they were not necessities. Their big feet were tough and wide. Probably no type of shoe could offer size or comfort to them.

Men and boys alike wore the conventional color-printed cotton wraps called lavalavas. A group of native Marine enlisted men came marching down the street in the regulation garrison cap and khaki shirt—with khaki lavalavas.

We returned to our ship at dusk that day and, soon after, found ourselves steaming out of the harbor for Ampolu, another island of the Samoan group, this one British-owned and administrated by New Zealand. It was only four hours away under normal cruising conditions, but we loafed along slowly so we would reach that point early the next day.

The ship steamed up the narrow, treacherous channel and dropped anchor in the port of Apia. Immediately, the Higgins lighters were lowered overboard, and the steam winches and cranes started operations as the freight from the ship's hold was unloaded.

This was the destination of the 2d Battalion, 2d Marine Regiment. From the deck we watched them disembark and took note of the crescent shoreline, which was ringed with neat buildings huddled together and composing the town of Apia. Very shortly, natives paddled their outrigger dugout canoes alongside our ship to sell bananas, baskets, and handmade souvenirs. The small, naked boys dived for coins that we tossed into the water.

The troops were now loading into the lighters, so a few of us went ashore with them. Apia was a clean little town. A hard-surfaced road followed close to the harbor.

Four miles inland were the home and grave of Robert Louis Stevenson. His large house sat upon a knoll at the base of a conical, 600-foot hill. Its name was Lea Lima, which means "water from the cup of the hand." That name was derived from the fact that Stevenson and his wife came upon this knoll after a long hike. Thirsty and tired, he sat down underneath a tree while his wife looked for water. She came upon a nearby stream, and, having no container, cupped her hand and drank the spring water—hence the name Lea Lima, from the native language.

Captain Claude Welch, Lt Thaddeus "Ted" Wojick, MG Bob Strain, and I—having steered clear of exertion since the beginning of the voyage—decided that exercise would do us good. So, on the only hard-surfaced road leading inland, we hiked the entire 4 miles to Stevenson's home. The surrounding countryside was fantastically beautiful. Tall coconut palms towered overhead, and hibiscus, crotons, and banana trees grew everywhere in profusion. The species of vegetation were reminiscent of those of Miami.

At last, we reached the grounds of the famous author's home. The narrow road that approached the lawns was canopied by huge elephant-ear trees. The driveway split at the front lawn and circled around to the front entrance of the house. The British ensign flew from a flagstaff on the roof, as this was now the governor's home. The area was meticulously groomed, its palm trees, hedges, and flowers in perfect order. A stream trickled along the sloping contours, which gently declined all the way to the sea.

Just as we arrived, the governor was leaving in his car. He directed two of his yard boys to guide us up the steep 600-foot hill, on the peak of which was the tomb of Stevenson and his wife.

A narrow, winding path zigzagged to the top. The foliage was extremely dense, with ferns, vines, and trees enveloping the path. Occasionally, we came across a banyan tree, its limbs spread out from the base and massed in every direction. It was the largest kind of tree on the island. After the exhausting climb, we slumped upon the benches there, stripped to the waist, and were delighted to feel the cool breezes blowing off the sea.

The tomb itself was merely two large concrete slabs—a small slab placed upon a larger one, about 10 feet long and 5 feet high. Bronze plaques bore inscriptions in both the native and English languages. An excerpt from the Book of Ruth was on one side of the tomb, and a quotation about the author's burial place was on the other. Stevenson's wish that he be buried on this mountain overlooking his home had been carried out.

The panoramic view over the vast area was superb. Far below, the author's house could be seen clearly. It was a splendid sight—fairly breathtaking in its startling beauty. The cool greens embellished everything, and the loftiness of the hilltop gave one an enchanting impression. Flying foxes flitted through the air, and white, long-tailed gulls floated slowly down below.

After a long rest, we began our descent and the long trip back to Apia. But first the native boys treated us to limeade and a tour of the house. In very serious and dramatic tones in broken English, the houseboy told the story of Stevenson's death in 1894.

It appeared that an interisland ferry service was being conducted, for the next day we weighed anchor and the *Heywood* steamed back to Pago Pago.

The next two days were spent loading the ship with more troops and supplies. In the meantime several of the officers drove 25 miles over a bumpy lava road to the Marine airfield. It had been a tedious and complicated construction job. This great tract had been cleared of dense jungle and mangrove swamp, until the final product was a fine, finished airfield with a superior surface.

There was a grand reunion of old aviation classmates, and we watched the Curtiss SBC-4 biplane dive-bombers land and take off.

July 5, 1942, was a bright, clear morning as we crept out of the harbor. This time there was an escort, the destroyer *Barker*. The sea was unusually choppy with strong winds, and huge waves dashed their spray over the ship. Our destination was unknown to us, but the ship was on a westerly heading.

The days at sea were uneventful. We crossed the international date line, which advanced our time ahead by one day. At long last came information of our destination from LtCol Hart. Originally, it was to have been New Zealand, but at Samoa the orders were changed to New Caledonia. Just off the Coral Sea, that location put us in the war zone. With a little research, we found that New Caledonia was French-owned, with the people speaking eighteen different dialects of French. The island was 260 miles long and 31 miles wide, the closest Australian port was 1,100 miles away, and the northern tip of New Zealand was 800 miles to the south. July 10 was the last day at sea; in the morning a patrol plane came out to escort us into the harbor.

The 1st Marine Raider Battalion was the first to disembark. Over the next forty-eight hours, the unloading activities kept up a constant hum. The shrill whistle of the boatswain's mate pierced the air, and the winches, pulleys, and booms rumbled continuously. The echoes of a hundred different noises accentuated the streams of cargo from ship to dock. The huge cranes lowered their rope nets, and a whole section of men immediately piled into it crates of ammunition, tents, folding bunks, and big tin boxes. Slowly the hoists lifted, swung over the side, and lowered the cargo where more men were waiting to carry it away. Along the entire length of the ship were mounds of crates, drums of gasoline, pyramids of ammunition, and hundreds of items ready to be reloaded onto trucks.

From the No. 3 hold, the wingless Grumman F4F-3P fighters were lifted one by one and set down carefully on the deck. Likewise were the two Grumman J2F-6 Duck biplane amphibians and the two North American SNJ-3 low-winged monoplanes. Then followed the wing crates for the eventual reassembly. In another hold the cranes were carrying big trucks, jeeps, and small tractors into space. Everybody was working like mad.

In the meantime, the system of dispersing supplies was grinding away at full speed. It was a picture of men and machines working together. From one stack of crates, a brigade of men passed crates from hand to hand toward the ten-wheeled Army trucks. Our planes were hoisted aboard huge trailers and were gone, as were the wing crates and propellers. All day long the work progressed at a feverish pitch until Captain Welch placed the last crate of ammunition on the truck.

That night the remainder of the working party piled into trucks and coursed their way over 50 miles of the "little Burma Road" to where an advanced party had set up camp. What a trek! The road was riddled with potholes and rippled in a series of sharp turns, downgrades, and steep hills. The trip to Camp Tontouta was slow and jolting.

Soon the planes were assembled, and at once a training program was instituted. The results of the Battle of Midway gave us a foreboding outlook as to our planes' ability in the event we were to tangle with Japanese Zeros. Tontouta Field was not yet completed, but there was one usable runway, and, as the wind was seldom over 5 mph, it made little difference whether we landed up, down, or across the wind.

Long days and weeks passed. Everyone was war conscious, even so far as the possibility of an attack on New Caledonia. The Japanese already had a firm foothold on New Guinea and the Solomon Islands, and it was more or less a race to see who would make the next jump first. It was told that a destroyer had spotted a Japanese submarine in Noumea Harbor and had sunk it. Our B-17s had started to bomb Japanese positions at a place called Guadalcanal—our squadron sent photo crews along to take pictures—and the Russians were getting set back in the Bonets Basin. Things as a whole looked rather grim.

* * *

Something was going on. You could feel it in the air. Suddenly one morning, our commanding officer, LtCol John N. Hart, and supply officer, Lt Frank Platt, left by plane, their destination unknown.

Then another surprise occurred: Without warning or arrangement, Capt William "Soupie" Campbell and Lts Todd Whitten, Roy T. Spurlock, William Kirby, and Carl Schuessler were ordered to pack bare essentials and were whisked away on some secret mission. This all happened during the last week in July.

Three days later, the CO returned and announced the relocation of the squadron to a forward area. This future base was to be Espiritu Santo, the northernmost island of the New Hebrides—a shared French-British possession. He brought back tales of scantily clad native women, cannibals, and tribal warfare. It appeared the squadron would be the buffer against the Japanese who occupied the Solomons, just a scant few hundred miles to the northwest.

There was a hush among the pilots huddled around a shortwave radio as news of the Guadalcanal invasion came in. The date was August 7, 1942. There appeared to be optimism in the news, as we heard about the 1st Marine Division setting up beachheads on the north shore of Guadalcanal and that the 1st Raiders had made a landing on a place called Tulagi. But the news was sketchy, and this aroused curiosity and a personal need to know inherent in us all. In fact, the lack of news was almost excruciatingly taunting.

On August 10 in a cloudy sky, the Grumman Wildcats took off—all fifteen of them—and proceeded on the flight to Espiritu Santo. The first leg was up 90 miles of New Caledonia to the red, dust-covered Plaine de Guiac. There, on the ground, I caught my first sight of a B-17 Flying Fortress. What a huge and beautiful airplane! I was impressed!

The second leg of the flight was over 200 miles of water to the recently built airstrip at Efate, the southernmost island of the New Hebrides. This few hundred miles made for a strange contrast in vegetation. This was strictly tropical. We pilots circled the airstrip and saw dense jungle and coconut plantations. The small town of Efate displayed the conspicuous red roofs indicative of its French occupants.

The final leg was 150 miles still farther north. We overflew many small jungle islands and, through the thick mists far to starboard, could see smoking volcanos. The airstrip was located beside the harbor on the southeast portion of the island. The runway, a swath cut through a coconut plantation, had been a monumental task for the Seabees, but it was now ready for operations. VMO-251 would be the first tactical air unit to oppose the Japanese to the north.

* * *

The horrors of war hit the squadron on August 13. That was the day Capt Soupie Campbell and Lts Roy Spurlock and Tod Whitten returned from the secret mission. Lieutenants Kirby and Schuessler were not with them. They had been killed in action.

Morale was low among the pilots on learning this disheartening news. We had become like brothers. Day in and day out for months, we pilots lived together, flew together, and became very involved with each other—like a fraternity. These two highly respected officers lost their lives during the invasion at Guadalcanal. At the first squadron inspection two days later, all heads were bowed for two minutes in a solemn tribute to these two brave souls.

We learned much later they had been involved in the Battle of Savo Island, located a few miles off the northeast tip of Guadalcanal. Campbell, Whitten, and Spurlock had been observers in the backseats of cruiser-based Curtiss SOC-1 biplanes on floats, flying from the USS *Astoria*. Kirby and Schuessler did likewise from aboard the USS *Vincennes*. They had taken part in the practice invasion of Zero Island, one of the Fiji group, and then finally the invasion of Guadalcanal on August 7, 1942.

At 0200 Sunday morning, August 9, a Japanese task force slipped in undetected and caught our ships by surprise. The U.S. cruisers *Astoria*, *Quincy*, and

Vincennes and the Australian cruiser HMAS *Canberra* were sunk. The *Chicago* sustained major damage.

The ships had been shot from underneath, and many lives were lost. The *Quincy* was the first to sink. Fatally hit, she went down in ten minutes with many casualties. The *Vincennes* was next, sinking one half hour after an explosion with great loss of life.

It was told how a Japanese bomber strafed the ship on the previous day when Carl Schuessler had returned from a flight. Schuessler immediately climbed into the rear cockpit of a Curtiss SOC-1 biplane, perched on the catapult, manned the .30-caliber machine gun, and riddled the bomber.

Whitten told how he had administered first aid during the sea battle and with his hunting knife had amputated a young sailor's foot that a shell had splintered and twisted.

There were other harrowing tales, and, although the invasion was successful, it was costly to the Navy.

* * *

Squadrons of planes—both fighter and dive-bomber—began phasing through Espiritu Santo on their way to "Cactus," the code name for Guadalcanal. It seemed VMO-251 was destined to sit it out for the duration.

VMO-251 should have been the first squadron into combat at Guadalcanal. Since VMO-251 was based at Espiritu Santo and VMF-212 was based at Efate, and they were the only two squadrons in the area opposing the Japanese to the north, the original plans had called for these two squadrons to operate as an initial land-based fighter defense. They were to fly to Guadalcanal once the airfields in the objective area were completed.

Rear Admiral Richmond Kelly Turner was in charge of planning and of the task force that would make the invasion. He determined, however, that since VMO-251 and VMF-212 were not carrier experienced and needed more tactical and gunnery training, they should remain at their present bases and away from Guadalcanal. But for this fluke of planning, VMO-251 would have been one of the first into battle.

On August 19 VMF-223 transited Santo on their way to Guadalcanal. Captain John L. Smith was the commanding officer and Capt Marion Carl the executive officer. My old classmate Howard K. "Bull" Marvin was with them. Next came VMF-224 with Capt Robert E. Galer as commanding officer. Two of his squadronmates were "Slim" Irwin and Stan Nicolay, my cadet classmates at Pensacola. Most of these pilots were to be future aces. This was only an overnight billet, and then they were whisked away to join combat. But how good it was to renew old friendships!

It was September 1, 1942, when I was about to experience my first carrier operation. The *Long Island* had steamed into Segond Channel the day before and dropped anchor in the harbor. Its hangar deck was loaded with the latest Grumman Wildcats off the assembly line: F4F-4s. Certain pilots were ordered to go aboard. With less than an hour's notice, the pilots boarded jeeps to take them from the coral strip just off Pelekula Peninsula to Segond Channel, just a few miles away. A launch was waiting at the dock and, with the pilots aboard, sped out to the sideboard ladder of the *Long Island.* We were to fly the Wildcats off the ship and back to the airstrip.

The briefing was short but we hung on to every word. It would be a catapult shot—at anchor! The deck crews brought the planes up the elevator to the flight deck and spotted them astern.

"Pilots, man your planes!" was blared over the bullhorn, and the pilots ran to their respective planes from the ready room.

"Start your engines!" In unison the propellers started turning over. The deck handlers waved forward each individual plane and spotted it in position on the catapult. The ship had swung into the wind on its anchor.

Wind? Was there enough? I was leery.

According to procedures the catapult crewman stood just off the starboard bow of the plane. He twirled his hand—the signal to push the throttle full forward. The engine wound up to full power; then he threw himself forward, pointing toward the bow. With the pilot's head back against the headrest, the catapult let go and slung the plane forward.

The plane cleared the bow then dipped, straining to gain airspeed. It struggled and, a couple of seconds later, became airborne. Thus a successful take-off was completed. Minutes later all the new Grummans landed back on the coral airstrip.

What an experience! That was the thrill of the day!

At 0430 on the morning of September 12, the pilots were awakened to assume an alert status at the ready tent. Intelligence had it that a Japanese carrier force was steaming our way. Normally, the lower echelons were not privy to much intelligence information, so rumors ran rampant and caused much confusion. About noon, however, the alert was called off, and half the officers drove to camp for midday chow.

Events happened fast. Right after lunch, notification came about going to Guadalcanal. The aircraft carriers *Wasp* and *Hornet* were steaming about 150 miles off Espiritu Santo to the east. Navy SBD Dauntless dive-bombers and Grumman TBF torpedo bombers had already flown in from those carriers and landed at the airstrip. The plan called for VMO-251 pilots to board these aircraft as passengers and fly aboard the respective carriers.

It was then an exercise in mobilizing personal gear and assembling at the right place at the right time. My flight consisted of Lts Robert "Doc" Livingston, Herb Peters, and Oscar "Curly" Rutledge. We were assigned to the carrier *Wasp*. The other eight pilots, under Captain Longley's leadership, went to the carrier *Hornet*.

We climbed aboard a TBF torpedo plane, the largest single-engine aircraft in the naval inventory. The cantilevered wings were folded. Then, as the huge plane taxied to the end of the runway, the wings were extended and locked into position. At 1330 the plane took off, climbed, and began a slow turn to port to rendezvous with four new Grumman Wildcats flown by Navy pilots.

The *Hornet* contingent carrying other members of the squadron launched in Douglas dive-bombers. One plane roared into the air and was in a climb when its engine faltered and then quit. The pilot made a water landing in the bay. A destroyer picked up the crew, which included our own Lt Eldon H. "Duke" Railsback, who had been in the rear cockpit.

The rendezvous was completed and the course set to 040 T. Low clouds and mist limited visibility. At the end of an hour and a half, the *Wasp* should have been sighted, but that time had elapsed and there was still no sign of her. The torpedo plane climbed to a higher altitude to obtain a ZB bearing. (ZB bearings were confidential compass cards issued to pilots and changed daily. The cards depicted the compass rose divided into sectors. From a station—be it an aircraft carrier or an airfield—alphabetical radio signals were emitted. Thus a pilot could home in on the station when using the proper alphabetical signal.) Finally, after another hour, she was sighted cruising—majestically and serenely—through the haze. Her escorts were destroyers and cruisers in concentric positions around her. Far in the mist, the battleship *North Carolina* could be discerned, and beyond that, the *Hornet*, staunch and foreboding.

The *Wasp* blinked her signals and, in response, a tight pylon turn was made—identification. The four Grumman fighters went first into the landing pattern. The first plane turned from downwind of the landing pattern onto the base leg, hanging on the prop, power on, nose high, just barely above stalling speed. Then the landing signal officer LSO gave his "cut," and the plane plunged to the heaving deck to grapple the athwartship cable. It was a hard landing, and the gear buckled under the impact and a wingtip was bent. But the crash crews were prepared for this sort of accident, and in a jiffy the deck was cleared for the next landing.

The other fighters landed in quick succession, then it was our turn. The tailhook grabbed, causing a counteraction to inertia that forced the body against the safety belt. Within the space of a few short feet, the plane came to a straining and abrupt but smooth halt. Thus terminated a three-and-a-half-hour flight. Flight-deck crewmen directed the taxiing plane to a position toward the bow and spotted it on the foredeck. In the meantime the other TBFs were landing.

Following our group into the landing pattern was a contingent from Marine Squadron VMF-212 with Maj Frederick "Beanie" Payne leading. They had also flown from Espiritu Santo in SBD dive-bombers. We Marines would fly the new Grumman Wildcats from the carriers to Guadalcanal in the morning. It would be a ferry hop only. Then we would return immediately to Santo by R4D, the military version of the DC-3 airliner.

*   *   *

What a contrast this was to jungle life! The carrier was a floating hotel, or was it just my mildewed imagination? After months of living in the hot, insect-infested jungle under primitive conditions, this was luxury in its purest form. The wardroom contained fans and floor lamps, overstuffed furniture, and comparatively recent stateside magazines. The temporary quarters were just off the officers' mess. Showers with hot and cold running water were just down the corridor.

Before dinner we strolled over the flight deck and down into the hangar deck to watch the huge elevators limberly lower the planes. Dinner that night was almost embarrassing, with linen tablecloths and napkins. The mess attendants in white coats served pork chops with all the trimmings. Then ice cream! This sudden thrust into the lap of luxury could be habit forming!

Three days later, September 15, 1942, the USS *Wasp* was torpedoed by a Japanese submarine and sunk. The USS *Hornet* met the same fate less than six weeks later, October 26. She went down after a bombing and torpedo attack in an area between Guadalcanal and the Santa Cruz Islands.

CHAPTER 4

Hell on Earth—Episode I

The bugle sounded over the loudspeaker at 0600. We ate a meager break-fast and then assembled in the ready room for a briefing—the pertinent information as to wind, weather, and course to fly. Once again the technicalities of a flyaway were stressed. This was to be my second carrier experience.

On the stern of the *Wasp*, the engines were warming up, preparatory to take-off. Everything worked with machinelike precision. Major "Beanie" Payne and his outfit of five F4F-4s took off first. I followed with my flight—each individual plane bumping along the flight deck with flaps cracked and throttle full. All nine planes effected good takeoffs.

Lieutenant Herb Peters was my wingman and, in the second section, Lt Robert "Doc" Livingston was leading with Lt Oscar "Curly" Rutledge as wing-man. The rendezvous was quick, and soon the entire flight of nine planes was heading northwest on a 310-degree course, toward the southern end of the Solomon Islands group. The *Wasp* had been plying the waters about 160 miles southeast of San Cristobal, the southernmost island of the group. The weather was bad all the way, with low scud and poor visibility. The formation flew between 500 and 1,000 feet. The island of San Cristobal finally loomed ahead, and our flight shifted course slightly to the starboard.

An hour passed. Soon I recognized Guadalcanal by the three islets that lay near the end of the larger island. To evade the Japanese antiaircraft guns, we flew slightly to seaward around the northern part of the island. In compliance with identification signals, the planes maneuvered in sharp left-hand turns. The vector was then toward the Marine encampment and the Henderson Field runway. This airstrip had been built by the Japanese and then, when elements of the 1st Marine Division under the command of MajGen Alexander Archer Vandegrift had driven them inland, was rehabilitated for Marine air operations.

These northern shores had flats that extended inland a few miles to the base of the mountains, which formed high ridges along the length of the island. Large plattes of grassland covered areas that were interspersed with hummocks of dense tropical vegetation. The Marine encampment was snuggled in and around a large, cleared coconut plantation.

The flights broke off, and my planes came in for a landing, followed by the flight from the *Hornet*. The devastation of the area was horrendous. The destructive force of shelling by a Japanese cruiser and destroyer the night before had left planes lying topsy-turvy around the field—a mass of debris. Grummans were wrecked and on their backs, Army Air Forces Bell P-39 and P-400 Airacobras were strewn in junk heaps, and shell craters were everywhere. It was an incredible sight.

The planes had no sooner landed than orders were given to take off immediately for a short flight to a fighter strip a few miles southward. It was hardly more than a green cow pasture, but all planes landed safely.

A couple of station wagons collected the pilots and baggage and drove us back to Henderson Field. Across the airstrip from the Pagoda operations center was a Japanese hangar with an armor-plated roof, where we deposited our baggage. We pilots stood outside, pondering our next move. A short while later, the hangar collapsed, burying the luggage.

The welcome back by the local Marine fliers was overwhelming. They had withstood assaults from land, sea, and air for days and nights on end. They had been obliged by superhuman strength and stamina to hang on. The previous night's shelling had lasted from 2200 until 0400. Three dive-bomber pilots had been killed as they lay in their slit trench. Palm trees all about had been denuded of their foliage. Yet these intrepid souls had maintained a rigid flight schedule, intercepting and downing flights of Japanese Zeros as well as Betty bombers. Some of the twin-engine Bettys had gotten through, however, dropping bombs and creating general havoc. It was awesome how these pilots, although edgy, were still in such noble spirits that they were ready to scramble on a moment's notice.

Stan Nicolay greeted me first. He was haggard and weary, but the meeting was one of elation. Then came lanky Darrell Irwin, all decked out in a bright red baseball cap. I didn't need convincing that this was a hell of a place. It was all too plain.

The welcome wore itself out in a hurry when the air raid siren started to wail. All pilots scrambled to available fighter planes. I jumped into a station wagon and bounced back to the cow pasture airstrip. Our planes had been refueled, but I observed the Grumman I had arrived in taxiing out for takeoff.

At Guadalcanal all pilots and planes were pooled. There was no distinction as to squadron identity for pilots. It was the same with the planes. Pilots never knew which plane they would fly until they saw it on the flight schedule just before takeoff. Your wingman might be a member of some other squadron. It was assumed that all pilots were equally skilled in gunnery and tactics. This was known as the "Cactus Air Force."

Several pilots were standing along the grass runway, watching the hurried takeoffs. Wendell Garton was one, and I heard him give a startled cry. I looked up just in time to see one of the planes go into a spin right after takeoff. It fell into the dense palm thicket at the end of the runway. Garton and I jumped into a nearby jeep with Captain Longley and bounded across the field to the crash scene. The plane was resting at an inverted angle against a palm tree. Then horror struck me: The pilot was Curly Rutledge, a member of my flight off the *Wasp*.

Curly was hanging unconscious with blood streaming down his scalp. I tried in vain to pull him from the cockpit, but the instrument panel and mapboard were pushed back and had pinned his leg. While I held Curly in my arms, Garton managed to unbuckle his parachute. Slowly his leg worked free and we laid him gently on the crumpled wing. My shirt was saturated with blood, but I hardly gave it a thought. The engine was smoking, so we frantically moved him a safe distance away. Soon a corpsman came with first aid. Curly's skull was laid open. The corpsman bound his head and a large cut on his chin. Curly's heart was beating, so we knew he was alive. An ammunition carrier had drawn up, and Curly was lifted aboard and driven to the hospital tent a short distance away, just inside the coconut plantation.

An air raid was imminent, but I looked frantically for a doctor. All hands were in the foxholes, waiting for the bombs to drop. A doctor was finally found and he examined Curly. He was in a coma but the diagnosis indicated that he would survive. Our thoughts turned next to finding a bomb shelter for ourselves.

A whine in the southern sky drew our attention upward. A Grumman fighter was in a spin. Its death throes rose to a deafening crescendo. Then it crashed. It was discovered later that it was Lt Herring, one of Maj Payne's boys who had been aboard the *Wasp* the night before. Evidently, the plane's oxygen equipment had not been functioning properly. The plane must have been at 20,000 feet before it began its fatal dive.

Another plane appeared in the sky. Its pilot was wounded, shot in the leg by a Zero fighter. He managed to land all right, and the ground crew helped him out of the cockpit and into the ambulance. A 20mm shell had done its damage.

No enemy planes dropped bombs. They were all Zero fighters. Two of these tried to make landings in a field adjacent to the airstrip. Captain John L. Smith was credited with having strafed them until they burst into flames.

From a higher altitude came another Grumman fighter with engine trouble. It circled around and around as it lost altitude. At a thousand feet, a 360-

degree turn was not feasible, and the pilot was killed when he crashed on the edge of the field. His name was Wildman. Erroneous identification among the circle of pilots indicated it was Weiland. I was quick to refute that claim.

From the Pagoda atop a barren hill, the white flag was raised—an all-clear signal. The planes returned to the field one by one. In the foray five Japanese Zeros had been shot down.

Darrell Irwin, Stan Nicolay, and I got together and decided to return to Henderson Field. About halfway there a jeepload of pilots came spinning back toward us—another air raid! So, back we went to the planes. This time my plane wasn't refueled, as the gas truck had sought out the nearest refuge, leaving many other planes grounded. I got into the Grumman anyway and taxied it back near a hummock for concealment purposes—to eliminate the threat of it being a target. I felt a loyalty toward that old bird.

Immediately, Darrell Irwin acquired a jeep, and we drove to the safety of the beach a short distance away. Many of the pilots were already there with radio equipment and earphones. Over this came the report of the distance of the enemy bombers by radar—42 miles, 30 miles—then a long pause. Soon we felt the explosion of bombs a safe enough distance away, but there was still a simultaneous dive for the trenches. We couldn't see the aerial activity for the palm trees, but we could hear the zooming and chattering of machine guns far above.

Once again the raiders were repelled, and we waited for the return of our planes. Some were riddled, but none was lost. On the other hand, four twin-engine Betty bombers and three Zeros were shot down. Once again everyone assumed the all-clear and viewed the situation with more or less casual apprehension.

If trends in Japanese operations proved correct, a relative calm could be expected later in the afternoon. Eight to ten pilots, including Stan Nicolay and me, got aboard a jeep to go down to the Lunga River for a swim, to wash away the grime of a hectic day. The jeep followed a winding path among rows of coconut trees. Then, like a flash of lightning, two Japanese Zeros on floats came roaring right over us at treetop level. The rising sun emblem was plainly visible on the side of the fuselage. The staccato of their machine guns was deafening.

The jump from the jeep was flat and bruising. I hugged a palm tree. Every bullet had my name on it! The two Zeros came out of their run, made another turn, and returned to strafe the field. It was over almost as quickly as it started.

It seemed to me that the old-timers had become impervious to the effects of this daily routine. Everyone rose from the ground, shook himself, got back aboard the jeep, and proceeded to the river.

As we dove into the water, a Marine SBD dive-bomber was entering the landing pattern to the west, wheels down, flaps down. Only an instant later did we detect the same two Zeros on floats closing in rapidly on the dive-bomber. This was happening right in front of our eyes. The unsuspecting crew of the dive-bomber was completely helpless. They were shot down, and the much-too-late antiaircraft batteries fired after the fleeing Zeros.

The Marine contingent that had flown the planes off the *Wasp* had completed the mission. The original plan had called for us to board an R4D for return to Espiritu Santo. Events of the day precluded any such immediate return, but a schedule had been set for takeoff at dusk. We stowed our flight gear aboard the big plane but, suddenly, the plans were altered. At the Pagoda, which served as the operations center, it was learned that the plane would not take off until 0300. Something ominous was going on. This was my first day in combat, but I was beginning to get war-weary already.

Is it always like this? I wondered.

But there was more to come—much more!

* * *

On the slope of the hill not far from the Pagoda, each officer picked for himself a slit trench in which to sleep. The evening was growing late. On a Japanese woven mat, I lay back, smoked a couple of cigarettes, and then tried to sleep. I had nearly dozed off when the shelling began.

Remnants of a Japanese force had regrouped and were coming down from the foothills to attack the field. They had broken through at a point along our lines just a few miles away, and they were now on the edge of the airfield. The artillery batteries opened fire and shattered the quiet atmosphere; Then the .50-caliber machine guns from every arc of the perimeter opened fire. The skies overhead were brilliant with tracers and flares, and the pounding was deafening.

I lay in the foxhole with my .45 at the ready. Tracers from Japanese gunfire enveloped us. Bullets sped over our heads, sounding like the faint squeak of a gopher. In the distance the sound came back much like an ignited string of firecrackers. The staccato of Japanese guns raked the air, then the response by our lower, heavier-sounding .50s. Generally, the opposition appeared silenced but, from another quarter, came repetition of the same thing.

The firing and explosions continued ceaselessly through the night. We could hear the gunners from the artillery batteries giving commands. Then came the roar of the 75mm and 105mm howitzers echoing and reverberating through the trees like the deep, hollow sound of a kettle drum. Seconds later, the still louder and deeper sounds came back as the shells impacted and exploded.

The 0300 takeoff by the R4D was completely out of the question. At one point I decided to crawl over to the blacked-out Pagoda for information. Suddenly, a flare illuminated the airfield. I lay there frozen in the open until the flare extinguished itself, and then retreated back to the slit trench.

When the half-light of dawn finally came, we pilots assembled to survey the situation. Japanese snipers were only a few hundred yards away, and, occasionally, the squeak of a bullet could be heard as it sped over our heads. A report came that two Marine battalions had encircled and were exterminating the Japanese force.

Just as the sun broke through the horizon, the air raid siren howled, and the Grumman fighters took off. They returned shortly, having reported that they had shot down two Zeros on floats that were attempting another strafing run.

A 0700 departure was scheduled, but the Japanese snipers were becoming more aggressive. After a couple of bullets dug up the turf near us, we huddled behind a 6-foot crate near the R4D. Once aboard, we took off from Guadalcanal, probably with a hail of bullets behind us. The plane set down at Espiritu Santo at 1200.

It wasn't until some time later that I learned I was involved in the biggest battle of the Guadalcanal campaign—"Bloody Ridge." It was the second attempt of the Japanese army to recapture Henderson Field. The Japanese force amounted to six thousand infantrymen. The thrust was to be a rugged approach from the jungle directly at the airfield.

A month earlier, after the battle for Tulagi, MajGen Vandegrift desperately needed additional infantry reinforcements on Guadalcanal. The 1st Raiders, the 1st Parachute Battalion, and the 2d Battalion, 5th Marines, were promptly transferred to Guadalcanal from Tulagi. Lieutenant Colonel Merritt "Red Mike" Edson and his Raiders, however, had been sent elsewhere on scouting missions involving Savo Island and destruction of Japanese supply bases. But now Edson was about to take up position in the expected attack area—on the slopes of "the ridge." He would be in command of both the 1st Raider and the 1st Parachute battalions.

The first Japanese attack came at 2100 that night with two thousand fanatical men, enough, according to their intelligence, to take the airfield. But they were mowed down. They came again and again, but were thrown back. All this was in coordination with shelling by ships at night and aircraft bombing by day. By early morning of the twelfth, it was obvious the attack had failed. This meant regrouping for an even bigger onslaught by a force of three thousand the next night. But Edson, reinforced by the 2d Battalion, 5th Marines, repelled the even greater enemy force. It was a fierce, all-night hand-to-hand encounter. By dawn, the Japanese force withered and withdrew with several hundred dead and wounded. On the following night, attempts to outflank the Marines were thwarted once again. The Battle of Bloody Ridge was over, and LtCol Edson received the Medal of Honor.

CHAPTER 5

The Waiting Game and Listening Watch

In early October 1942, a new coral airstrip was being completed about eleven miles up the line at Turtle Bay. This would be the new area of operations for the squadron. The Seabees had cut a swath through the coconut plantation right to the edge of Turtle Bay and paved it with crushed white coral. The move was made and camp set up on a point of land just a few feet from the seashore.

It was at about this time that I received the belated news of my promotion to captain. The time element between Headquarters, Washington, D.C., and the forward area made it about two months late, but that didn't seem to affect the elation I experienced. This meant that I was now ranking officer next to Captains Yeaman, Campbell, and Longley in the squadron. But I really never was the rank-conscious type. Lieutenant George S. Kobler was to underscore that attitude when he said, "Ho, ho, ho, you'll never be a captain to me. You'll just be the same good ol' Pat Weiland." Needless to say, what superiority complex I may have had dropped a few notches. My first captain's bars were forged out of two silver fifty-cent pieces by a PX steward.

Later in October, things started to heat up again. Lieutenant Colonel Joe Bauer, commanding officer of VMF-212 from Efate, came through with his outfit on the way to Guadalcanal. It was the same with Joe Foss, another friend from the Pensacola days. Then, suddenly, Capt Soupie Campbell, Lts Doc Livingston, Herb Peters, and Mike Yunck, and Sgt Andy Anderson got orders to proceed to the combat zone.

Heroic stories began to trickle back—also heartfelt losses. Joe Foss became the top ace of the war with twenty-six planes to his credit. Likable Joe Bauer had tallied up ten enemy aircraft, but Bauer became a fatality, failing to return after an air raid. Our own Andy Anderson was shot down behind enemy lines on his third hop and presumed lost. Jack Conger and many others became aces in short order while others, whose fate was not destined for such glory, went down gallantly and heroically. Our other four squadronmates fared particularly well. Doc Livingston and Herb Peters were credited with having bombed and sunk a Japanese destroyer. Soupie Campbell shot down three Zeros, and Herb Peters was credited with four and a half.

We were always eager for news of the Guadalcanal campaign. Trickle-down information was usually sketchy and unreliable. It was sometimes months, even years, later that history provided us with the real facts. But, eventually, we learned what was really going on. The Japanese were determined to recapture Henderson Field, and they came close many times. For instance, in the latter days of August, about eight Japanese destroyers made successful night runs to Guadalcanal to land thousands of troops. Submarines had also off-loaded troops and supplies—all under cover of darkness.

In early October the U.S. Army 164th Infantry Regiment was sent to the island to reinforce the hard-pressed 1st Marine Division. The Marines mounted an offensive to prevent the Japanese from establishing artillery positions that could bombard Henderson Field. On October 8 several Japanese cruisers and destroyers shelled Henderson Field while eight of their transport ships simultaneously disembarked troops and equipment.

Two days later a U.S. Navy task force intercepted a Japanese naval squadron en route to bombard Henderson Field. Our task force sank a cruiser and a destroyer and crippled two other cruisers.

These were crucial times at Guadalcanal. On October 15, a well-planned coordinated attack by two Japanese cruisers, bomber aircraft, and long-range howitzers knocked out Henderson Field and the new fighter airstrip No. 1. Most of the Cactus Air Force was destroyed, too. The shelling continued for three days, blowing up ammunition and gasoline dumps.

Resupply of aircraft was effected by dive-bombers and fighters flying in from Espiritu Santo. The gasoline supply was critical. It was only by the superhuman efforts of all personnel that the runways were repaired and gasoline salvaged from destroyed aircraft. R4D cargo flights and destroyers also helped alleviate the gasoline situation. But the Cactus Air Force had dwindled to only thirty-four operational aircraft by this point.

It was also on this day, October 15, that a Japanese convoy of six ships unloaded five thousand troops and their supplies in broad daylight only 10 miles from the American beachhead.

As Brigadier General Roy Stanley Geiger's aide and personal pilot, Maj Jack Cram flew a PBY-5, a Consolidated Catalina flying boat. He devised a scheme to hang two torpedoes under the wings of the Catalina. It was purely a jury-rigged affair, as Jack had no experience in torpedo tactics whatsoever. I watched this hanging operation on Espiritu Santo just before he took off for Guadalcanal. Jack got permission to make two twin torpedo runs on that six-ship convoy landing troops on October 15.

He made his run in the lumbering old Catalina and scored a hit on one of the three passenger-cargo ships, which burned all day. The Zeros pounced on him but, despite the bullet holes, he made it back to fighter field No. 1.

Intelligence indicated that a battle was looming both on land and sea for the seizure of Guadalcanal by the Japanese. A fleet of four carriers and other units were moving into position for this decisive battle.

Vice Admiral William Halsey's task force included only one carrier, the *Hornet*. At the last minute, another task force, with the carrier *Enterprise*, joined up.

Early on the morning of October 26, the Battle of the Santa Cruz Islands began. Three successive enemy air attacks dropped bombs and torpedoes on the *Hornet*, dealing her a mortal blow. All efforts to save her were to no avail. Procedures for abandoning ship were under way. She was taken under tow temporarily, but a Japanese pilot dropped a final bomb on her flight deck, and the ship was enveloped by fire, so the tow was cut loose. To prevent her from falling into enemy hands, our own destroyers attempted to sink her. This failed even though she was burning from stem to stern. The Japanese were closing in, and she was finally sunk by torpedoes from Japanese destroyers.

The *Enterprise* was damaged by two bomb hits. Others of our fleet suffered major damage, and only one Japanese ship was sunk. *Hornet* pilots seriously damaged the huge carrier *Shikoku*, however, and it would be months before she again became operational. The Japanese fleet withdrew, postponing the big push to recapture Guadalcanal.

In preparation for the big push, air attacks on Henderson Field had accelerated. Combat and operational accidents had taken their toll, and the Cactus Air Force, under the command of Gen Geiger, now had only thirty operational aircraft remaining to confront the Japanese.

The U.S. Army Air Force was hard-pressed by Gen Douglas MacArthur to lend a hand to Gen Geiger's Cactus Air Force at Guadalcanal. We watched increments of the 67th Pursuit squadron out of Brisbane, Australia, stage through Espiritu Santo on August 22, 1942, with the first five Bell P-400 Airacobras. This was followed shortly by the 68th Pursuit squadron with P-39 Airacobras. Then the first eight of twenty-five Lockheed P-38 Lightnings came through on November 12, part of the 339th Fighter Squadron. This was followed up immediately by Curtiss P-40s.

Once again in November, a small group of Airacobras of the 67th Pursuit Squadron set down at Espiritu Santo and stayed overnight. I became acquainted with one of their pilots, a Lt Hansen, and we engaged in a lively conversation about airplanes. The conversation grew serious as we conspired to swap airplanes the following day. Secretly, I would fly his Airacobra and, in turn, he would fly my Grumman Wildcat.

The next morning I taxied the Airacobra down the coral strip into takeoff position. I gave it the gun, and it started tearing down the runway. It was only natural to ease the stick forward to lift the tail. It was beginning to trot to the left toward the palm trees. Hell! This plane had a tricycle landing gear—the tail was already up. When I eased back on the stick, it fairly leaped into the air.

This was a beautiful little airplane with a cockpit so compact that it fit me to a tee. This Bell P-39 had 1,150 horsepower, with its liquid-cooled, V-12 Allison engine placed aft of the pilot's seat. The propeller driveshaft ran forward under the pilot's seat to the nose. In the nose cone, a 20mm cannon was mounted in the propeller shaft.

The plane was highly maneuverable and, with its engine placement aft, it afforded unobstructed visibility. I came in for a landing, and the roll-out was fine.

Then it was Lieutenant Hansen's turn. It worried me somewhat as those Army Air Corps pilots had the reputation of landing hot and long. I had cautioned him about this the night before; the airstrip wasn't all that big. I had also cautioned him about it on the takeoff.

"Be sure to keep your eyes glued on the horizon. The instant the nose moves past the line of sight, correct immediately."

Because the wheels of the Wildcat's retractable landing gear— unlike most planes—were so close together, this caused an instability that ended up in a ground loop. Many pilots checking out in the Grumman learned the hard way, which resulted in bent wingtips and propellers.

I observed Hansen's takeoff and it was near perfect. Then came the landing. On the approach he was slow and dragging it in. He landed in the sand among the tree stumps, just before the lip of the runway. I cringed at the prospect of a court-martial; but the Grumman missed the stumps and bounced up on the runway, and his roll-out was okay. What a sweat!

The Airacobras left the next day for Guadalcanal. Three days later, Lieutenant Hansen was killed.

*   *   *

Those were exciting times on Guadalcanal, yet the remainder of VMO-251 waited, trained, and hoped to get a crack at the Japanese. It seemed that destiny was dictating that we sit it out for the duration on Santo.

But the orders came.

MARINE OBSERVATION SQUADRON TWO FIFTY-ONE
FIRST MARINE AIRCRAFT WING,
FLEET MARINE FORCE, IN THE FIELD

1 December 1942

From: The Commanding Officer
To: Maj Charles H. Hayes, U.S. Marine Corps
Subject: Orders to Temporary Aviation Duty

1. In accordance with verbal instructions from the Commanding General, First Marine Aircraft Wing, you will take charge of the below named officers and proceed by first available government transportation to Guadalcanal for temporary aviation duty:

> Captain Charles P. Weiland, USMCR
> 1st Lieutenant Blaine H. Baesler, USMCR
> 1st Lieutenant Kenneth J. Kirk, USMCR
> 1st Lieutenant George S. Kobler, USMCR
> 1st Lieutenant Joe H. McGlothlin, USMCR
> 1st Lieutenant Eldon H. Railsback, USMCR
> 1st Lieutenant Roy T. Spurlock, USMCR
> 2nd Lieutenant Harry F. Schwethelm, USMCR
> 2nd Lieutenant Thaddeus Wojick, USMCR
> MG Wendell P. Garton, USMC

2. Upon arrival at Guadalcanal you will report with your detail to the senior First Marine Aircraft Wing officer present.

3. Flight orders for personnel are continued in force for this duty.

Charles H. Hayes

It is to be noted that the above set of orders were actually postwritten. The verbal orders received on November 30—and verbal orders alone—are what set the pace and energized this small contingent of VMO-251 pilots into a frenzy of action. Early the next morning, we found ourselves winging our way in an

R4D-1 (DC-3) on the five-hour trip to Guadalcanal. The written orders, as defined above, were received weeks later. In fact, written orders in or out of Guadalcanal did not become routine until after the first of the year 1943. In the meantime, checking into the Cactus Air Force at Guadalcanal was merely a handshake with the appropriate wing staff officer.

CHAPTER 6

Hell on Earth—Episode II

How can one describe activities in a combat zone? Days that alternate between mud and dust; suffocating heat and pesky mosquitoes; and daily flight operations with fear of the outcome were all part of the routine. The pressures, tensions, and pent-up emotions under adverse conditions were the order of the day—a kaleidoscope of emotions run amok. Funny little happenings during the daily routine, which under normal conditions would evoke only a grin or perhaps a chuckle, would turn into hilarious events. Psychologically—and in retrospect—I suppose these were sanity-saving devices. Daily combat air patrols, nightly enemy bombings, and the tormenting wait for a scramble at the ready tent were constant.

The fury of battle had lessened somewhat by the time we reached Cactus. Even though the Japanese were reinforcing their troops by submarine and other means, the 1st Marine Division had pushed them back farther and farther into the jungle. The enemy air raids were not as frequent as before, but there was always enough activity to keep one edgy.

The Slot was now a well-known term to all our people—in the air and on the ground as well as on the sea. To those in the southern Solomons, it was a direction toward the northwest whence the Japanese threat would come. A wary eye and a discerning ear were already posted to check those enemy forces emanating from Rabaul and Truk. But by either sea or air, the enemy seemed committed to the flow of the Solomon Islands chain in a southeast direction in an effort to reinforce their beleaguered troops, deposit their goods, and retake Henderson Field. Like the bombers and fighters, they came from right down "the Slot."

It was interesting to learn of the plight of our squadronmate Lt Mike Yunck, who had been ordered to Guadalcanal a little earlier than the rest of us and had become involved in the following incident.

It was toward the end of November, and it was Mike's first mission. The attack was to be on Rekata Bay—up the Slot—where the Japanese had amassed troop concentrations of approximately a thousand men as well anti-aircraft batteries.

Mike Yunck had made a strafing run with all six .50-caliber machine guns blazing. Big, black puffs of AA fire saturated the skies. The Grumman was hit, but not enough to immediately put it out of commission. Mike pulled out of the strafing run and tried to gain altitude, but one of the bursts had hit his oil line. Slowly, the plane settled as it lost rpm. Mike was heading south above the islands when the engine froze, and he had to make a water landing.

Many days later Mike was recovered, and we gleaned the exciting details of his story. He said that after the water landing, he looked at the altimeter and it read 25 feet below sea level. He gurgled to the surface and swam the 200 yards to a small islet near where his plane went down. There were apparently no inhabitants, and he was hungry, so he contented himself with wild bananas. He swam back to the submerged aircraft and dove for the rubber life raft. He also cut the bureau number off the rudder section of the plane as a souvenir.

Contemplating his next move, Mike ensconced himself upon a rock. With an eye toward where the coastline of Santa Isabel intercepted the horizon, he set course in the life raft. A rubber life raft, like a barrel, is hard to negotiate in a straight course. The first, second, and third days passed—and still no sign of life. On the fourth day, he noticed smoke threading slowly from a jungle hummock. Mike was suspicious—could be Japanese. He hid himself in the bushes, waiting for something to develop. Shortly, some natives appeared in a dugout canoe. They seemed friendly, so Mike attracted their attention, sign language being the only recourse for communication. He found himself en route to their village, where he was led to their chief.

In highly excited gestures, Mike proceeded to demonstrate his status. He jumped up and down and waved his arms.

"See, me bird man—me Jap-killer—me need help—me need go back—Guadalcanal!"

The chief sat stern and silent, and Mike had reached the point of futility.

Then the chief rose, smiled, and he said in perfect English, "Yes, yes, I understand very well. We will make immediate arrangements for your return to Guadalcanal. Incidentally, I went to medical school in Suva."

Mike's mouth was agape. He was awestruck and stared wide-eyed at this remarkable species of intelligentsia. The chief was missionary-educated and had gone to the medical school in the Fijis.

The next day the chief ordered a dugout canoe with husky paddlers to take Mike to the coast watcher near Rekata Bay. They traveled swiftly and covered as much distance in a half day as Mike did in the four days he was adrift in the rubber life raft. The coast watcher took Mike into hiding and, with his portable short-wave radio, sent a dispatch to headquarters indicating the safety of "Mad Mike."

(The various coast watchers were indispensable to American security. They were generally men long familiar with the islands. They had lived previously on these islands as plantation owners and were of Australian, French, or English descent. They dotted points along the Solomon Islands, watched Japanese movements, and relayed pertinent information by shortwave radio. They were always one jump ahead of enemy bloodhounds, which constantly harassed them. On one occasion a coast watcher sent a dispatch to thank head-quarters for the dive-bomber pilot who had made a direct hit on a kennel of bloodhounds—bloodhounds that had been trailing him all week! Indeed, they were essential keys to vaults of intelligence supplied to our forces' security.)

But, getting back to Lieutenant Mike Yunck, a week had passed since Mike's association with the coast watcher. During that time he lived off the fat of the land, eating wild fowl and fruit. To the natives he was something of a wonder, but life among the silver-glinted palms that fringed deep, azure pools was getting monotonous. Mike sent a dispatch to the commanding general, 1st Marine Air Wing, stating: "Request your advisability on my building a boat and returning to Guadalcanal." No answer was received.

Eventually, a large dugout canoe with burly oarsmen transported Mike the distance from Santa Isabel Island to Tulagi, where a PT boat delivered him to Guadalcanal.

After this ordeal Mike could have been evacuated to the rear area, but he was bent on getting at least one Japanese Zero. So, on December 3, when he lead a flight of Grummans on an escort mission to intercept eleven Japanese destroyers coming down the Slot, he shot down three Japanese float biplanes.

Mike came home happy, everybody else was happy, and the next day he left Guadalcanal for a rest.

The days that followed became more and more tedious. No Tojo—day after day, except at night. The continuous patrols were becoming boring and the scrambles disconcerting, as the bogeys always turned out to be our own planes. On the night of December 7, however, Tojo sent down seven more destroyers at the same time and place as before. (Hideki Tojo, leader of the upper hierarchy of warlords in Tokyo, was often a symbolic reference to the threat that emanat-ed from the Japanese-controlled areas to the north.) To intercept them we flew out at dusk. The balance was in our favor, but our greatest loss was that of Maj Joe Sailer, commanding officer of the dive-bombing squadron, who lost his life.

December 8, 1942, marked the beginning of the second year of the war with Japan. This occasion would have been significant to the squadronmates of VMO-251 had not an overriding event of a personal nature occurred: the loss of Lt George Kobler.

Communications and intelligence can be decisive in winning or losing battles, but sometimes things go awry. Channels of communication can be misconstrued or confused. This was obviously what happened the night of the anniversary of Pearl Harbor, when word was received of another Japanese task force steaming down the Slot – the usual route from the New Georgia group southeasterly to Guadalcanal.

My flight was alerted in the early-morning hours. It had been a night of bad weather as thunderstorms had poured rain down on the short strip and left it riddled with water-filled potholes. Because the strip had recently been hewn out of a coconut plantation, there was still no provision for installation of navigational or instrument aids; the runway lights consisted of beer bottles placed at intervals on each side of the strip and lighted with flares.

Just before 0430 I taxied out with my flight of four. Kobler was tail-end Charlie—wingman in the second section. It really was an instrument takeoff, even though the rain had subsided. The cloud scud remained low, and visibility was nil. I poured the throttle to the Wildcat, and it moved slowly down the muddy runway. I eased the stick forward and the tail came up; flying speed was almost attained. But then the plane hit a pothole and lurched and staggered. I popped the flaps to get everything I could out of the Grumman. The palm trees were dead ahead in the darkness, and there wasn't much runway left. Slowly, the plane left the ground and I made a gentle arc to starboard. It was pitch black, and concentration was on "needle/ball and airspeed"—instruments.

The takeoff accomplished, I concentrated on rendezvous. As I sharpened the gentle turn to starboard, my peripheral vision picked up the navigational lights of two other planes cutting inside the circle—a good rendezvous. But then, out of the rearview mirror at the top of the canopy, I saw a white light. My first thought was Kobler's plane. The red diffuser must have fallen off the left wing and now the light being emitted was white.

I gained altitude and eased throttle so the other planes could join up. I made a port turn out to sea, charged the six .50s, and let go with a short burst to test the guns. The other planes widened their pattern and did likewise. The tracers split the air in the darkness. The fourth plane had not joined up. We continued the turn to a northwesterly heading, still climbing. Once abeam of the runway, I saw the white light again. It appeared on the ground.

While the dive-bombers were taking off from another field, we leveled off at 12,000 feet. We stayed in contact with Cactus, awaiting orders to switch frequencies, but Cactus radio was ominously quiet. An hour went by and then I heard my call sign and, with it, "Abort mission. Return to base. Repeat. Abort mission. Return to base."

I executed a 180-degree turn and maintained altitude back to base. Dawn was breaking now, and we soon found ourselves about to enter the traffic pattern. The other flights had been recalled earlier and were already in the traffic pattern.

The sun was just above the horizon and the airstrip was highly visible in the brightness. About halfway down the runway was a pall of black smoke billowing upward and outward. Realization struck: the white light in the rearview mirror, the absence of second-section wingman George Kobler. It all added up—a collision on takeoff with planes parked on the left-hand side of the runway.

Because the wind was listless and had shifted somewhat, we landed opposite the direction of takeoff. At the end of the roll-out, I passed the wreckage on my right side. There lay the smoking wreckage of George's plane and the one with which he had collided. The remains of the cockpit were clearly visible, and so was the hipbone of the charred remains of a crewman trapped inside.

The pilots stood outside the operations tent. Nothing was said, but it was obvious by their troubled expressions that an explanation was necessary. Had the situation really required those drastic measures in view of questionable communications, inadequate field lighting, and sodden runways? It was only conjecture that Kobler's plane had taken off diagonally because of the lights, or because of striking a pothole, but the fact remained – there were three casualties, all dead.

It was a sad day for the squadron.

War was like that. It offered no conveniences and contributed only to heartfelt losses. It was especially so with fellows one had daily nudged elbows with for months on end. So today it was Lt Kobler. In August it had been Lts Kirby and Schuessler, and in October, Sgt Anderson, the Naval Aviation Pilot. And there would be more. There was nothing romantic about war.

*   *   *

One day our reconnaissance planes uncovered a carefully concealed construction job that the Japanese were undertaking. It was an airstrip being built under the camouflage of palm groves at Lambete. This was farther up the Solomon chain, about 189 miles away, in the New Georgia group. It was a crafty operation. Two days later, observation indicated that the palm trees and stumps had been removed and replaced by fill. A full-fledged airstrip was operational.

This news stirred the adrenaline in all the pilots. The point of land where the airstrip reached the water's edge was called Munda Point. It was obvious that missions to Munda would be come a daily routine, and soon B-17 bombing formations headed for Munda at regular intervals. Marine fighters escorted dive-bombers, which blasted the runway and installations. The Japanese repaired the damage overnight. Reports flashed back that camouflaged Zeros were seen in hidden revetments. Perhaps the Japanese would stage a last-ditch comeback after all.

It was on just such a mission, late on the afternoon of December 23, 1942, that Major Don Yost's and Lt Pete McGlothlin's flights flushed the first Zeros. Ten Zeros were in the air at the time, and they became prey for the mighty Grumman Wildcats. In the foray there were triumphs and losses. Five Zeros were shot down; Yost got two, and McGlothlin, Irwin Carter, and Benjamin Wisner got one each. But we lost two of our own planes.

During the dogfight, Lt Blaine Baesler's plane was shot up, but a Grumman is tough, and it served only to make it air-conditioned. Dave Andre, who was a rival fraternity brother, went down. His engine was shot up, but he made a safe water landing near a small island that was not under Japanese control. The coast watcher and friendly natives rescued him.

When back from the mission, the boys told a real thriller, and the rest of us just sat back and looked envious. When asked for a statement, McGlothlin modestly replied, "I just seen my duty and so I do'd it."

Other comments included, "Every way the wind hits a Grumman, it strikes it at right angles" and, as Garton remarked, "I've never seen an airplane so reluctant to fly!"

The next day was Christmas Eve. Early in the morning, Major Don Yost, who obviously made the most out of "rank has its privileges," took off again with his flight on a mission to Munda Point. Our own Ken Kirk was his wingman. During the climb Yost discovered that the wing-tank release ring had fallen down to the bottom of the cockpit. Unbuckling his safety belt, he squirmed down to reach the ring, holding the stick with his left hand and flying by instruments. Kirk glanced over to the apparently unoccupied cockpit and decided he was hallucinating. Much to his relief, Yost's ghost appeared, and the flight continued to Munda.

Douglas SBD dive-bombers also participated in this flight. The cover consisted of Grummans flying at 10,000 feet, P-39 Airacobras at 15,000 feet, and Lockheed P-38 Lightnings at 20,000 feet.

It turned out to be a field day. They caught the Zeros just taking off. Don Yost shot down four. Kirk got three, as did the other boys. The Airacobras shot down several, and even the dive-bombers got two in the air and four on the ground. The remarkable score was twenty-seven Zeros! This time all our planes returned safely.

The Japanese were now resupplying their new base with antiaircraft guns brought in by barges and tankers at night. So in the days that followed, two or three missions per day would sally forth to strafe and blast them out.

*   *   *

Dawn broke on the twenty-seventh day of December 1942 with a little scud cloud in the sky but nothing really to worry about. The plan of the day showed me scheduled for a combat-air-patrol mission early that morning. I was also scheduled later that afternoon to lead a flight of sixteen Grumman Wildcat fighters on a mission to Munda Point. Needless to say, during the whole two-hour patrol, my mind was filled with all the contingencies of the mission. I was well prepped. I would use the same Grumman Wildcat, for it checked out with precision. The six .50-caliber machine guns also test-fired in accordance with standard operating procedures. I was well equipped for any eventuality.

Just prior to our 1500 takeoff, all sixteen Wildcats were strung along the taxiway leading to the runway. I began my takeoff run down the dusty runway precisely at 1500; the others following closely in a climbing left turn around the field to effect the rendezvous. We continued the climbing turn but leveled off at 12,000 feet, our assigned altitude. The P-38 Lightnings and the P-39 Airacobras had taken off earlier and were already at their assigned altitude of 20,000 feet top cover and 16,000 feet medium cover, respectively. The formation headed out to sea and spread out to test the machine guns.

We began the long overwater flight of 189 miles to Lambete, one of the islands in the New Georgia group where Munda Point and the new Japanese airstrip was located. This large flight was droning northwestward now without a falter. I couldn't help but marvel at our engineering and ordnance crews, who were responsible for keeping these machines squared away and always on the go. All the Marine pilots in this flight were tried and true as well, and of course they were a mix of the Cactus Air Force. In other words, all the pilots and planes were pooled, but they consisted mostly of VMF-121 pilots who had just arrived three days before Christmas. These new arrivals were not green pilots, however; they were on their second tour at Guadalcanal, having tallied up a spectacular record between October 13 and November 15 of 110 Japanese planes. In my immediate formation, Lieutenant Harold "Fateye" Gardner was wingman. Lieutenant Roy Spurlock was leading my second section, and his wingman was Lt Alexander "Sandy" Hearn. Only Spurlock and I were members of VMO-251.

It seemed an interminable length of time en route, but I'm sure it was less than two hours before I sighted the Japanese airstrip at Munda Point. I began a wide arc to port and noticed several shiny objects just below and in the not-too-far distance. I was about to caution the flight about barrage balloons when suddenly we were enveloped by big black puffs of antiaircraft fire. The black puffs seen earlier had been perceived as balloons because of the light shining though them with a silver glint. This illusion dramatically changed into a very real threat.

Just as we were about to push over into a strafing run, I saw three planes strung out in the distance, heading perpendicular to my line of flight. They were unmistakably Japanese Zeros. My wits sharpened a few degrees at this realization, and I instinctively pushed the throttle full forward, checked the rich mixture and rpm, and eased the stick forward just a hair for an intercept with the leader. This would give me a little bit of speed advantage. The six .50-caliber machine guns were now charged, and my finger was on the trigger. I doubt that the leader saw me first. Perhaps we saw each other at the same time. But I didn't have time to think about that now. The only thinking involved was that of flying the airplane, and this was mostly done by reflex action. Any other analysis of the situation would have to wait.

The Japanese leader seemed indecisive in his direction of flight at first, but then suddenly turned toward me. We were closing in microseconds, but I was able to fire a quick burst, which I realized immediately was too long in lead. He made a diving turn to the right. I stood the Grumman up on the left wing to follow him down, but decided not to get suckered into a situation like that, considering the maneuverability of his airplane. I was in a shallow dive in his direction when he abruptly came straight up in a veering turn; but then just as abrutly, he changed to a backing turn with a wingover to the left. By now I had cut across his circle and had the advantage. He had just set himself up in that left wingover. I was now in a wingover myself, about a hundred yards just inside and below his left side. My long burst penetrated the Zero at the most vital places. I was near vertical by now and fell off to the right. When I gained control, I spotted the Zero in an inverted spin. He was windmilling slowly downward and hit the water just off the end of the Japanese airstrip. When the geyser subsided, I studied the water for a moment in sober reflection.

I was completely oblivious to what was going on elsewhere in the air. It turned out that Roy Spurlock shot down the second Zero, and Hearn got the third. Lieutenant Gardner had been circling above, watching the show.

We regrouped, Gardner still with me, and Spurlock's section closed in behind. We were flushed with victory, and there was more to be had. We climbed for altitude and then pushed over on a strafing run on an installation near the middle of the runway. The formation spread out and then each plane raked the area, pumping thousands of rounds of those high-powered .50s into sensitive targets. The stalwart Grummans then pulled upward and outward in a gentle turn to the right. Coming about, I saw raging fires and smoke starting to billow high, which may have been the result of hitting either a gasoline dump or some camouflaged Zeros. This was not the time to find out for sure. We had to get out of the hot zone, our fuel and ammunition now very low. The flight joined up and headed for home. The afternoon was late, but we might just make it before dark.

About halfway home, I came to full realization of what had happened. God, that was for real! My legs began beating like trip-hammers against the floorboards. What in the world was going on? Was this the withdrawal phase of a psyched-up proficiency peak? Obviously, the adrenaline pump was also slowing down. So that's what combat is all about, I mused.

I thought about that Japanese pilot. This would be the beginning of an ongoing analysis of why things happened the way they did. Why did he set himself up like that? Why did he go into that steep dive and then zoom up into that undecided wingover? If he'd fallen off to the right instead of the left, maybe he would have gotten away with it. Didn't he know I was there? Had the sun blinded him? It was a proven fact that the Zero was much more maneuverable than the Grumman Wildcat. Perhaps the Zero pilot was overconfident in this knowledge. On the other hand, maybe Lady Luck was riding with me that day.

That night back at camp was a festive occasion. The combat maneuvers were rehashed over and over again. There were backslapping and guffaws, and the air was rife with jubilation. Eventually, it became obvious that we were boring our listeners. And so the night dragged on.

Lieutenant Gardner, my wingman on that memorable day, was not so fortunate a short time later. He was killed on a mission to Munda.

A few days later, my flight had patrol duty. Roy Spurlock was once again second-section leader. This was an uneventful three-hour hop, enduring the tortures of the jungle pack. Just before landing, we performed the usual loop in formation. Spurlock was the third plane to land. As he set down, the plane's wheels dug deep into a soft spot; the plane cartwheeled, flipped over on its back, and strewed wreckage along the runway. Spurlock emerged with only a few bruises and a cut cranium. The whole top of his head had to be bandaged by Dr. R. D. Little. The next day Spurlock found that piece of paper we claimed he had been looking for: the orders evacuating him to the rear area.

* * *

In the days that followed, we took turns flying missions to Rekata Bay, Munda Point, or Wickham Anchorage. At Rekata, planes strafed float Zeros hidden in coves, as well as antiaircraft batteries. At Munda pilots caught Japanese planes on the ground and set them afire while dive-bombers blasted more antiaircraft batteries. At Wickham Anchorage, we flew top cover while Airacobras strafed and bombed Japanese barges and tankers.

On one such mission I was returning from Munda down the Slot toward Guadalcanal. It was dusk. We closed in on the coast at an angle. I homed in on where I was positive the airfield was located. No lights. My heart sank. We made a wide orbit to port, out to sea, and tried it again. There was still a little light remaining in the western sky, but the jungle below was dark. As we traversed the coast again, the runway lights came on. Thank God! We all landed safely. It was discovered later that an impending enemy air raid had caused blackout conditions.

* * *

There were times of relative calm at Guadalcanal, which allowed some off-duty hours for many of us pilots. Normally, we would go back to the tent camp area overlooking Sailer Field to do chores such as laundry, working the jury-rigged shower, or writing letters. Sailer field was named for Maj Joe Sailer, commanding officer of VMSB-132, which commenced operations from Guadalcanal in the SBD Dauntless dive-bombers on November 1, 1942. Joe had built up an amazing reputation in a short time. On December 7, while on a mission 200 miles up the Slot to counter eleven incoming Japanese destroyers, he was hit by antiaircraft fire. He had been nursing his damaged plane back home when he was attacked by a Japanese float fighter, shot down, and killed. Thus Sailer Field was our monument to this famous hero.

The tent camp was located on a low ridge overlooking Sailer Field to the northeast. In a line down in front was a row of three refueling trucks and about six Airacobras; not far over were the parked Grummans and P-38s. Of course there was also enough time in off-hours to indulge in the usual bull sessions or airing of little annoyances. Some of the musings might include the girl back home, or scorn about the way things were run and who was running them. And then, if that wasn't enough to vent frustration, it could easily degenerate into the bashing of our own airplanes in a friendly sort of way.

The Grumman F4F Wildcat was always subject to many uncomplimentary remarks. Sharp barbs and satire were always in evidence. We reviled it. On the flight line, one of the pilots would look admiringly at an Army P-38.

"Look at that beautiful thing!" he'd say with unconcealed admiration. "It's sleek, it's clean, and it's deadly!"

Then, taking a glance over at a Grumman, he'd say disgustedly, "Yes, and look at that abortion."

Wendell Garton, with animation, demonstrated the prowess of the Airacobra. "At first sight of an Airacobra flying toward you, one observes a speck in the sky. "You say, 'Here it comes!' in anticipation. Only seconds later it comes streaking by.

"At the first sight of a Grumman flying toward you, one observes a speck in the sky. You say, 'Here it comes! [pause] Here it comes!' [a longer pause], then [in a fading voice], 'Oh, to hell with it!' "

Despite the indignities the Grumman suffered, it was a stubborn airplane in its determination to keep going. Unlike the Zero, the Grumman was a tough old bird and, in most cases, resisted the enemy efforts to shoot it down. The Zero was much more maneuverable than the Grumman but lacked its armor and armament. The Zero did not have puncture-proof gas tanks and so, once hit, would invariably go down in flames. The Grumman had a personality all its own. It was truly a friend and, deep in our hearts, we loved that grand old bird.

It was now January 1, 1943. My flight took off with the hopes of starting the New Year right. The rendezvous was effected along with Airacobras and P-38 Lightnings. Soon the flight was winging its way to Munda Point through sparkling clear and sunny skies. General Geiger told us this would be a fighter sweep—Zeros were to be encountered. We maintained a wary eye and a swivel head as we approached the Japanese base. The antiaircraft fire was intense, but there were no signs of Zeros. We made a third circuit around Munda and then swept around the north portion of the New Georgia group, looking for any sign of combat. None was found. It was an uneventful way to begin the New Year.

Two days later Zeros came into spotlight prominence once more. It turned out to be anything but a triumph for us. In fact, two of our pilots were lost: my Lambda Chi Alpha brother, Joe Crum, and Robert "Pete" Peterson. It was due to a bitter mistake in the planning of the mission. Coordination was lacking among the dive-bombers, Grummans, and Army pursuits right from the beginning; the rendezvous was never completely effected. When this weakly proportioned force reached Munda, twelve Zeros slashed at them from above. At no time could Irwin Carter's flight maneuver into an offensive position. Wounded and riddled, Irwin Carter and Jack Foeller escaped into the clouds and limped back to Sailer Field. Joe Crum and Pete Peterson failed to return.

Tragedy struck Irwin Carter's flight again the next day, when Irwin himself failed to return. They were poised as ship's cover for the task force proceeding to shell Munda Point. At dusk the flight secured the cover and started home. The weather was bad. That plus darkness is in itself one of flying's greatest hazards. Two planes returned and two didn't. Their fate? No one knows.

The U.S. cruisers and destroyers that shelled Munda on the night of January 5 evidently ripped it asunder, because our next mission was seemingly a routine flight. There was no activity—nor any sign of life.

Not so at Rekata Bay, however. During the dark nights of the month, the Japanese had infiltrated men and materiel to reinforce the small garrison there. One day a flight of Martin B-26 medium bombers flew low over the Japanese base. Heavy antiaircraft fire raked the air, and a bomber shuddered, pulled helplessly upward, then collapsed and fell into the bay. Two other B-26s were also severely hit. They limped back to Henderson Field, but the crew members of one bailed out, and the remaining bomber made a crash landing. It was an expensive day for the Army.

On the return of the task force from the shelling of Munda, flights once more assumed the role of fighter protection above the slow-moving ships. Each flight relieved another at four-hour intervals.

It was Greg Loesch's flight that caught the Japanese bombers and fighters attacking the ships. Banzai, what a day! In the maelstrom, the crews of six Japanese dive-bombers and one Zero were granted the supreme sacrifice. Later, I wondered if those Japanese pilots were so keen on their ancestral and emperor-god loyalty when it came face-to-face with death. I wondered if they remembered the inscription that was said to have hung above a certain head-quarters door: "Remember that death is lighter than a feather, but duty is heavier than a mountain." I wondered if they said, "Boy, if the hometown folks could only see me now!" I wondered—but I doubted it.

* * *

The morning of January 9 seemed to roll around early. We knew we were to go on a mission to Gizo Bay at 0630, but that was no particular reason why the jeep driver should rush into camp and breathlessly shout at the top of his lungs for Weiland's flight. I lunged out of bed—maybe we had overslept or perhaps they had set the schedule ahead. I met the jeep driver and he was grinning.

"Hurry up and pack," he said. "You're leaving Guadalcanal for Santo on the next transport!"

The reaction could have registered a reading on the Richter scale. This new twist was beyond belief. Those few words were an elixir that swept the boys into action. All other sleepers in the camp who didn't give a damn whether we left or not just fussed and cussed.

A truck pulled up, and it took only seconds before luggage, souvenirs, and pilots were aboard, winding our way down the "Little Burma Road" for the last time. We waved good-bye to the men and thumbed our noses at the airstrip and airplanes and Army camps and artillery batteries through which we passed. Jubilation was running rampant!

The transport plane rose higher and higher above Guadalcanal. It made a 180-degree turn and I got a good view of that godforsaken island from the port window. There it lay, half submerged, like a hippo bathing in the sun. My emotions were a mixture of anger and elation. I stared down at that seething hulk. I felt testy: You beast! You tried to get me, but you didn't!

I almost blurted it out.

1st Lieutenant Pat Weiland at Espiritu Santo. August 1942.

A Grumman F4F-3 Wildcat Fighter.

VMO-251 Grumman Wildcat on the flight line.

The officers of VMO-251 at Espiritu Santo. Summer of 1942.

TOP ROW (left to right) Lt George Kobler, Capt Pat Weiland, Capt Carl Longley, Capt Ralph Yeaman, Capt "Soupie" Campbell, Maj "Frog" Hayes, Capt John Collins, Capt Claude Welch, Doc Little, Doc Ray Wallenborn, Lt Doc Livingston. MIDDLE ROW (left to right) MTSgt Witt, GySgt Merle Davis, Lt Blaine Baseler, Lt Frank Platt, Lt Eldon Railsback, Lt Ken Kirk, Lt Harry Schwethelm, Lt Bob Straine, MTSgt Gilbert. BOTTOM ROW (left to right) Australian Coast Watcher, MTSgt Mussacio, Lt Ted Wojick, Lt Pete McGlothlin, Lt Herb Peters, Lt Roy Spurlock, Lt Tod Whitten, GySgt Wendell Garton, MG Pardee. NOT SHOWN: LtCol John Hart, 1stLt Michael Yunck, Doc Kalez, Capt J.P. Adams.

A VMO-251 Wildcat over the jungle.

A Marine Wildcat taking off for a mission
from Fighter-1 at Guadalcanal.

This photo of VMF-121 fighter pilots at Guadalcanal includes a sprinkling of eight VMO-251 who flew with them. Notice how tired everyone looks.

A Douglas SBD Dauntless dive-bomber.

A Mitsubishi A6M2 Zero, code-named Zeke. This captured Zero shows
an American star, somewhat washed out to reveal the Rising Sun insignia.

CHAPTER 7

Routine at Turtle Bay

In the familiar but primitive surroundings of Espiritu Santo, we eventually sank into a deep sense of complacency. There was no motivation to hurry or be constantly alert, but our long-pent-up tensions were slow to fade away.

It took a while for the tenacity of our stress to disappear completely. A case in point was the time "Pop" Flaherty and I were standing outside the mess tent beneath a coconut palm, deep in conversation. A coconut fell and hit the ground immediately behind us. Bombs! Simple reflex action caused us to jump and cower for an instant.

Reflecting back on those revelations in the combat area, I recall that emotions never really showed. They were ever present, but it was something subconscious, hidden under the guise of the job at hand.

* * *

After a sojourn to Sydney, Australia, we settled down to routine at Turtle Bay, and I became operations officer for the squadron. It was in early February 1943 when Greg "Pappy" Boyington drifted into my office. Greg and I were old friends from the pre–Pearl Harbor days in Pensacola. We both had been instructors there, he in primary trainers and I in instruments. At that time he had been conscripting pilots, both Navy and Marine, for the Flying Tigers. Slim Irwin and I were about to sign up, but the quota had already been filled. Greg went to China, made a hero out of himself, and then returned to the States. He was made a major and then shot back out to the South Pacific.

It was about this time when he walked into my office. It was good renewing the friendship. He needed flight time, so I looked at the flight board and saw that old Number 7 was available. Greg indicated that he was a little rusty and asked me to come out to refresh his memory. While he sat in the cockpit, I bantered with that old pro by pointing to "stick, rudder pedals, airspeed indicator, altimeter . . ."

He had taken off, tooled around for two hours, and then landed before I found out that he'd never flown this airplane before! Little did I realize that I had "checked him out" in the Grumman Wildcat.

Long, wearisome days passed with scarcely an eventful happening. VMO-251 had been torn apart. The majority of ground personnel were on

Guadalcanal; other remnants were in Headquarters and Service squadrons. We had previously sent our photographers on Army B-17 bombers to accurately assess damage on their bombing missions. Now we remaining pilots, much to our dismay, found ourselves thrust into a new fighter unit. It was hard to start over for it meant the same old routine—more training and then, undoubtedly, back to Guadalcanal. New casuals just out of the States had to be taught, and so we gritted our teeth and set the pace.

Stan Bailey, my old roommate at Pensacola, showed up one day. He was later dubbed "Captain Jerry Colonna" for his long, turned-up mustache. That pesky little Vermonter even got in my same outfit, same tent, and same flight. Stan was, indeed, a character.

Saint Valentine's Day sparked new zeal to our spirits when BriGen Ross Rowell announced that the whole of VMO-251 would very shortly return to the States. With more vigor and ardor than ever, we set forth on the training program of gunnery, strafing, formation tactics, dawn and dusk patrols, and night flying. It wasn't half bad.

Weeks passed quickly, and then we suddenly transferred into another squadron. More pilots needed training. The talk of going home was waning, and an ominous feeling of suspicion crept over us. Something snapped, something that killed the old spirit. Months passed. It was no joke now, trying our patience like this.

The last of the Grumman Wildcats were sent to Guadalcanal. Now came a newer, swifter, more sophisticated aircraft—the Vought F4U Corsair. It was sleek and beautiful with that inverted gull wing. Comparing the Wildcat to the Corsair was like comparing a Model T to a Cadillac.

News came out of a small town in Minnesota that Ted "One-Shot" Wojick was the proud father of Thaddeus, Jr. We had left the States exactly nine months earlier.

Mike Yunck, Blaine Baesler, and Ken Kirk transferred themselves into another squadron, relinquishing the hopes of ever going home. Sometime later, I discovered the reason for this sudden change of heart: Blaine had fallen hopelessly in love with Poppy, an exotic, rapturously beautiful brunette in Sydney, Australia. Blaine and I had met her at about the same time during the rest period there following our Guadalcanal tour. Once back in the battle zone, he insisted that his buddies Mike and Ken hang on for an extension in order to be part of the wedding party on a subsequent rest trip to Sydney. This event eventually took place.

Things were picking up at Turtle Bay. The first Coca-Colas arrived on Santo, and there was even talk of the USO eventually coming in. Instead of taking a jeep to Cape Esperance Bay to do business with the ships, we now used the remaining squadron SNJ-5 to fly the 11 miles to the bomber strip. Most of the time, two people rode piggyback in the rear cockpit. Also, we had one remaining Grumman biplane amphibian Duck, the other having been ditched in the ocean west of Santo sometime earlier. On one occasion, a pilot flew the Duck on the long trip to Sydney to pick up dozens of cartons of beer and booze. The officers' club tent was now in full operation. Things were really getting up-to-date.

* * *

On April 17, 1943, the news that we'd been waiting for finally arrived. It was like a thunderbolt out of the heavens: We had two hours to pack all personal gear and board the USS *Chandeleur*. The orders stated, "You will stand detached from your present duties and proceed to the United States."

Just like that—simple and quick. Only one who had been in the combat zone with yearning, longing hopes of getting back home again could fully understand the impact of that news.

Although the ship was fast and new and the staterooms modern and roomy, the voyage was excruciatingly long. The ship's officers were friendly, especially Dr. Gould, who was a most interesting companion. A short stop at Efate, in the southern New Hebrides, and one at Noumea, New Caledonia, were the only respites until Pearl Harbor.

The pleasure of the 24-hour stop in Hawaii was secondary only to that of getting home, and the most was made of that temporary sojourn! In the late afternoon, Dr. Gould, Doc Livingston, Pete McGlothlin, and I went to what might be termed a "swimfest"—the bar adjoined the hotel swimming pool. Then the next morning, through the generosity of a friend, we toured the island, saw the picturesque mountains and valleys, the upside-down falls, and the wind-torn precipice of the Pali, which dropped sheerly for hundreds of feet. We investigated Waikiki Beach and the beautiful Royal Hawaiian Hotel. We drove through Honolulu and then back to the ship for the last leg home.

Point Loma appeared darkly out of the fog. There it was—Stateside! We'd briefly reflect back to life in the jungle, where one lived like an animal—a tense and wary sort of life. But that was gone now. Ahead lay comfort at its best, and a long leave period to make the best of it. Stateside—that's for me! I didn't realize it before, but I would certainly appreciate it more in the future.

My mind was running rampant now. I could foresee the immediate future—a trip to the old homestead in South Dakota where I was born and raised. I visualized my mother greeting me with open arms; my father, Uncle Bill, my four younger sisters, and my little five-year-old brother—all waiting anxiously. Also there would be my next-younger brother, Dan, smiling and bronzed, now one of the key figures in operation of the farm. He would be looking forward to another challenge in wrestling—ready to topple me from the status of wrestling champion earned at the University of Miami. He could probably do it now, too, because of the daily rigors of farm life, giving him the advantage of endurance and stamina—unlike my recent routine.

I could visualize the river that meanders through the farm to the east, now full after the spring thaw and the hundreds of acres of corn and wheat now beginning to sprout through the rich, black loam. It would be nice to feel and smell the refreshing countryside with the Hereford cattle grazing the green pastures. Even the Percheron horses won't be objectionable to see as they once were, when it was my duty to feed and groom them and clean the horse barn.

Then it would be nice to see all the hometown folks in the little town of Ashton, which had grown up alongside the farm in the late 1800s. There would be Charlie McCrossen, who was the dealer for the International Harvester Implement Company; Billy Francis, the old-timer who cut everyone's hair at his barbershop; Otho Jones, who owned the drugstore; Jack Druley, who ran the post office; Herman Kragenbrink and Garret Bymers at the filling station; Mr. Perry at the grocery store; and many, many others. Yes, it's going to be good to get back home.

Point Loma grew more dominating now—like a watchdog peering out to sea. It gave no hint of the gaiety in the land that lay just beyond. I thought of the dreadful existence of the men still fighting the war. I remembered some of the boys who would never make it back.

But enough of that—bring on stateside! Bring on those favorite old haunts and those fond acquaintances. Hurry, too, for this respite may be just a calm before another storm.

CHAPTER 8

Strange Twists at Stateside

Fourteen of the original thirty VMO-251 officers arrived at the San Diego port on May 9, 1943. Our group reported in to Fleet Air West Coast, which in turn directed us to report to Service Group, Marine Corps Aviation Base, Kearney Mesa, California (now Miramar).

In the meantime we took advantage of a thirty-day leave period. Josie and I took the train via an indirect route to South Dakota to visit the folks at the old homestead. Then we boarded a plane to see her family in Roanoke Rapids, North Carolina. Finally, we took a side trip by air to Jacksonville, Florida, to see my uncle, Dr. Weiland. By now he had been recalled into the Navy at the naval air station there and was made captain, Medical Corps, USNR.

The return trip to San Diego by air? Impossible! Our only recourse was a coal-burning train, which we were convinced was left over from the Civil War and which exuded smoke and grime along the entire southern route.

Back at Kearney Mesa, I received orders to report in to MCAS El Toro, and almost immediately after our arrival there, on to MCAS El Centro.

El Centro was located about 80 miles east of San Diego. It lay in the Imperial Valley on a barren desert that was approximately 100 feet below sea level. It had a hot, sticky climate—and, I'm sure, every insect known to man. Scorpions overran the place, as did the crickets, which at certain seasons of the year blackened the facades of buildings under the canopied archways covering the sidewalks downtown.

A small cadre of seasoned pilots assembled at El Centro to train new pilots in gunnery, aerobatics, bombing, strafing, and night flying in Grumman Wildcats. Of the original VMO-251 members, only Capt Joe "Pete" McGlothlin, Lt Robert "Doc" Livingston, and I reported in to Maj Pete Haines, commanding officer of VMO-155. To the east of El Centro lay the Chocolate Mountains, where our bombing and gunnery ranges were. Here we taught the fledgling pilots to hone their skills in practice, which was a seven-day-per-week work regimen.

It was over the Chocolate Mountains one day that I almost met my demise. As flight leader, I peeled over and headed straight down on a bombing run to the target. I made a pretty hard pullout and blacked out. Actually, it was a little bit more than a blackout—I was only semiconscious. As I slowly regained my senses, I found the plane flying straight and level just above the terrain. My head was spinning; the whole world was going around and around.

I headed back to the field and landed with difficulty, taxiing up to the flight line and cutting the engine. The crew chief knew something was wrong the minute he saw me. I needed help getting out of the cockpit. An ambulance was called, and away I went to the hospital. It was my first attack of malaria.

To combat malaria overseas, the doctors had prescribed quinine for all hands. Then in August 1942, a new little pill called atabrine came out, and we switched to that medication. I took those little yellow pills religiously throughout the whole tour. When I left the South Pacific, there seemed no need to take the medicine any longer. Apparently, I had been carrying the disease all this time and didn't know it.

The impact of malaria was a double whammy. I alternated between bone-chilling cold and severe night sweats. Even though it was summertime on that hot desert, no amount of blankets could keep me warm. I boiled and sweated deliriously. This alternated day and night until a few days later, after intense medication, when the attacks gradually subsided. But just like clockwork, it came back every other month. Each successive attack was less horrible than the one before. Gradually, the attacks tapered off completely, but it took years.

Lieutenant "Doc" Livingston was one of our leading instructor pilots. It was during one of those bombing runs over the Chocolate Mountains that he plowed into a mountain and was killed. The board of inquiry decided it was pilot error, but deep in my own mind I often wondered whether he might have suffered a malarial attack similar to mine.

On September 24, 1943, I was ordered back to MCAS El Toro, California, to assume command of Fighter Training Unit 2 (FTU-2). I headed up this squadron to train new pilots in the Grumman Wildcat. Major Hank Ellis commanded Fighter Training Unit 1 and headed up this squadron to train new pilots in the F4U Corsair. Lieutenant Colonel Luther S. "Sad Sam" Moore was overall commander of both units.

It seemed as though all the Marine first and second lieutenants who had been commissioned during the past year were being funneled into the fighter training units at El Toro. There was, however, a "holding bin" at Kearney Mesa for many Marine pilots either arriving or departing for overseas. The new pilots had originally graduated from Elimination or Primary Flight Training at schools all over the country. They had then graduated from Advanced Flight Training at either Pensacola, Corpus Christi, or Jacksonville. Some of those graduates went to NAS Opa Locka, Florida, where they flew the Curtiss SBC-

4 Helldiver biplane bombers, and the Brewster F2A Buffalo low-winged fighters. Some even received training in the Grumman Torpedo bomber and the
Vought OS2U-2 Kingfisher seaplane. But now this great assemblage of fledgling pilots was being taught at the El Toro FTUs by captains and majors fresh
out of the combat area, and then shipped out to the forward areas as quickly as
possible.

The Corsair, newly integrated into the FTU system, was considered the
Cadillac of all fighter aircraft, which now made the Wildcat the Model T. The
sleek Corsair was faster, more maneuverable, and easier to land than the
Grumman. It was a pleasure to fly and had a comfortable cockpit and a big,
powerful engine. The bent-wing bird was one of a kind.

The Corsair did have its quirks, however. We usually referred to it as the
"birdcage" model, because of the number of reinforcing bars in its sliding
cockpit canopy, which restricted the pilot's visibility somewhat. It also had
poor visibility in a three-point landing attitude because of the long nose that
poked up ahead. And then, just before touchdown, the plane had a tendency to
shudder and shake at stalling speed, especially during deceleration. The port
wing was stalling out before the starboard wing. I noticed this when on occasion I was able to borrow a plane from Hank Ellis for checkout.

In the meantime, Grumman F6F Hellcats manned by Navy pilots had taken
command of the skies. This plane was the Navy's choice over the Corsair for
carrier operations. The Corsair had the ability to fly 20 knots faster and climb
800 feet per minute faster than the Hellcat, but the Corsair had a 20-degree
blind spot dead ahead and a landing-gear problem for carrier landings. For this
reason the Navy rejected it in favor of the Hellcat. At least this is the way we
Marine pilots at the lower echelon sized up the situation. Much later, we would
also like to think, we taught the Navy how to operate Corsairs off carriers.

But, in reality, there was a little bit more to it than that. The Navy conjured up a
compelling argument to justify its choice of the Hellcat. Logistics was one deter-
mining factor and mechanics another. Initially, the Navy didn't want to have two
logistics systems aboard carriers, one for the Corsair and one for the Hellcat. To deal
with the procurement of spare parts and trained groundcrews for both would be to
lose economy of effort on a grand scale. But the Navy pilots loved the Hellcat, and
there was no doubt that it was a fine carrier airplane. The Corsair was a real bouncy plane aboard a carrier, and the Vought engineers had a real shock absorber problem to solve. The stiff landing gear and the bounce characteristics were finally eliminated by the installation of a redesigned Schrader valve in the oleo and an increase
of air pressure in the struts. It was not until after all this was eventually accomplished that the Corsair would distinguish itself aboard carriers with a flair.

* * *

MCAS El Toro was almost completely surrounded by orange groves owned by the Irvine Company. They stretched as far as the town of Santa Ana a few miles away and to the foothills going into Laguna Beach and beyond to Corona Del Mar. The main gate was on the north side of the air station. The road led out, then made an abrupt westerly turn to the little hamlet of Irvine. The crossroads at Irvine consisted of no more than a filling station and corner grocery store. Those of us who lived in Laguna Beach coursed our way from Irvine through the orange groves and Laguna Canyon. It was a matter of routine to stop on occasion beside an orange grove, form a hand-to-hand brigade, and toss oranges into the backseat of the car. (We found out later there was a $50 fine for each orange picked—if you were caught.)

The new pilots we were training were an eager bunch, but there were many accidents—some fatal. It happened more than once that an airplane experienced engine failure or spun in after takeoff; many would wipe out an acre or so of orange trees on the Irvine ranch. At times I would be appointed the investigative officer, responsible for conferring with the Irvine people on the claim forms. Not once to my knowledge did the Irvine people ever file a claim. They knew the sacrifices of war and would simply write off the damage with no claims against the government.

Night flying was another ordeal, with which we had to contend. There were many ground loops on night takeoffs and many crash landings at night. If an engine quit on takeoff, there was no room for return to the field, nor was there altitude to effect a bailout.

Once, when my brother Dan was visiting me from South Dakota, his fascination with aircraft operations left him immediately agog. One night I took him out to the end of the runway to observe night-flying operations. On this night there were a horrendous number of incidents—especially crash landings. To Dan, the airplane had no visible means of support. He wasn't about to entertain any notion of being an aviator—especially a military one.

Fog was always a problem at El Toro. On many mornings the field would be enveloped and zero-zero visibility was the norm. But then by midmorning it would burn off. The fog could cause problems during night flying too. It was a phenomenal experience to watch the fog banks move in off the ocean on a moonlit night. In minutes a quiet, wind-free evening would be usurped by a thick fog that hugged the ground and galloped like a horse. It moved in fast, and more than once it trapped airborne flights without a place to land.

I had the officer-of-the-day duty in the tower one night when this happened. As soon as Aerology alerted me, I got on the microphone to recall all aircraft.

There must have been a couple dozen planes in the air. One by one they came in for landings. It was too late for one four-plane division, for the fog had enshrouded the airfield completely. I contacted the leader of the flight and told him to head for MCAS El Centro. I gave him the vector and phoned El Centro to alert them about the incoming flight. They promised to return the call as soon as all aircraft had landed. I waited and waited an interminable amount of time. An hour went by, but still no phone call. I felt responsible. I called El Centro and was told that a flight of planes had flown over but had continued on an easterly course. Much later I was finally able to relax when I received word that the flight had landed at Yuma, Arizona!

* * *

On December 6, 1943, as I walked out of the squadron office building on an errand to the hangar, I noticed that all eyes of squadron personnel in the area were turned upward. I immediately caught sight of a Corsair in an inverted spin high above the field. It seemed to be windmilling ever so slowly on its way downward. Soon I heard screams of people near me, "Jump! Jump!" There was no visible exit from the plane, nor a blossoming parachute. In seconds the plane hit with a resounding crash in the plowed field just outside the main gate. The pilot, 1stLt Andy Elenor, was killed.

I was assigned investigative officer for the accident and was also detailed to notify next of kin. Lieutenant Andy Elenor and his wife lived in Laguna Beach. To notify next of kin with news of such magnitude was foreign to me. How would I go about leveling with the truth in such a delicate situation? How does one inform a wife that "your husband has just been killed"?

My mind raced in a search for answers and I was grasping at straws. At the moment the only resources available would be my presence and my genuine feelings of compassion. My next thoughts were to find a standard procedure of conduct in such matters if one was available. But time was of the essence. I quickly resorted to two courses of action: One was to contact the group chaplain immediately—someone experienced in consoling the bereaved when such tragedies occur. Next, to direct the most intimate of Andy's friends and their wives to hasten to the Elenor house as follow-up visitors immediately upon my departure.

The Navy lieutenant chaplain, dressed in his Marine greens, followed me in the gray staff car to the quiet street in South Laguna. We parked the cars and proceeded up the steps of the house. Apparently, the slamming of car doors alerted Mrs. Elenor that guests were arriving, for as the chaplain and I mounted the steps, I caught sight of a face peering from the window. It was not possible to hide the steely expression on our faces, and she met us at the door before I had a chance to ring the bell. Her expression was solemn too as she searched our faces for some compelling reason for the visit. She had already seen the cross on the chaplain's collar, and she knew me as the CO of the squadron. Mrs. Elenor sensed something wrong immediately. Her suspicions had been aroused the minute we parked the cars.

"Is it Andy?" she asked plaintively.

"Yes," I said.

"Is he OK?"

The silence lasted for only a second before I shook my head and softly said, "no". Then she collapsed in my arms. The chaplain and I guided her to the sofa, where we three sat, waiting for the right moment to speak, grasping for the right words.

Through tears and with an almost inaudible voice, she asked, "What happened?" I tried to couch my answer in acceptable terms, but felt very clumsy. I was very thankful when the chaplain finally interjected with consoling words and my attention was momentarily diverted from the grief-stricken wife. Shortly, I heard activity and hastened to the door to meet the arriving guests.

This was the first in a long series of my notifying next of kin. As a squadron commander over the years, it was a duty that befell me often, and it never got any less traumatic.

The investigation revealed that Lt Elenor had been on a tactics flight. As bad luck would have it, he encountered an Army P-38 on the way home. The temptation was too great and a mock dog fight ensued. While in a tight maneuver, Lieutenant Elenor fell out in an inverted spin.

At times likes these I questioned the sanity of my being a fighter pilot. Perhaps orthopedic surgery wouldn't have been so bad after all.

Josie and I had by now moved to more suitable quarters in Corona Del Mar— a duplex apartment shared with Dr. Brad Bradbury and his wife. Brad was an Army Air Corps doctor serving at the Santa Ana base. This area was very pleasant, a nice place to live. Just around the curve of the paved road lived Harry Carey, the movie actor. To our right was a view of Balboa Island and the pleasure boats—a scene that would have been an artist's delight. But we also had some undesirable neighbors to contend with: a nest of skunks that had taken up quarters under the house. At times their malodorous presence became unendurable. Our affable landlord tried without success to eradicate them.

In the meantime, back at the El Toro Air Station, operations continued as usual, along with some unusual twists. Lieutenant Colonel Luther "Sad Sam" Moore came over to my office one day, carrying an exciting bundle of papers: It was a promotion list. He had not yet looked at it, so we both got down to scan the list. Suddenly, my gaze came to an abrupt halt. I looked at my name three times before I began to believe it—promoted to major, retroactive to October 10, 1943. This exciting news made me quiver; in fact, I began trembling all over! Although I was ecstatic at the news, this sudden shaking seemed a bit much. Something was wrong. Soon my suspicions were confirmed: I was having my second attack of malaria. So it was back to the hospital, with blankets piled high to keep me from freezing to death—and then came the dreaded fever. About three days later, Dr. Kenny said I could go home to recuperate.

Being housebound was not without its merits. It wasn't long before my old Guadalcanal mate Blaine Baesler and his new wife, Poppy, came by to see me. Poppy had just arrived in the States from Australia, her ship having caught fire en route. Her arm was in a cast, but that didn't stop her from planting a kiss on my cheek. We reminisced about these fond times we all had shared during the memorable leave in Sydney.

A few days later, I felt well enough to participate in a little promotion celebration. Dr. Brad and his wife decided we should go to the new Hurley Belle bar and restaurant in Corona Del Mar. Josie had just retrieved my new greens from the cleaners, so I put them on for the first time since the malaria attack. I was dismayed at the weight I had apparently lost—the pants seemed extremely baggy—but there was nothing I could do about it at the moment. We entered the bar at the Hurley Belle and had a drink. There was only one other customer at the bar and he was dressed in civilian clothes. After we adjourned to the dining room, the drinks kept flowing, compliments of the gentleman at the bar. Apparently, he was celebrating my promotion, too. Dr. Brad said he knew the man slightly out at the Santa Ana Air Base. We invited him in to join us and soon learned more about this extraordinary character.

He called himself Mac, and it turned out that he was a sergeant in the Army. Although middle-aged, he had insisted on joining up to help do his part for the war effort. He had a son who was a bombardier on a B-17. We learned that he owned a couple of nightclubs, one being the Trionon in Hollywood. Before the evening ended, the sergeant had invited all of us to be his guests for a night on the town in Hollywood. He would take us in his car to Earl Carrol's and his own nightspots. As far as he was concerned, it would be a tax write-off—wouldn't cost him a cent. Thus ended a mighty fine promotion party.

Even though I was still on sick leave, Josie and I drove to Santa Ana to do a little shopping. I still had on the baggy britches. Josie went into a jewelry store while I walked across the street to another store. Suddenly, I was confronted by an Army military policeman (MP).

"Sir, may I see your identification card?" It was obvious to the MP that this skinny young kid with brand-new, shiny major's leaves and not exactly form-fitting uniform trousers was an imposter. It hadn't been many months earlier that a major was viewed as a distinguished-looking gentleman with slightly graying temples. But *this* kid?

I was caught flatfooted. I didn't have a major's ID card. I didn't even have a captain's or first lieutenant's ID card. The only one I carried said I was a second lieutenant. It was useless to show him that. The MP allowed as how it was embarrassing to him, but that it was a necessary precaution to check up on phonies who portrayed themselves as officers and heroes. He cited a case the night before, when he picked up a couple of civilian boys wearing stolen uniforms.

"Sir, would you accompany me to MP headquarters?" I was irked, but I was also hamstrung. We walked into the station, and the MP said to the sergeant at the desk, "Sergeant, here's a major who has only a second lieutenant's ID card. Wonder if you'd call up El Toro to verify his authenticity?"

The sergeant at the desk promptly and indignantly stood up and answered, "I know this major; I know 'im! He's OK!" I blinked, and then came the dawn. It was Mac, the man in civilian clothes at the Hurley Belle. I was a friend in need, and he was a friend indeed.

It should be noted that the mystery of the baggy britches also resolved itself when we discovered there was a mixup at the cleaners. Identification on one of the pockets revealed them to be someone else's uniform trousers.

* * *

The relatively new Marine Corps Air Station at El Toro had just been commissioned in May 1943. It lay in low flatlands between the hills to the west and the mountains to the east, with Saddle Back Mountain the most imposing. Almost everyone lived in either Santa Ana or on the ocean in Laguna Beach. I immediately fell in love with Laguna Beach. There was a scent in the air of eucalyptus and orange blossoms that lent an appealing aura to this extraordinary artists' colony. There was nothing commercial about it. The small-town ambience was obvious in the day-to-day routine. Even though Route 101 coursed its way through the main street, the traffic was never overwhelming. I remember in particular a fat, grizzled old artist who set up his easel on the centerline of the highway to paint. He was barefoot and wore only khaki shorts, displaying a hairy chest and beard. In my mind, he will always be a symbol of the unrushed society that was Laguna Beach in the forties.

It was now November 1943, and somehow it seemed appropriate to purchase a house in the area; something that would serve as a home base. Even though orders could send me anyplace on the globe at any time, it just seemed the right thing to do. I had already decided that Laguna Beach was my kind of place. My sights were set on something for around $7,500, a very modest figure considering my rank and status. You could obtain a very fine home for that price in those days. So the search began. One house in particular seemed to fit the bill, but then we came across another in South Laguna that was like a Cape Cod cottage; we immediately fell in love with it. The problem was the price tag: $10,000—way beyond my means. But just like one who gets the itch to buy a new car, it became a matter of throwing caution to the wind and taking the plunge. This was a charming little house one would keep forever. It was located up the gently sloping hill from Highway 101 and overlooked the Pacific Ocean within walking distance of the coves and sandy, rock-strewn beach.

Back at Corona Del Mar, we bandied about names for our dream house with Dr. Bradbury and his wife, Dorothy. It finally came down to "CAVU," which had a catchy ring to it and was very appropriate in view of my being a pilot. *CAVU* is actually an aerological term, an acronym for ceiling and visibility unlimited. Weather teletypes used the term *CAVU*, denoting fine weather at cities across the country. In filing a flight plan, one had to get it cleared by the weatherman. If the weather during a cross-country flight was cloud-free with clear skies, he simply scribbled *CAVU* across the face of the flight plan and one was cleared to make the flight. CAVU was definitely a fine name for a dream house. In December 1943, we moved into CAVU in South Laguna Beach.

Our new abode was to accumulate many memories in a short span of time. It would be the scene of many squadron parties as well as reunions of old friends coming from and going overseas. House guests were a common occurrence, such as Capt Hank Schriver and his wife, Katie. Hank was not a pilot but commander of an amphibian tractor company (LVT) at Camp Pendleton. Katie was a svelte brunette, who had just brought the records of the new Broadway musical *Oklahoma!* with her from the East Coast. It wasn't long before we knew all those whimsical tunes by heart.

One Sunday afternoon before Hank was shipped out overseas, he indoctrinated me in the "ins and outs" of amphibian tractor operation. At Camp Pendleton I'd driven that old bear through the surf and out into the ocean. It was a strange element for a fighter pilot to experience. But all these were memories I wouldn't soon forget.

In the meantime, we kept abreast of a world in turmoil. These were exciting times, driven by the building tension of the all-out war effort. Keeping up with the news seemed to salve the situation somewhat, conjuring up in us the will to win and end the war. When the censors permitted, newspaper headlines blared the latest events, and the radio news broadcasts held us all in rapt attention.

Gabriel Heatter came on the air at seven o'clock, and I listened to his fifteen-minute news program every night with devotion. I liked his manner of presentation. The news was delivered in a humble, soft-spoken, trustworthy manner. I never missed his forthright portrayal of events. It had been only a month earlier, on November 20, 1943, that he had apprised me of the Tarawa Atoll invasion in the Gilbert Islands. Later we learned how the 2d Marine Division, under command of MajGen Julian C. Smith, stormed ashore on Betio Island. The taking of Tarawa would be the first crack in the outer ring of the Japanese defense lines.

In this same time frame, halfway around the world in the Central Pacific, another scene was unfolding, this one of gigantic proportions. It was a further cracking of that outer ring of Japanese defense lines. The Marine V Amphibian Corps, under LtGen Holland M. Smith, began landings at various atolls in the Marshall Islands. The first landing would be at Roi-Namur on January 31, 1944. Then the next day, February 1 and 220 miles to the northwest of Roi-Namur, a landing would be made on the biggest atoll in the world—Kwajalein. Still later, February 17 and 330 miles to the northwest of Kwajalein, Eniwetok would be taken. Once rehabilitated, Eniwetok would prove to be a vital U.S. Navy supply and maintenance facility. The American industrial and military potential was gathering steam, and this was just the beginning.

Not only were events abroad happening rapidly, but news was breaking quickly at home as well. I received new orders, directing me to report to the Marine Corps Air Station, Mojave, California, in the middle of February.

My name was included on a blanket Change of Station orders dated January 22, 1944. It emanated from the commanding general, Marine Fleet Air, San Diego, and listed the names of 246 officers, ranking from major on down through second lieutenant. All these were pilots, both instructors and students, at the fighter training units at El Toro.

Five days later I received another set of orders, which actually delineated the first. These orders essentially specified that a new squadron would be formed, designated VMF-452. It further listed, by name, the two majors, three captains, seven first lieutenants, and thirty second lieutenants who would compose its officer ranks.

In quieter moments I reflected upon the impact of this order and the news it contained. I was one of those two majors—and also the senior. I would be the commanding officer!

The prospect of running a tactical squadron stirred up mixed emotions. I began to muse on the challenges, the obstacles, and the hurdles. They all lay out there in one form or another.

Then I thought of those unruly college kids. How would I handle them? Of course, I was once a college kid myself, and it takes one to know one. In fact, at twenty-five, I was hardly more than a step or two ahead of them in age. Yes, being a squadron commander was going to be a challenge.

In my musings, I recollected one hard charger who represented my idea of an outstanding squadron commander. He was a Navy lieutenant whom I'd known down at Opa Locka about the time I was getting my wings: Lt "Jumpin' Joe" Clifton was then gaining a reputation as a hard taskmaster and a superior Navy flier.

Jumpin' Joe was loud and boisterous, and people could feel his presence for a mile around. How would he handle an unruly college kid? I could imagine a scenario involving a young ensign's confrontation with Jumpin' Joe Clifton: The young ensign is in his office behind a closed door, yet no door will bar the decibels of an enraged Jumpin' Joe.

"Godammit, Smitty, I'm not asking you, I'm telling you! What do you think this is? A question-and-answer period? It's not! I'm telling you! You're going to be doing it this way from now on—or else. Understand?"

The voice on the other side of the door slackens from its crescendo, and the tirade ends. Conciliatory tones then prevail. and there is an obvious meeting of the minds. Shortly, a chastened young officer emerges and beats a hasty retreat to the ready room.

Yes, that's the way Jumpin' Joe would do it. On the other hand, there is a lot to be said for good old horse sense, and since I was no Jumpin' Joe Clifton, I'd have to resort to some other tack. It seemed like a pretty good approach to me to consider horse sense. I think I'll go that way, I told myself.

PART III

The Desert

VOUGHT F4U CORSAIR

CHAPTER 9

Genesis on the Desert

The Great Mojave Desert is a land of cacti, rattlesnakes, lizards, and jackrabbits. It is a great expansive plateau with some elevations of more than 2,000 feet above sea level. Pilots flying at this altitude find the air is thin—and even thinner in the hot summer sun.

This was the scene in February 1944, when VMF-452 became a reality at the Marine Corps Air Station, Mojave, California. I was assigned commanding officer of that squadron, commissioned February 15, 1944.

A year and a half earlier, contractors had begun building the new air station. By late in the year, a Marine headquarters had been installed and, many weeks later, the runways had been completed. Then certain Marine air support elements moved in. This would be the beginning of a gigantic step by Marine Corps aviation to supplement the juggernaut necessary to destroy the enemy.

Now the large transfer order was taking effect, and the influx of personnel from El Toro began. This move doubled the population at Mojave but depleted the strength of the fighter training units back at El Toro. Another squadron, VMF-451, received orders identical to ours and set up shop on the sandy ramp next door to us. Its commanding officer was Maj Hank Ellis. I now, more than ever, thanked Hank for that Corsair checkout back at El Toro when he was running that FTU Corsair squadron.

It was immediately after February 15 that men and materiel began flowing into the squadron. Forty-six officers and 250 enlisted men would eventually bring us up to strength. What was most encouraging was the quality of the non-commissioned officers. For all intents and purposes, these would be the people running the shops. We were extremely fortunate in obtaining leading chiefs who were battle-tried. Someone was looking out for us, for about a half-dozen master sergeants and a dozen technical sergeants checked into the squadron. They would be doing double duty over the next few months in the training of their underlings.

The town of Mojave was small, and quarters for married people were almost nonexistent. It was a stark contrast to the lush orange groves of Santa Ana and the eucalyptus of Laguna Beach whence we all had come. Twelve of our officers were married. Captains Robert Bryson and John Rumbold "Jack" Stack and Lt Walter B. "Walt" Hurst lived in the town of Tehachapi, about 18 miles west of Mojave. Some of the others who had families, such as Lts Charles W. Weitzel, Jr. and Lanman T. "Lanny" Holmes, found places in the town of Mojave. For Lt Donald R. "Don" Phillips and his wife, Gerre, home was an old house with a potbellied stove in the middle of the living room and a tin flue pipe through the ceiling; at the ready, the coal scuttle sat nearby. Josie and I lived in half of a Quonset hut on the air station—replete with bedbugs, roaches, and other such amenities. It was primitive but bearable.

The desert was now to be our home, and here we would train for that next confrontation with the enemy. The big question was this: Where precisely would that confrontation be? Which island out there on that vast Pacific Ocean would be our next base of operations? The Japanese outer defense ring was now being cracked in the Marshall Islands, and it was only sage to believe that there would be many more Marine amphibian landings requiring close air support. I viewed the long road ahead with mixed emotions; it appeared both dismally formidable and extremely exciting.

But there were immediate problems closer to home: A brand-new squadron had to be organized.

Out there on the sandy lot just off the ramp where the hangars were located, the squadron offices were being set up. Warrant Officer Donald Adgee was now the adjutant of the squadron, and he performed like a whirling dervish to whip everything into shape. Warrant Officer Adgee first entered the Marine Corps in 1936 and became an administrator. Now, under his directions, the desks, files, map boards, and other paraphernalia were being assembled in accordance with standard operating procedures. It was obvious he was a fussbudget when it came to attention to detail. Under him was MTSgt Robert D. Ragan, acting as sergeant major, and, under him was Sgt Theodore K. "Ted" Gore, the first sergeant. They didn't consider the haranguing by the adjutant as harassment, for they were eager to please, aware that this was a new adventure. In the not-too-distant future, this squadron would be involved in combat.

The first order of squadron business was an orientation drill. All department heads toured the hangar shops and became familiar with locations and the inner workings of the squadron. Unlike peacetime routine, there was no formal squadron commissioning ceremony. In these times of strife, it was pretty much business as usual throughout the squadron area.

The officers' club was really the only social center for miles around, so it held a captive audience. It was a low frame building painted almost the same color as the sand that surrounded it. It had a large bar and a long dining room. Slot machines lined one wall of the barroom. The foyer was large, and it was obvious that it would become part of the dance floor on party nights.

It was here at the "O Club" that we all gathered in a relaxed mode for the first time, to eat, drink, and get acquainted. The wives of those few who were married enhanced the spirit of living by their presence and added prestige to the squadron. There was Gerre, the flaxen-haired wife of Lt Don Phillips, from Oklahoma City. There was Joan, an Australian, who had married Jack Stack on his third trip to Sydney from Guadalcanal. And there was Naomi, a very friendly yet serious dark-haired, brown-eyed woman who had married Capt Bob Bryson. And of course there was Marcia Hill and Ruth Hurst, and Elizabeth, Claire, Frances, Elva Mae, and the others. All beautiful. Anyone could tell at a glance that each of these women was a cut above—strictly first-class. Josie entered into the camaraderie, too, and this unofficial sorority assisted in the making of a cohesive, distinctive outfit.

Very few of the enlisted men were married; and for those who were, it was almost impossible to find suitable quarters in the area. Therefore, those wives stayed back in the hometown, and their husbands lived in the barracks with the greater percentage of the other enlisted men.

Of immediate concern were the tools at hand—specifically the experience of the pilots. Back at El Toro, I knew almost every Marine combat pilot who had returned from the South Pacific, if not personally, at least by name. Now, with the rapid expansion of Marine aviation and the commissioning of new squadrons, these resources would be spread thin among them. Each reorganized squadron and each new squadron would be given its cut of the wealth, small though it might be. Unfortunately, a newly appointed squadron commander was not given the opportunity to choose from the skill pool. He took what was given to him, which obviously eliminated the greed factor. I could not complain, however, for the assets available to me were more than satisfactory. Including myself, five of our most senior pilots were combat-qualified.

Major Phillip L. Crawford became executive officer of the squadron. Phil had trained at Pensacola and then received his commission at Opa Locka in the fall of 1941. He was shipped overseas shortly thereafter.

Captain Robert L. "Bulgy" Bryson had gone to flight school at Corpus Christi, Texas, and received his commission February 12, 1942. By May, he found himself at Tutuila, Samoa, flying Curtiss SBC-4 fabric-covered biplane dive-bombers with VMO-151. Then, by December 1942, he was flying Grumman Wildcats with VMO-251 at Espiritu Santo and later the new Corsairs at Guadalcanal. Having returned to the States and being, then, assistant flight officer at the fighter training units at El Toro, he was a natural to join VMF-452 at Mojave.

Captain John "Jack" Stack joined the squadron shortly after it was commissioning. He was another South Pacific veteran. During the Battle of Guadalcanal, specifically on November 13-14, 1942, Jack Stack shot down a Japanese Zero that was one among several Zeros and Bettys attacking our American transports on those days. On February 1, 1943, he shot down his second Zero. Air activity was extremely intense at this point.

Captain Harold Trenchard was a lieutenant with VMF-121 and participated in the Central Solomons invasion in the New Georgia group. On June 30, 1943, he shot down two Zeros and one probable. On July 7, he shot down another Zero and damaged still another. So he came to the squadron with three kills, one damaged, and one probable.

The age difference was so trivial between us seniors and our fledgling juniors that a distinction was obvious only in rank and experience. We never flaunted our superiority, because we really were never aware of it, despite the fact that we were now battle-tried veterans. We came out of Guadalcanal with new tactics and perhaps a new philosophy on life. The realization that we had acquired certain skills as experienced combat pilots started to sink in. At this point it became clear to some of us that we were part of the nucleus of what was to become the modern Marine Corps air arm. We were the pioneers/teachers from that point on. As green as we felt, we had more experience than most pilots on active duty. When we formed the squadron, we had very little experience with troops, administration, discipline, and so on. We were now assigned key squadron positions: commanding officer, executive officer, operations officer, and so on down the line. Our responsibilities and inexperience suddenly became apparent. It goes without saying that when a problem came up and the answer was not readily available, we probably faked it.

In the hunt for one good revealing feature in the way of experience among the junior pilots was the revelation that most had already checked out in the Vought F4U Corsair. The seven first lieutenants had been commissioned not much more than six to eight months earlier; the second lieutenants, probably three to five months. After commissioning, many of these pilots had received further advanced training down at Opa Locka, flying the Curtiss SBC-4 biplane dive-bomber and the Brewster F2A Buffalo fighter. Some had then been transferred to the Marine Corps Aviation Base at Kearney Mesa, California. Kearney Mesa acted as a kind of holding area for the transfer of pilots arriving from and departing for overseas. Most of these, however, ended up at the fighter training units at El Toro.

One by one, each first and second lieutenant was interviewed during this initial indoctrination period. There was a healthy mix of Corsair experience among them. For instance, 1stLt Peter Schaefer had already logged upward of

50 hours in the bird. Pete was raised in Wilmette, Illinois, and had received his commission just seven months earlier. He would be pegged as a tutor and flight leader immediately. Close on his heels were 1stLts Baxter R. "Bo" Little and Kenneth "Kenny" Bennett. The value of the other first lieutenants such as Ernest D. "Dale" Oakes, Gerald J. "Gerry" Vetter, Stanford E. "Stan" Cooley, and Donald L. DeCelles consisted of quality time spent in other fighter aircraft.

Second Lieutenant Emmons S. "Mal" Maloney was born and raised in Green Bay, Wisconsin, and had received his commission the August before. He had logged fifteen hours in the Corsair. Close behind him were Lts Eugene S. "Rocky" Staples and John E. Lawrence. But Joseph R. Warren was recognized immediately with the buildup of twenty hours he had acquired. He would be ensured of a good billet in the squadron.

At the end of the interviews, we concluded that there couldn't have been a better conglomeration of human flesh and spirit assembled anywhere in the land. It was refreshing to see these high-spirited dynamos ready to go. They were eager and robust. All they needed was the signal. They seemed to have already developed that traditional Marine gung ho attitude. I was beginning to think that the only problem I might have with them would be a matter of constraint.

Chief Warrant Officer Clayton W. "Smitty" Smith would be our engineering officer. His service record book showed him to be an old mustang. This was good. The Marine Corps couldn't have survived the war so far without the old mustangs. These "hangers-on" originated in the 1920s and the 1930s when a corporal received $21 per month pay and stayed in grade for years at a time before a normal promotion. Some of these old-timers had seen action in Nicaragua and Haiti. Chief Warrant Officer Smith would later enthrall us with stories of how the U.S. Marines chased the bandit Sandino in Nicaragua for five years without catching him. It was an interesting story of how Augusto César Sandino had been a soldier in the liberal army but broke away after accusing Gen José Maria Moncada of having sold out Nicaraguan independence to the Americans in 1927. Sandino formed a small army of his own and always seemed to be just one step ahead of the Marines. What was most interesting about Smith's stories was how the Chance-Vought Corsair biplanes engaged in aerial bombardment. These were small bombs dropped by hand from the rear cockpit of the Corsairs. Although officially recognized as a warrant officer, Clayton Smith was more appropriately addressed as "Gunner," a title denoting honor, praise, and respect. And once the warmth of his personality became apparent, all hands in the squadron started to call him "Smitty." Smitty was in his early forties, and although he had never married, it soon became obvious that he had accumulated no small number of girlfriends. I could tell immediately that Smitty would be a great asset to the squadron.

The ordnance officer was next on the interview agenda. His name was Carl Omasta and he was also a warrant officer in the Marine Corps. Carl was not of the same vintage as Clayton Smith, but still, by the standards of the time, he was regarded as an old-timer. He had entered the service of the Marine Corps in 1939, undergoing recruit training at Parris Island, South Carolina. His original intention was to join the Army Air Corps, but that was stymied when the policy of that service dictated a year-long delay. His goal was to get into aviation, and he achieved this at a later date when he became a tail gunner in Douglas SBD dive-bombers. Then, due to his expertise in matters of ordnance, he became attached to aviation units in that area.

The only other warrant officer on our roster was Francis I. Taylor, who was well experienced in matters of materiel and supply. He would play a very important part in some future deployment if we were relegated to some remote island out there in the vast Pacific. Although a bit older than most of the other officers in the squadron, Francis was tall, slender, and ramrod straight.

First Lieutenant Fred Olson checked in as intelligence officer. He was also a little older than most of us. It hadn't been many months earlier that he had been walking a beat as a policeman in a small town in Michigan. His entire demeanor screamed military. Everything about Olson was spit and polish. When he stood at attention, his tall frame was erect and he spoke with an air of determination. This no-nonsense Marine exemplified all that was proper and dignified. I made a mental note that this trait would be useful in the subsequent training of the troops. We needed a role model for the young Marines in the squadron. Olson was just one more cog in what would soon become a strong, cohesive machine.

Lieutenant William D. McDowell was the last ground officer on the roster, and he came in well qualified as a communications officer. This was a very important billet, for the success of an air mission was very much dependent on how well communications served among aircraft.

Our other assets included two civilians, Donald H. "Don" Russell and Bob Graham. Don was the technical representative for the Vought Company. He, in conjunction with our engineering section, would be dedicated to keeping the Corsairs not only in the air but airworthy as well. Don was a studious-looking man with a medium build, glasses, and slightly tousled hair.

Bob Graham was the Pratt & Whitney tech rep, a slender towhead with a crew cut. He would be working hand-in-hand with the engineering section—especially the single-engine mechanics with the 752 Military Occupational specialties.

The enlisted contingent comprised about 250 people. It was interesting to note that many of the noncommissioned officers in that group were battle-proven veterans. Still, it would be a complicated job in every department, for at least 80 percent of their charges were fresh Marines. Theirs would be a formidable task, a challenge demanding much time and energy.

Private First Class D. W. "Douglas" Frederick was typical of the enlisted men complementing VMF-452 early in 1944. He was, as were many young American boys wrested from school, work, or other activities, called in to serve his country during World War II. Frederick was born and raised in Gillette, Wyoming. He graduated from Campbell High School and took a job with the Gulf Oil Company as a member of a party searching for oil in Texas. His wages were 68 cents per hour. He was called up for duty, given the physical, and asked his preference of duty. Frederick had a sister who had joined the Women Marines so, of course, it would be the Marine Corps.

At Fort Bliss, Texas, Frederick was sworn in and told to wait for a troop train headed west for boot camp at the San Diego Recruit Depot. At Fort Bliss the inductees were given the inevitable head shave and then liberty. A last fling prior to boarding the troop train meant an excursion to the border town of Juarez, Mexico, to see the sights. The "boneheads" caused quite a stir in Juarez, because the Mexicans thought they were escaped felons. The sordid stories of prisons in Mexico were enough to make these new Marines reevaluate their presence there. With a bottle of peach brandy in each hand, they returned to El Paso.

The contingent of future Marines boarded the troop train and headed west. Immediately, the question arose: What is the difference between a troop train and a cattle car? The answer? "Very, very little." The train traveled close to the Mexican border, and stops were frequent. Guards prevented anyone from leaving the train. The boredom of many hours of travel led large groups to play cards and crap games. Wristwatches and rings were laid down as last-ditch stakes. Tempers exploded into scuffling and rowdiness. Most of these boys were Texans—big bruisers. The MPs had a tough time keeping everything under control.

The troop train entered California, and at each stop Mexicans would appear beside the open windows, selling souvenirs, cigarettes, and rings. Frederick bought cigarettes and a heavy brass ring with the Marine Corps emblem on it. The Mexicans told him it was good for barroom fighting, but in the back of his mind, Frederick thought perhaps it would be a good weapon on an enemy soldier's jaw.

At the Marine Corps Recruit Depot, San Diego, Platoon Number 339 was formed. Their drill instructor (DI) was called Stonebreaker and he was mean. His idea of training was to break down a man's spirit and self-esteem, harass him into committing the unthinkable, then eliminate the SOB, branding him "not Marine material." Obviously, Stonebreaker overstepped the bounds of DI propriety, and he was relieved of his duties a short time later. From then on things went well with Texan DIs calling the shots.

At boot camp Frederick asked for aviation duty, because he figured that was the wave of the future. He was transferred to the Marine Corps Air Depot at Miramar, California, and assigned mess duty.

In early 1944 Frederick joined VMF-452 at Mojave. He was always perplexed about his constant assignment to mess duty and desperately wanted to do something different. When he checked into the squadron, he kept his mess experience a secret. His record book revealed his military occupational specialty, however, so he was assigned to the NCO mess.

At least Frederick knew his way around the scullery. The day started at 0400 and ended at 1400. This mess was, in a sense, a promotion. The noncommissioned officers (NCOs) ate off china, and the food was better prepared. I was to learn later that there was one thing you could say about PFC Douglas Frederick: He never shirked his duty. He was the kind of man you'd want in your outfit—trusting and loyal, and, when given an order, he carried it out to the best of his ability.

Another one of those boys who was ready to lick the world was Cpl Robert E. "Bob" Eggleston. Like so many other young men of that era, it was almost providential that graduation from high school occurred just before Pearl Harbor. These people fit the exact profile of what Uncle Sam was looking for in time of crisis: energetic, healthy, young men, perfect for combat duty.

Bob Eggleston was born in Omaha, Nebraska, on March 15, 1923. His family had moved to Kansas City, where Bob grew up into a 6-foot, 3 1/2-inch athlete. He played center on the Westport High School basketball team. During his senior year, the team won the Missouri state championship.

His coach told Eggleston that he could get a full scholarship to college because of his athletic talents. He was recruited by several colleges in the Midwest, but decided to attend Creighton University in Nebraska. Suddenly, our country was in the throes of World War II, and those plans were cut short. Bob decided to join the U. S. Marine Corps. He enlisted on June 10, 1942, at Kansas City. His college education would simply have to wait until after the war, at which time he would either become an athletic coach or go into engineering.

Bob had a 16-year-old brother named Jack and a six-year-old sister named

Monica. These two were both enamored of their big brother—especially Monica, who adored and idolized him.

I remember Bob marching on Ninth and Walnut streets in downtown Kansas City with lots of other young men who had enlisted to go to war. Relatives and friends were lined along the street, watching as the boys marched south to Union Station to be sent off. I thought it was fun. My brother was in a parade. I called to him, and he turned toward us—I thought he heard me. I said to Mama that I wanted him to come home with us now. She said he couldn't. I insisted over and over again, sensing something terrible happening. Both my father and my mother were crying. Soon I was, too, as I began to understand. My brother was a Marine in World War II.

Our whole world was turned upside down. Mama cried and waited for letters and hung a star in the window.

In December 1942, PFC Robert Eggleston joined VMF-124 at Kearney Mesa, California, as an ordnanceman. That squadron was transported to the South Pacific aboard the *Lurline* the following January and saw combat duty at Guadalcanal. In August 1943, Eggleston, now a corporal, returned to the States. It was upon the commissioning date of February 15, 1944, that he became a member of VMF-452.

CHAPTER 10

Integration of Experience

The time had arrived to mold this motley assembly of disoriented attendants into first-class combatants. At this point, however, that vision seemed hopelessly far off. Even though most of the pilots had checked out in the Corsair, their accumulation of hours ranged from less than a handful to a dozen or so. Building up time was the same as building up confidence, so it was a matter of concentrating on flight hours and squeezing every bit of time possible out of both plane and pilot.

Captain Bob Bryson was the squadron operations officer, and his flight officer assistant was Capt Wallace S. "Wally" Wethe. These two would make an outstanding team as leaders in the most active department of the squadron. Bob Bryson was twenty-three years old and brought an enviable reputation out of the South Pacific, where time with the Corsair was tried and true. He would soon be tagged with the nickname "Bulgy," which had more to do with his generous personality, I think, than his size.

Wally Wethe was a young, energetic officer, unmarried at the time, and dedicated to the perfection of Corsair proficiency. He had a suave, soft-spoken manner and instilled confidence in those lieutenants who were trying so desperately to absorb every technical detail of that flying machine. Among many assigned tasks, he made up the written test. During this indoctrination period, Wally gave lectures day after day and, with the assistance of his helper, 1stLt "Bo" Little, saw to it that these eager young people took to the air one after the other.

An inventory of Corsairs was on the ramp almost immediately. Some were F4U-1s built by the Vought Company, but most were FG-1s built by the Goodyear Company. The airplanes were identical in every respect. The Pratt & Whitney R-2800 engine developed 2,000 horsepower. All the pilots glowed with anticipation of flying this best-of-all-airplanes.

The Corsair designation was the same name as an earlier Chance-Vought biplane, which was first-line in the early 1930s. That Corsair biplane was still in service in Pensacola for basic training in 1940. In fact, when I was a cadet, I made my first cross-country flight in that biplane.

The progress in modification of the inverted-gull-wing Corsair was always positive. Its evolution from the experimental model to the F4U-1D made it more or less a bug-free bird. The Vought engineers had rectified the quirk that caused the Corsair to shudder and shake just before touchdown on landing. They mounted a little six-inch wood spoiler on the inboard edge of the starboard wing, which caused both wings to stall at the same time. This fix cost the company $3.67 per plane.

Other changes were made that eventually eliminated all the quirks. The Vought engineers came up with the raised-seat modification and the bubble canopy, providing the pilot much better visibility. There were also improvements in armor protection, instrument panel, and gun sight. The Corsair was now an even greater pleasure to fly.

But a Corsair's personality, piqued by a whim, could have devastating consequences. Like almost any other fighter airplane, it demanded constant attention—to the point of endangering the pilot who ignored it.

A case in point involved Ken Kirk, a Guadalcanal squadronmate. The Corsair was interesting in its proclivity for encountering compressibility. At El Toro, Ken took a Corsair up to 30,000 feet and put it in a terminal dive with full power on. He frantically tried to pull out of the dive and at first was unsuccessful. Seconds later the air was thicker and the plane gradually obeyed the command of the stick. When Ken landed, he discovered that the fabric on the tail elevators and the rudder had been shredded. This happened to another pilot, with fatal results.

Charles A. Lindbergh was technical adviser for the Vought Company. He visited El Toro and came over to the squadron one day to give a lecture and explain the compressibility factor. In essence, he said that the plane in a dive was approaching the speed of sound and this set up harmonics untenable to the structure of the airplane. This backed up the theory that no aircraft could ever break the sound barrier without shattering.

Boone Guyton was the chief test pilot for the Vought Company. He gave lectures at El Toro to the squadrons receiving the first Corsairs. In his book *Whistling Death: The Test Pilot's Story of the F4U Corsair*, Guyton emphasized that "stalls were one thing—spins something else." When asked about spinning the new fighter, he offered sage advice with a blunt answer: "Don't."

A one turn could usually be corrected within a quarter turn, but into the third or fourth gyration the Corsair wanted to poke its long nose down and wrap up even tighter. A related problem was the inability of some pilots to recognize an inverted spin soon enough to correct it. As usual, experience was the best teacher—if one survived to learn the lesson.

Once understood, the stall/spin characteristics were but part of the U-bird's personality. As an aircraft and a weapon, it offered exceptional range of performance and mission options. Fast, robust, long-legged, and hardworking, it was tremendously versatile.

It was calculated that the Corsair could fly 20 knots faster and climb 800 feet per minute more than the new Grumman F6F Hellcat.

The Corsair handbook was the pilot's bible; a prospective pilot had to memorize the entire thing before he took the plane into the air. He had to know the mechanics of the engine as well as the aerodynamics of the plane itself. The Corsair was a complicated machine, unlike anything previously manufactured. Many of the pilots of VMF-452 had already checked out in the plane at El Toro.

Appendix C to the pilot's handbook listed the following checkoff list for landing and takeoff of the Corsair:

TAKEOFF

Wings	—Spread and locked
Arresting hook control	—UP
Fuel tank selector	—RESERVE
Mixture	—Automatic RICH
Supercharger control	—NEUTRAL
Propeller control	—Max RPM (down)
Cowl flaps	—2/3 open
Intercooler flaps	—CLOSED
Oil cooler flap	—Open as required
Rudder tab	—6 degrees, nose
Aileron tab	—RIGHT
Elevator tab	—1 degree, nose UP
Alternate air control	—Direct (in)
Wing flaps	—Set as required
Tail wheel	—LOCKED
Manifold pressure	—53.3" Hg

LANDING

Stall warning switch	—ON
Tail wheel	—LOCKED for field
	—FREE for carrier
Fuel tank selector	—RESERVE
Mixture	—Automatic RICH

Supercharger control	—2300 RPM
Cowl flaps	—CLOSED
Alternate air control	—Direct (in)
Landing gear	—EXTENDED
Wing flaps	—Set 30° or as required
Arresting hook	—DOWN for carrier
	—UP for field

Perhaps the best training aid ever invented was the bull session. It's a well-known fact that wherever pilots congregate, their conversations always gravitate toward what is first and foremost in their minds—flying (although women come in a close second). There don't seem to be any work hour restrictions nor any holds barred on weekends where airplane talk is concerned. It goes on morning, noon, and night, over a meal or a beer at the club, even in the wee hours of the morning at the bachelor officers' quarters (BOQ). Any pilot who is that interested in airplanes has to be that interested in learning; as a result, it becomes an unsolicited dividend in the learning process. A pilot can sort out bum dope from good dope and then later apply the sound principles in the air. In almost every case, this incongruous yet effective type of education, in combination with the lectures he receives and the textbooks he studies, will make him a well-rounded, reputable pilot.

Bull sessions can be even more valuable in combat. Among the old-timers who had been to Guadalcanal, it was agreed that bull sessions were, in fact, worth many hours of normal training flights. One of my old friends who embraced this phenomenon was Maj Herbert H. "Trigger" Long, an ace with ten planes to his credit. Before he entered combat, he mentioned the talks he had had with VMF-221 pilots and what a great opportunity they had been to exchange views. Then, just before the transfer to Guadalcanal, were the bull sessions with Joe Renner and Soupie Campbell, who passed on valuable information concerning the characteristics of the Zero. Following this, and after arriving at Guadalcanal, again those pilots were briefed by Joe Foss, who told them the best way to shoot down a Japanese Zero: "You fly toward the target until a midair seems inevitable, then fire all six guns and fly through the wreckage." Obviously, there was no real way to train for this eventuality.

* * *

The status board stretched across one wall of the ready room. It displayed each phase of the F4U Corsair flight syllabus, which each new pilot would have to accomplish over the months. Once filled in, it would reflect more than 200 hours of flying time per pilot. The names of the pilots were listed in the left column in order of rank. In a horizontal line opposite each man's name were squares that, when checked off, would represent the number of hours he'd accumulated toward accomplishing that phase of the syllabus.

The first fifteen squares on the status board came under the heading *Familiarization*. A pilot checking out in the Corsair would get the feel of the airplane in this stage. Captain Wally Wethe conducted many lectures on the flight characteristics of the Corsair with particular emphasis on spins and stalls. Once in the air, if a pilot inadvertently entered a stall, he had to resort to his training on the ground in order to recover from his problem—and do it instantaneously! This meant pushing that stick hard forward and the rudder hard over in the direction opposite the roll tendency of the airplane.

In the preflight briefing, a pilot would be assigned an air-space area designated on his chart in which to perform his maneuvers. Normally, a young pilot's timid beginning soon turned into a bold exhibition of radical moves. Much time was spent on acrobatics, and this would be the key to precision formation flying later.

Second Lieutenant Jimbo Ormond, one of our more aggressive young pilots in the squadron, was now well into the familiarization stage of the syllabus, having accumulated upward of twenty hours. It was a nice day high above the Mojave Desert when he was giving that Corsair a "wringing out." Jimbo really had the feel of that airplane—or so he thought. The stunts were getting tighter and tighter, then suddenly there was a jerk and a hair-raising sensation of something wrong as the plane fell out in a left spin. He heard a loud warning inside his mind: *"Do something—quick!"* Jimbo was going through the recovery procedures when, suddenly, another jerk produced still another unnerving sensation and the plane began spinning to the right. The adrenaline was pumping, but he caught himself, saying, "Now come on, Jimbo—take it easy—and make a smooth recovery." Happily, he did, and a little shaken but more conservative Lt Jim Ormond landed safely.

Second Lieutenant John F. "Johnny" Cox was one of about a half-dozen of our pilots who had not flown the Corsair before. Johnny had received his preflight training in Iowa City, Iowa, and then primary at Olathe, Kansas. He finished his advanced training at Pensacola, where he was commissioned in August 1943. He was able to build up time in the Curtiss SBC-4 biplane at Opa Locka, as well as the Brewster F2A Buffalo. The F4U checkout eluded him at El Toro, but he did get time in the Grumman Wildcat.

Johnny Cox passed the written test and then was taken out to the flight line to sit in the cockpit of the Corsair for the blindfold test. Wally Wethe and Bo Little stood on the wing on either side, observing the procedure. They ignored the sweat rolling down his brow. Next was to learn how to start the engine. Johnny was allowed only two shells, ten-gauge shotgun shells, to be specific, which the mechanic inserted in the breech of the engine access compartment. (A Jack and Heintz electric starter would eventually be installed in place of the starter cartridge system.) So far, so good. Johnny got a thumbs-up.

On the following day, Johnny was scheduled for his maiden flight in the Corsair. But first came a short briefing. It accentuated what had been drilled into his head time and time again. Airspeeds were stressed and the gentle maneuvers were once again reviewed. Wally and Bo watched Johnny slowly weave his way out to the end of the runway and into position for takeoff. A chase plane did not accompany a solo plane in those days.

There always seemed to be a significant wind blowing on the Mojave Desert, and on this day it was blowing down the east/west runway. But that runway was closed for repair, so the duty runway was 32, the one to the northwest. The crosswind was something to be concerned about. Besides that, on the approach end, a Corsair was lying upside down just off the runway to the right. A pilot from another squadron had been checking out in the plane earlier that morning and, upon landing, had not been able to cope with the crosswind and gusty situation. Upon observing this bad omen, Johnny thought, Is this a portent of things to come? But Johnny's brow was as determined as it was furrowed, so he pushed the throttle full forward and gathered speed down the runway. He knew he could do it—and he did.

After Cox there was a quick succession of checkouts. Second Lieutenants Raleigh E. "Blimpo" Fletcher, Norwood R. "Norry" Hanson, and others flew the Corsair successfully the first time. Fletcher had been commissioned only six months earlier. As a brand-new second lieutenant, he was transferred to Jacksonville, Florida, for training in the Grumman torpedo bomber. Then it was a move to Santa Barbara, California, to join a Marine torpedo squadron. But then, in the bureaucratic way the service sometimes handles things, he was abruptly directed to join a fighter squadron in the Mojave Desert. Fletcher seemed just like any other ordinary second lieutenant when he checked into VMF-452. In a quiet, unassuming way, he had a penchant for fully understanding the Corsair, and it soon became conspicuous. From an engineering point of view, he beheld it with awe and soon learned every technical facet of this complicated machine. Of course, this was true of almost all our new pilots. The eagerness with which they learned to fly was phenomenal.

Once through the familiarization phase, a pilot would progress to the "formation" stage, flying two-plane section formations at first and then, later, four-plane division formations. During these initial training phases, a section leader had to be especially alert during the join-ups. It could be a harrowing experience watching a new pilot slide into position for the first time. But his leader would be anticipating such an eventuality and would adjust accordingly. His wingman soon learned that any sudden movements were taboo—that all turns and adjustments were to be conservative and calculated. Depth perception was tied in with keen judgment of acceleration and deceleration. There was a way to do it with precision, and this is what the new pilot had to learn. Most often, speed control on join-ups was manipulation of the cowl flaps or the oil cooler flaps—opening when overrunning or closing for acceleration on a join-up. Sometimes the speed brakes on a Corsair were the landing gear. There was a position on the gear quadrant that indicated dive brakes. The gear trailed but the tail wheel remained retracted. Resorting to this device was seldom necessary, however, for most often the cowl flaps did the trick.

In the formative stages of flying together at Mojave, the pilots were getting the feel of the Corsair and learning the rudiments of formation flying and tactics. One day I was leading a flight, and Lt Johnny Cox appeared to be all over the sky; he just couldn't seem to get it right. After we landed, I called him in and told him, in no uncertain terms, that that was the worst exhibition of formation flying I had ever seen. I berated and castigated him, and I don't think Johnny ever forgot it. Privately, I felt a little bad about it later.

Once some semblance of formation flying had been achieved, at least ten flights involving division tactics were on the agenda. Because each pilot had individually gained proficiency in acrobatics, flying with multiple airplanes was demonstrated. The flight leader had to have the utmost confidence in his wingman and the whole flight behind him. The many hours of climbing, diving, and tail chasing earned him that trust. Because these young lieutenants lived and breathed the Corsair day in and day out, and because they flew together so much, they learned to understand and react to a leader's intentions.

Captain Bulgy Bryson, our operations officer, sized up the way he wanted his four-plane division to fly: "If I plow in, I want three more plowing in with me—in perfect formation!"

Once a pilot began formation flying, he would continue to do so regularly for as long as he was part of the active fighter squadron. With luck and longevity, he would eventually be promoted to the position of flight leader.

* * *

Probably one of the most important tactics to come out of the early

Guadalcanal era was the "Thach Weave." This was an offensive/defensive maneuver that a two-plane section, or multiples thereof, used in achieving their own security en route to and from a target. In horizontal flight, a section leader and his wingman would make continuous S-turns—opposite each other as they proceeded on their mission. The logic behind this sort of maneuvering was that if one plane had his tail exposed to an attacking enemy plane, the other had the capacity to make a near head-on run on the adversary. This security had a ripple effect in that it would extend likewise to the second section of the same division—or to the whole flight, if need be.

Lieutenant Commander John S. Thach sparked the idea for this innovative maneuver while flying from the carrier *Enterprise*. He and LCdr Jimmy Flatley, commanding officer of VF-10, fine-tuned it just in time for the October 26, 1942, Battle of the Santa Cruz Islands. Soon the Marine fliers on Guadalcanal adopted this unique twist, and it was doctrine from then on.

The Thach Weave was a radical departure from the way aircraft elements had traditionally been composed. The departure from the old three-plane section to the two-plane and, likewise, the nine-plane division to the four-plane division, was a giant step in achieving agility in formation flying. The old three-plane section was unwieldy because the inside pilot was always in trouble—sliding in too fast and trying to put the brakes on.

Once the pilots of VMF-452 began formation flying, the Thach Weave was common fare throughout the syllabus. We Guadalcanal veterans who picked up the tactic during the Solomons campaign liked to think that we refined and improved on it. We flew this formation hour after hour until we could maintain it in all kinds of circumstances. Even in mock dogfights, when two or more divisions would become a ball of airplanes—diving, climbing, and tail chasing—we were ever mindful of always turning toward, in protecting a friendly. Later on when the squadron began gunnery, bombing, and rocketry, division tactics dictated that the Thach Weave be practiced to and from the gunnery ranges. Even on cross-country navigational hops, the practice was demanded where practical.

Whenever there was an air-group exercise, the Thach Weave was practiced. We would cover the dive-bombers and torpedo planes en route to the target. We would move our elements close abreast and loosely enough that they could turn in to each other. In this kind of exercise, there was another advantage in using the Thach Weave: It enabled the fighters to fly slowly enough to stay with the air group when acting as an escort. We were always striving for perfection.

At this stage of squadron training, it was very important to monitor each new pilot's proficiency. It was a personal sort of thing and had to be done in kind of a clandestine way. The evaluation was to protect the pilot—and others—from danger. There had been specific cases in the past involving slow reflex, mechanical response, a general timid approach, or just simply a lack of proficiency. In each case, a transfer to flying duty involving less frequent employment of the calculated risk was a necessary course of action. This was a responsibility we had to take seriously. Fortunately, we had only two cases in the squadron that fit that category.

CHAPTER 11

Routine with Punctuations

Above my office door was a wood sign painted red and inscribed with bold yellow letters. Somewhere along the line I had picked up these words by an unknown author:

Flying in itself is not inherently dangerous,
but, to a greater degree than the sea,
is unrelentingly unforgiving of carelessness.

This somber message was supposed to have a sobering effect on the sometimes blindly enthusiastic squadron members. During the war the fatalities that a resulted from operational accidents far outnumbered those suffered as a result of enemy action. Almost every squadron had its toll of catastrophic operational mishaps at one time or another. VMF-452 was no exception.

Captain Hal Trenchard was a model pilot. He was tall and handsome with a very pleasant demeanor, the type of Marine who would have served well on a recruiting poster. Coming from Ambler, Pennsylvania, Harold was a letterman who had gained recognition in football, basketball, and track. He had gone to college and then flight training, and had distinguished himself in the Southwest Pacific by being officially credited with having shot down three Japanese planes. On one occasion, he had been forced down on a deserted island and remained there ten days before being picked up. Later, he was again shot down and landed in the jungle—painfully wounded. He was rescued by friendly natives who cared for him until he could be taken to an American hospital for treatment.

It is my recollection that Harold was a penny-ante poker enthusiast. During lulls in flying activity, we all had sessions playing the game. He played it dumb like a fox and wiped us out many times.

Being one of the senior pilots, Harold led many of the training flights. He was now beginning his second tour.

Captain Trenchard was leading a formation of four Corsairs on March 8, 1944, when the accident occurred. Second Lieutenant Mal Maloney was his wingman; Lt Rocky Staples led the second section with Lt John Lawrence as his wingman. They had been practicing formation flying, changing formations, climbing and descending turns, wingovers, and then a tail chase. About 15 miles northeast of Mojave, the formation joined up for return to the field. Maloney was on Trenchard's right wing, and the second section flew in formation to his left. Trenchard announced over the radio that he would like to try a four-plane, simultaneously executed, in-place slow roll. It was attempted once to no avail, with planes falling out in all directions. The formation reassembled and Trenchard radioed with considerable force and anger that they were going to accomplish this maneuver. The formation was now at about 2,500 feet, and Trenchard began his slow roll to the left. Maloney rolled over until they were on their backs. As they went past 180 degrees, Maloney lost sight of Trenchard, then pulled out to regain control and orientation.

Meanwhile Staples and his wingman had finished their roll well off to the left. They saw a smoke-and-dust plume rise from the desert. The three planes joined up, returned to base, and reported the accident. It is only conjecture that Trenchard dove straight into the ground for lack of altitude or that he entered an accelerated stall.

A board of inquiry was presided over by the base commander, and all pilots involved testified. The board was extremely upset but saw no fault to be laid. Privately, we all agreed that it was an impossible maneuver, considering the airplanes they had as well as their level of experience and skill.

These new pilots had not been briefed on this particular aspect of the flight that day. They were just beginning to get the feel of the Corsair. Only experienced pilots could accomplish such a dangerous maneuver in formation.

On March 23, two weeks after Trenchard's death, the squadron suffered another casualty. Second Lieutenant Arthur D. "Don" Boyd was returning to the Mojave base after a training exercise when he spun in on the approach for landing. The turn coming in was much too tight and he lost control. The Corsair crashed just before the head of the runway, and Boyd was killed.

Second Lieutenant Rocky Staples, who had been a great friend and drinking buddy of Boyd, accompanied the body back to Flint, Michigan, where he escorted Boyd's folks and girlfriend to the funeral.

We did a great deal of soul searching after these accidents. How would we go about pulling in the reins? How could these tragedies have been prevented? The bereavement period may not have been long enough for conservative flying tactics to continue. Still, every member of the squadron was conscious of the loss, so there might have been some lessons learned. We all perhaps speculated, but resisted the thought that there would be more losses.

Night flying was a very important part of Corsair proficiency. The syllabus called for night flights to be scheduled at regular intervals throughout the year. At first, each pilot made individual flights, then section and division formation flights became mandatory. Later, when night-flying proficiency had been achieved, the whole squadron of twenty-four aircraft would take off, rendezvous, and fly in formation on prescribed routes before returning to base.

Night flying was almost synonymous with instrument flying. Preparation was crucial. Night vision had to be acquired by all pilots, and this was done in the squadron ready room under red-light visibility for a period of adjustment time before takeoff. And of course, depth perception was tied in with keen vision in landings, takeoffs, and formation flying.

The Corsair had once had a bad reputation as a bouncy airplane. But a recent fix to the oleo strut was a big help upon landing, especially at night. It eliminated much of the bounce, so when the plane hit the deck, it normally stuck there for the rest of the roll-out. Once the pilot was in the traffic pattern and was lined up with the runway ahead, he could see the two narrow rows of lights that converged in pinpoints at the far end. His timing was such that as he decreased his altitude and neared the head of the runway, the lights suddenly spread apart and he was close to the deck. Flaring out in time at near stalling speed was the adjustment he strived for. With good night vision, this was normally no problem. But here again it was always practice and experience that made the difference.

All did not go well on some of those first attempts at night flying. On March 20, Lt Thomas D. "Tom" Pace had an accident. He was coming in for a landing, and somehow the plane flipped over on its back. Of course, most of the impact was on the bubble canopy which, unfortunately, included Tom's head. As the inverted plane skidded down the runway, Tom was almost scalped. There were no broken bones, so he returned to flight status a few weeks later after the head wounds had healed.

And there were other jittery moments. Night flying had progressed to the division formation stage, and 1stLt Gerry Vetter was leading a section with Lt Jimbo Ormond as wingman. There had been breaks and join-ups and, at one point, Gerry opened up on the radio and asked, "Jimbo, where are you?" Simultaneously, Jimbo's plane shook as Gerry passed immediately in front. The plumes of his exhaust flames were startlingly visible—at about the same time the navigation lights were. Although shaken, all pilots joined up and returned to base safely.

* * *

Gunnery would be an exciting phase of the training program for the pilots, who had never experienced the level of efficiency in Corsair performance as a stable gun platform. The six 50-caliber machine guns fired through ports in the leading edge of the wings—three on each side. The ammunition was fed to each machine gun from its individual ammunition pans, located in the outer wing panels just aft of the guns. The mass of lead, calibrated to converge and concentrate on a small area 400 to 500 yards ahead, was devastating. That range was normally considered the optimum distance for firing at an enemy airplane.

Before the squadron pilots could practice firing the guns at a tow target— a banner being towed by another Corsair—they had to accomplish about ten flights of dummy runs.

Normally, a flight of two divisions would climb to 18,000 feet en route to the gunnery range. The tow target would set up for its run about 3,000 feet below and proceed on a straight and level course. The eight attacking Corsairs would peel off one at a time for the overhead run at the target. As the pilots gained experience, their techniques improved. These runs would be near vertical, but the set patterns were not realistic in a combat sense. In later phases of gunnery the pilots learned other techniques as well.

Our eager lieutenants were always trying to outdo each other. Joe Warren is a case in point. One day during a dummy run flight, he was the one who was right on target—literally. He hit it. The lead weight on the end of the banner hit the oil cooler at the base of the Corsair's left wing. The plane began losing oil fast, and it wasn't long before all the oil was gone. The inevitable happened: The engine froze up. Joe decided to make a wheels-up landing on a dry lakebed. He discovered too late that the bed was so hard a B-17 could have landed wheels down with no trouble. The flight leader buzzed him for a while and then returned to base.

Joe cooled his heels in the hot, sizzling sun. Quite sometime later a yellow Piper Cub sat down on the dry lakebed beside the Corsair. Joe couldn't believe it when he saw his squadronmate Lt Bruce A. "The Ox" Guetzloe climb out of the cub with a Coke in his hand for Joe. The Ox left sometime later, but Joe had been ordered to stay with the plane. Much later a flatbed truck and a jeep showed up, and Joe and the Corsair were brought back to base.

Next morning came the confrontation with me. Joe stood at attention while the expletives flew and he heard what a stupid thing he'd done . . . again. Years later, when he confided in me about the incident, Joe said he was sure I was going to make him pay for that Corsair!

* * *

The flight syllabus was a rigorous grind that began to mold these pilots into first-class combatants. It was a seven-day-a-week regimen, but we did try to stagger the schedule so that a pilot would get at least two successive days off per month. Most of the time, he could count on a day off during the week as well. Time was passing quickly up and the squares on the left side of the status board were filling up fast. The months of March and April flew by, and we were entering the ordnance phase of the syllabus along with some night flying.

* * *

Competition was rife among the eager squadrons at the Mojave base. Earlier, one of the first orders of business for our squadron had been to design an insignia. Lieutenant Norwood Hanson was elected to develop the idea we had in mind: It was to be the image of a bearded, rugged-looking individual waving an extremely large scimitar above his head, the famed "corsair," or thief Ali Baba of *Arabian Nights* fame. The swashbuckling name *Skyraiders* was pinned on the squadron patch and emblazoned on the leather flight jackets of all the pilots in the squadron. In view of the rivalry among the squadrons at Mojave, this indeed enhanced our prestige. But it wasn't until May 24, 1944, that the squadron insignia was finally approved by the Navy Department in Washington, D.C.

Although the training and preparation of the five tactical squadrons based on Mojave differed little from one to the other, our squadron spirit indicated otherwise. On the sandy approach to the VMF-452 office building was a wood archway through which all our pilots entered. Above it was the huge squadron insignia and below it a sign that read: THROUGH THESE PORTALS PASS THE BEST DAMN FIGHTER PILOTS ON THIS STATION.

Liberty on the Mojave Desert left a lot to be desired. It was not like El Toro, which had within a 30-mile radius a plethora of sights to be seen, luxurious nightclubs, exotic dining rooms, and theaters to attend. From the cultural ambience of Laguna Beach to the glitter and excitement of the big cities, everything was right at hand. Los Angeles and Hollywood were almost 100 miles away from Mojave, and gas rationing was an inhibiting factor for those who had automobiles. In fact, being assigned to Mojave was tantamount to being relegated to the boondocks.

Of course, one could find recreational outlets on the Mojave Desert if he looked for them. Many people became amateur geologists, for the desert abounded in minerals. It was a fascinating place to explore and perhaps find beautiful jade glass shale. I envisioned the back patio of my house in Laguna Beach paved with this shale, polished and laid down like flagstone.

The lack of recreational facilities off base was compensated for by intense intrasquadron sports such as baseball, basketball, and swimming events in the indoor pool. Second Lieutenant Alex Dutkin was a sports enthusiast, and it wasn't long before he had conscripted from the officer and enlisted talent pool some very competitive athletes. He was able to organize these into teams to be reckoned with by the other squadrons on the base. We all supported these athletic events, which was obvious by our loyal attendance.

I suppose the motorcycle could also be considered a form of recreation. In view of gas rationing, it was a really economical way of getting around. Lieutenants Norry Hanson, Paul Piana, Blimpo Fletcher, Ox Guetzloe, and Frank T. Morrison each had one, and I suppose there was not a man among them who didn't have an accident at one time or another.

Once on his day off, Frank Morrison took off aboard his motorcycle on an exploring excursion up in the Tehachapi Mountains. This turned out to be a bonanza for the squadron, for he met and later became fast friends with old man Duntley, owner of a ranch there. It wasn't long before Mr. Duntley gave carte blanche to the whole squadron, along with a standing invitation to all the barbecues and picnics he hosted on his beautiful property.

Mr. Duntley's ranch was in the foothills of the Tehachapi Mountains about 18 miles west of Mojave. His establishment epitomized a real working ranch. The herds of cattle, the cowboys and horses, the ranch buildings, and trappings indeed gave new meaning to the phrase *local color*. And Mr. Duntley himself was an interesting character, dressed in cowboy boots and broad-brimmed hat—a true westerner. He was a little stout, with a friendly face. And, best of all, he loved the Marines.

CHAPTER 12

Boys Will Be Boys

It was early June 1944, and things were going along almost too well. The progress in accomplishing the syllabus had been pretty much incident-free in recent weeks, despite the normal mechanical problems that harried the engineering department. So long as we had Corsairs on the line, we had pilots in the air. There were no slackers here, for the program would not allow it. It was designed to wring out the best a young pilot had to offer. Also, it was seen to that a junior officer's collateral duties did not interfere with his primary function as an up-and-coming skilled fighter pilot. So now these young officers were deeply involved in absorbing the lessons being taught by their mentors—Bryson, Stack, Wethe, and Weiland. Very slowly and methodically, the phases of dive-bombing, strafing, gunnery, and tactics were being driven home in a cogent, enlightening sort of way.

Because things were going almost too smoothly, something was bound to give. It did. Some overzealous pilots went beyond the envelope of tactical propriety.

Probably all red-blooded American pilots found it hard to resist the temptation of "flathatting," which referred to illegal, hazardous, low-level flying. To vent frustration and seek thrills this way was something of which no landlubber could boast. Much like flying under the Golden Gate Bridge, flathatting lent prestige to the pilot—it was an achievement of sorts. In other areas, flying at 200 to 300 miles per hour a few feet above the ground over undulating terrain produced an adrenaline high. Good 20/20 vision and depth perception were essential.

Flathatting was strictly against the rules, but, if an honest poll could be taken of all pilots since the advent of the airplane, I'm sure it would reflect 100 percent culpability. It was almost expected that any young pilot worth his salt would indulge in just a little innocent flathatting—unless he was sure that the powers that be were watching. The idea, of course, was to never get caught. Getting caught could lead to grounding—the ultimate humiliation. It could also possibly affect the officer's fitness report. Understandably, the irrefutable evidence of a nicked prop or sagebrush in the oil intakes led to some rather hairy explanations. Second Lieutenant Emmons "Mal" Maloney, having been caught in the act, rationalized it this way: "We kept it safe and kept it at about ten feet."

Once a pilot matures, he generally understands the life-threatening nature of flathatting. As the old saying goes: There are old pilots and there are bold pilots, but there are no old, bold pilots. Unfortunately, you *can* keep a good man down—permanently, as too many accidents proved in those days.

A flathatting incident occurred on a particularly hot June day in 1944. I was in the office when the phone rang.

"Major Weiland here."

"This is Colonel Torrey. Pat, I want you to come to my office immediately."

"Yes, sir, Colonel."

The receiver slammed down on the other end. Colonel Dan Torrey was our air-group commander. Something had happened. I jumped into the jeep and wheeled over to group headquarters.

"Pat, I just want to know what in hell happened over at Muroc Dry Lake!" Torrey said. "I just got a call from Colonel Adams and he says a couple of your boys practically took the cover off the whole installation. He has the fuselage numbers and the time it happened. And he wants to see them immediately!"

Colonel Joseph P. Adams was in command of the Marine Corps Air Station at Mojave. He had received a phone call from the Muroc Army Air Corps commander, who was in a huff over the flathatting at Muroc. There were big, lumbering B-24 bombers based there, along with a secret aircraft test program. Muroc's group had to curtail operations while our planes harassed their installation.

Torrey wasn't about to let this pass.

"Pat, climb in your Corsair and go over there and find out what in hell exactly went on," he said. "Let me know as soon as you get back."

"Yes, sir, Colonel."

I wheeled about without hesitation and hurried back to the squadron. I called in Capts Wally Wethe and Bob Bryson.

"Wally, tell the flight line to get a couple of planes ready. You and I are flying over to Muroc Dry Lake.

"Bob, find out who was flying Numbers 10-A and 16-A between 1030 and 1100. They've been harassing the hell out of Muroc. Colonel Adams wants to see them immediately. You take them to see him at the Mojave Administration Building."

When Wally and I landed at Muroc, a staff car was waiting to take us to the commanding officer. The colonel confronted us and told us in no uncertain terms of the disturbance the flathatting had caused. I waffled a little bit with what I thought was a proper demeanor and promised that nothing like this would ever happen again.

"Sir," I began, "those two pilots were very young and immature—"

The colonel exploded.

"Two pilots? There was a whole goddamn flight! A B-24 was landing from the opposite direction and had to take a wave-off. An evasive maneuver like that can kill people, you know."

I was puzzled. I had been told only two planes were involved and we had both pilots' names and side numbers. But now two more? What in the world was going on? It stymied me. What more could I say to appease the commanding officer at Muroc Dry Lake?

Wally and I drove on to Muroc Operations. It wasn't all a lost cause; while there I recognized two Army Air Corps pilots who had been friends of mine at Guadalcanal. Originally based in Australia, in those days they had flown with the 67th and 68th Pursuit squadrons, flying Airacobras. In December 1942 and January 1943, they flew medium cover on our missions to Munda and other targets in the New Georgia Island group. It was on one such occasion that I shot down a Japanese Zero in a dogfight over Munda. I was pleased to see these two test pilots at Muroc, even though this wasn't exactly the time for a happy reunion.

Meanwhile, back at Mojave, 1stLts Rocky Staples and Bo Little were in deep trouble. Before Capt Bryson escorted them up to see Col Adams, Rocky and Bo changed out of their flight suits into appropriate military attire. They wouldn't have considered wearing their flight suits beyond the confines of the squadron area.

In the ready room, Rocky said to Bo, "You let me do the talking. You just agree with everything I have to say." But during the confrontation, Col Adams was not impressed.

Lieutenants Staples and Little were sentenced to ten days confined to quarters for a lesser offense. Many months later, Rocky tried to explain it: "I won't pretend we were taunted or provoked into doing it—seduced might be a more accurate word."

The other two planes flathatting over Muroc were flown by 2ndLts Raleigh "Blimpo" Fletcher and Norwood Hanson. Whether it was contrived or a mere coincidence, I'll never know. Always eager to fly, as Fletcher put it, "We had sweated and sniveled two maintenance test flights that particular morning." After checking out the aircraft in the air, they took turns getting on each other's tails in dogfights. At one point Fletcher was on Hanson's tail when an Army P-38 Lightning came zooming into them. Hanson immediately hopped on the P-38. This tearing up of the skies went on for some time and the next thing they knew, they were down on the deck over Muroc Dry Lake.

The investigation showed that they flew down the service runway at below minimum, maybe 200 feet, with one aircraft inverted (Hanson, of course).

Lieutenants Fletcher and Hanson were offered a choice of either a general court-martial or six months' delay in promotion. Because of the exigencies of wartime, this was really no choice at all. Naturally, they accepted the six months' delay in promotion. Fletcher later caught up with his class when he made captain, then moved ahead of some when he made major in Korea. After the war Hanson elected to return to civilian life.

I thought we had the problem licked, but that ol' devil temptation struck again. Sometime later a couple of our Corsairs came home flying so low that they had tumbleweeds in their oil coolers and stains on the propeller blades. I suspected that the culprits were Lts Rudolph J. "Rudy" Collett and Bruce "The Ox" Guetzloe—they were just the types. It was all hushed up pretty well. There were certain things the Old Man wasn't supposed to know about. I won't say I turned my head exactly, but since there was really no damage, I didn't press the issue. The squadron was already in enough trouble as it was.

* * *

Out in that vast Pacific Ocean where islands were spaced hundreds of miles apart, it was safe to assume that someday, in the not too distant future, VMF-452 would find its niche in the order of battle and be placed there opposing the Japanese. It was also a safe assumption that we would have to be prepared for the island hopping that had been characteristic earlier in the war. Therefore, we needed the experience to cope with such an eventuality.

The element of navigational training was introduced into the squadron system, and this called for many cross-country flights. Quite often a cross-country flight led to an RON, which was a pilot's delight. Most often, these were under visual flight rules, but the calculations of fuel consumption and times en route and arrival were a mathematical chore. The pilot was kept busy with the ever-present chart and knee pad.

A section or division would fly a loose formation for reason of fuel economy. A pilot would normally use "automatic lean" on his fuel mixture control; but on a long cross-country flight, he would adjust it to "manual lean"—which was to "lean" it out until a drop of 50 to 75 rpm was observed—then add one click to the control. Around 1,450 rpm in manual lean provided maximum endurance. In view of all the fuel carried internally, plus that in the belly tanks, it was pretty much the consensus of all pilots that the maximum endurance of the Corsair was far greater than that of a pilot's ass.

Furthermore, the Corsair had taken on a more versatile role as a fighter-bomber. The F4U-1D's offensive capability had also been supplemented at the factory with four rocket rails under each wing. New production models would come equipped with these rocket rails. We in the squadron would have to wait months before the timetable of overhaul and repair would permit installation and our eventual use in rocket practice. The rails carried eight 5-inch HVAR rockets, which, in combat, would be common fare in attacking ground targets.

Two pylons were also fitted to the Corsair's stub wings just inboard of the wing-fold mechanism and were capable of carrying either two drop tanks or two 1,000-pound bombs. A droppable fuel tank could be hung from a centerline pylon.

* * *

At about this time, in early June 1944, the capability of the F4U-1D was being demonstrated in the South Pacific by Charles A. Lindbergh, the technical representative for the Corsair. Unlike the regular bomb load of 1,500 pounds that the Marine pilots were carrying, Lindbergh proved that it was possible for the Corsair to carry 3,000 pounds. He later he went a step farther and took off with a 4,000-pound bomb load. The Vought Company could now tout the Corsair as a very versatile machine.

The squadron was building up time and experience in the Corsair at an accelerated pace. We couldn't help but notice an innovative twist that our sister squadron next door was smugly performing out on the desert. VMF-451 had an intelligence officer by the name of Lieutenant Nayman, who envisioned strafing targets of parked Zeros right at their doorstep. He selected a site about ten miles west of the air station and well out in the desert. He bulldozed a landing strip and revetments and built dummy aircraft of scrap lumber. Below each dummy he placed a five-gallon can of gasoline, and herein was a great training aid. For three days those pilots strafed the field and destroyed all of the aircraft. At the end of the third day, Nayman drove to the site and replaced the destroyed gas cans and the simulated airplanes. The simulated Japanese airfield was now ready for renewed attacks. An Army Air Corps B-25 unit based at Muroc Dry Lake somehow got wind of this target arrangement and, when VMF-451 wasn't looking, they came over and destroyed the targets the very next day.

Not to be outdone, and in an attempt to emulate that good idea, our squadron found a suitable target just inside the boundary of one of the gunnery ranges, over the mountains just to the northeast. The targets were old mining shacks that had long ago outlived their usefulness and were within the restricted area.

The flight schedule in the ready room reflected the day's flight operations on that hot June afternoon. Two divisions of Corsairs would practice strafing runs with live ammunition on the mining shacks. The flight of eight planes took off, led by 1stLt Kenny Bennett. At 20,000 feet each pilot peeled off and made his run, firing the six .50-caliber machine guns at the targets. It was good training for the pilots and they did a terrific job of blasting the shacks.

A few days later a grizzled old prospector (aren't all prospectors "grizzled"?) came on foot to the main gate at MCAS Mojave. He was furious. He demanded to see "the fella that runs this place." He was so adamant about it that the MPs drove him up to headquarters to see Colonel Adams. They ushered the old prospector into the colonel's office, catching him flatfooted.

The old man ranted and raved. "Those durn fools tried to kill me!" he yelled. "At first I hid under my bed, but then the bullets got closer so I hid behind the stove. Those airyplanes got so close they blew down my house. They killed my mule and shot up everything else they could find. I want to know what's going on and who's going to pay for my mule."

Colonel Adams listened patiently to the prospector's story, then led him to the wall chart where a map of the Mojave Desert showed the magenta-colored outlines of the bombing and gunnery ranges. They pinpointed the exact location of the prospector's recent residence. Sure enough, it was right in the middle of the gunnery range. He was now even more grizzled and disgruntled as he trekked his way off the air station.

Compensation for the mule? It is only conjecture that he ever received it.

Captain Pat Weiland. Late 1942.

Lieutenant Colonel Luther S. "Sad Sam" Moore (center),
the commanding officer of Marine Fighter Training Units, El Toro, California.
He is flanked on his right by Major Hank Ellis (FTU-1, Corsairs),
and on his left by Major Pat Weiland (FTU-2, Wildcats). Fall 1943.

The "Skyraiders" of VMF-452.

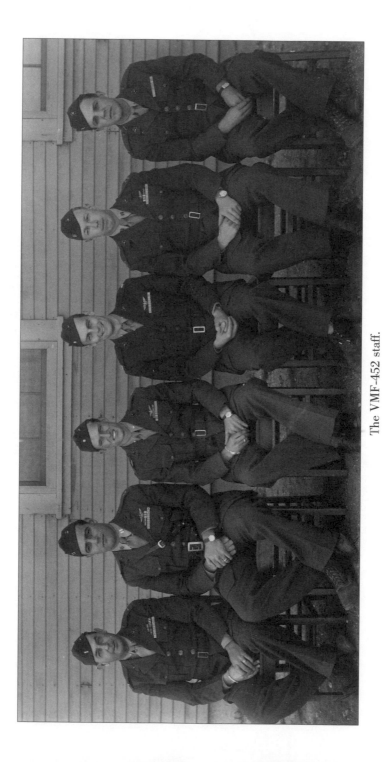

The VMF-452 staff.

An aerial view of Marine Corps Air Station Mojave. August 1944.

A flight of VMF-452 Vought F4U-1D Corsairs.

Above and Beyond: Major Pat Weiland and a Corsair.

COMPLIMENTS OF COLONEL HERBERT A. LONG

A Corsair over the Tehachapi Mountains.

The crash of this
VMF-452 Corsair killed
Capt Hal Trenchard.
March 8, 1944.

COMPLIMENTS OF BAXTER LITTLE

CHAPTER 13

Incidents Home and Abroad

June 15, 1944, was D day of the amphibious landing on Saipan. I had known of this operation almost immediately upon its happening, because it was the duty of 1stLt Fred Olson to bring in the latest intelligence bulletins and lay them on my desk for perusal. It was interesting to note in that bulletin that the Marines' amphibious landing at Saipan was supported by Navy pilots flying F6F Hellcats from escort carriers.

Olson had sorted out the intelligence information and disseminated pertinent items to those persons on a "need to know" list to read and initial. It was fascinating to read the discreet, confidential reports that analyzed the accuracy of the news already broadcast by the media. No one outside a small, privileged military circle was privy to these intelligence bulletins.

Each subsequent bulletin seemed more interesting than the one before. About four days after the Saipan landing, one arrived that struck me as particularly riveting. It was captioned "Marianas Turkey Shoot." I sat up at attention while reading this one. It appeared to be a last-ditch effort by the Japanese to retain the Marianas Island group after all.

The Japanese correctly reasoned that this would be a crucial battle. This was their outer defense ring and included the main islands of Saipan, Tinian, and Guam. The Japanese fleet, which included nine aircraft carriers, was hell-bent on equalizing the debacle it suffered at Midway and the Solomons. Two of its carriers were immediately sunk by our submarines, but the remaining seven continued on their do-or-die mission. By 0800 on June 19, huge flights of Japanese airplanes were winging their way on an easterly course toward Guam and our own fleet. Detection had been made early enough, so our own planes were prepared for the attack. Within an hour and a half, thirty-five Japanese planes had been shot down. But all day long the Japanese planes kept coming, and the Navy pilots in their F6F Hellcats kept shooting them down. At the end of the day, the tally amounted to 383 enemy planes. Another Japanese carrier had been sunk by American aircraft; later in the day, the remaining six carriers, plus five battleships, began to flee to the west. Vice Admiral Marc A. Mitscher ordered hot pursuit by our aircraft off the fast carriers, but the distances were overextended and, as a result, eighty aircraft were lost by pilots trying to find their way back home.

This was exciting news, but there was one big question that hovered over the whole story: Where were the Marine fliers? Holy smoke! I could see the guys up at Headquarters Marine Corps in a tizzy. This news must have stirred up a hornet's nest! Where *were* the Marine fliers? Why didn't they get a slice of the action? From our little keyhole of observation at the lower level, it was obviously an unjust exclusion. With only island airfields from which to operate, Marine pilots and their planes were landlocked in areas to the rear.

Subsequent bulletins indicated that the close air support that had been provided by the Navy and the Army Air Corps was extremely insufficient. It seems the only answer to this dilemma would be to put Marine flyers aboard escort carriers in order to support the Marine troops on the ground.

Of course, we at the lower level were not allowed to reason why. All we could do was get the squadron trained and out into combat.

News of combat casualties in the South Pacific trickled down slowly at Mojave. When someone particularly close was on the list, it was like a stab in the heart. Captain Hank Schriver was one of those casualties. He was killed in the first wave during the invasion of Saipan. Hank's death brought memories flooding back. It was probably his same amphibian tractor with which I had invaded the surf at Camp Pendleton earlier that sealed his doom at Saipan.

Now that early summer was upon us, conditions were almost perfect for keeping pace with our projected schedules. This was especially true for night-flying schedules. Every pilot in the squadron had mastered a fair degree of proficiency in it and could now advance to flying in formations of multiple divisions. The anxieties of preflight preparedness and night vision were pretty much routine now, so a mass squadron exercise at night was programmed.

It was envisioned that once the squadron got out to one of those Pacific island outposts, predawn missions would be a necessary part of the tour. At least that's the way we did it at Guadalcanal when taking off at night for targets up the Slot.

So now, the preflight briefings became routine. The pilots knew in advance the rendezvous points for each section and division and, finally, for the whole flight of twenty-four Corsairs—if we could manage to get that many in the air. Throttle settings and rpm adjustments had been predetermined, considering fuel economy. The pivotal points in navigation had also been stressed, as well as times en route and times of arrival at a target area. The time element was critical in terms of coordination with other flights involved in the same mission.

All did not work well on one of those first attempts at formation flying with the whole squadron in the air. Still it was considered a real feat for our engineering department to have all twenty-four Corsairs in commission at the same time. On this particular night, there were a few wispy clouds at the 5,000-foot level; otherwise it was considered a fair night for the exercise. The planes took off in rapid succession and started to form up on their division leaders. The division leaders maintained a slow climb and then a leisurely orbit at their respective rendezvous sectors. Their navigation lights were on bright—red to port, green to starboard, white to stern. The others were on dim. The whole flight of divisions was about to merge into one formation when the last division, led by 2dLt Johnny Cox, realized he had a missing man. First Lieutenant Kenny Bennett was not among the division. Kenny had overshot the rendezvous and gotten messed up in the wispy clouds somewhere. He opened up on the radio with "Where are you?" Johnny came back with, "We are circling the dry lake." Suddenly somebody shouted over the radio, "Look out, here he comes!"

It was like the burst of a giant skyrocket, with planes flying in every direction. The skies were filled with twenty-four shooting airplanes—luckily not fragmented!

The initial flight plan had to be scrubbed due to the confusion. After that mixed-up mess in the sky, it must have taken a full thirty minutes to get reorganized and re-formed. By then it was too late to satisfy the schedule. All planes landed safely and the pilots assembled in the ready room. Lieutenant Kenny Bennett was a very conspicuous culprit among them. He suffered through the indignities of good-natured taunts and jibes with a half-smile. But the best part was when he became the squadron "Dilbert of the Month," a dubious honor not exactly relished by the recipient. Kenny really didn't deserve that distinction, but, after all, somebody had to get it...

There was another night-flying incident of particular note that stirred us all. Sometimes more than one squadron would be scheduled for night-flying operations at Mojave. The time/space factor had to be considered when so many airplanes were in the air. Generally, coordination and good planning made for smooth operations. But if Murphy's Law stepped in and it became a matter of aircraft and engine reliability verses pilot skill, a clash usually occurred. Major Lou Smunk had to reckon with this phenomenon on one occasion. He was another old friend from the Guadalcanal days who had been conscripted to help organize and train new pilots in a squadron on the Mojave base. Lou now served under Maj William A. Millington, commanding officer of VMF-124.

It was a very dark night, but otherwise conditions were quite good for Lou's familiarization flight. Within the confines of the blue-lighted taxiway boundaries, he made his way to the far end and stopped just shy of the runway to check the magnetos. He revved up the engine and checked first the right and then the left magneto. The right one fell off about 300 rpm. This was on the borderline but, he felt, within safe limits. He asked for and received clearance for takeoff from the tower. Once lined up with the runway, he pushed the throttle full forward, and the Corsair gathered speed. Just as he was becoming airborne, a pilot's worse-case scenario unfolded: The engine sputtered with a loss of power. Seconds later it quit altogether. Lou's only alternative now was to squash the plane in—wherever that might be—as flying speed was now reduced to the stalling point.

Following a roller-coaster sensation, there came the resounding crunch of metal on earth. The inertial energy attenuator was the raised bed of the railroad tracks just north of the town of Mojave. The Corsair teetered on the tracks, and Lou, although in mild shock, was uninjured, so far as he knew at the moment.

About that time, a bum came walking down the railroad tracks. He was about as scared as Lou was! He was able to detect movement in the cockpit and finally climbed up on the jagged wing to inquire, "What's going on here?"

Lou slowly extricated himself from the cockpit, got to the ground, and braced himself against the crumpled fuselage. The bum figured that Lou could use a drink, so he pulled a bottle of Old Ripple from his hip pocket and gave the shaken pilot a big swig.

In the meantime the Mojave tower had observed the malfunctioning plane go down, and a search party was immediately dispatched to the scene. By the time the searchers found the crash site, Maj Lou Smunk was in need of no further medical attention—and the bottle was empty!

*   *   *

In view of the absence of recreational facilities in the area, and in the interest of maintaining high morale, one of the housekeeping functions of the air station at Mojave was to provide the troops as much entertainment as possible. The various clubs and the station theater were adequate facilities to handle the run-of-the-mill events, but every once in a while, a shot of big-league entertainment was necessary to stimulate the soul. After all, it was only a matter of time before the majority of all personnel on the base would be cast into dismal confrontation with the enemy under the most trying conditions.

All of the clubs had banks of slot machines, and these were pretty well attended by all the troops. One whole wall in the barroom at the officers' club was lined with them. The club made about $6,000 per month off these machines. I knew about them firsthand, for at the end of the month, I came out relatively solvent. The calluses on my right hand reflected my winnings of at least one nickel jackpot a day, a dime jackpot once a week, and a quarter about once a month.

One of the more notable events at the officers' club happened on the second of July when Hollywood entered the scene. This was its contribution to the war effort. It was only a coincidence that the gala event fell on my birthday. But there was another reason for all of us to celebrate: Bulgy Bryson had just learned of his promotion to major effective two weeks earlier.

Almost overnight one Hollywood studio transformed the club's outdoor patio (which was actually a sand pit) into a veritable oasis. Setting the scene was a portable dance floor surrounded by artificial grass mats. This was embellished by floodlit palm trees and lanterns glowing on each of the tables.

Evening came and so did the ladies dressed in their flowing evening gowns. (I had to fly down to Laguna Beach earlier to retrieve Josie's gowns.) A fine Hollywood band enhanced the atmosphere. The food was stacked high for a free buffet dinner. At midnight the orchestra played "Happy Birthday," and I was recognized.

That evening a brilliant moon bathed the desert with its luminance. The wind abated, so the canvas enclosing the patio rippled ever so slightly. This event was definitely one of the highlights during the tour of the Mojave Desert. The exotic setting was reminiscent of the Coral Gables Country Club in Miami, where I had gone to the university. This was, indeed, a fine birthday.

Birthday celebrations were going on concurrently at the Weiland homestead in South Dakota. Basic family values came to the fore. My sisters had all written me fine letters. My brother Tommy, who was born the day after I left home to go away to college, honored me by having his first Holy Communion on my birthday. There was a spiritual bouquet by Sister Maria Daniel; she was one of the Catholic nuns who came to the diocese at this time of year to teach catechism. My mother convened a novena with the rest of the family. I'm sure it was the prayers and the tears on her pillow that got me through. My morale was higher than it had ever been.

Celebrations were going on as well in the staff NCO club and the enlisted club. There had been many promotions in the lower enlisted ranks. Corporal Bob Eggleston, in the VMF-452 ordnance section, was one of those promoted to sergeant. It was effective as of July 1, 1944. This called for a rousing good time.

The Fourth of July was two days later and was of no less significance. The focus of this celebration was mainly the war bond drive. All flying was secured at noon and a big field day commenced. All hands assembled on the baseball diamond, including the wives and kids. Civilian spectators swelled the crowd. Competition was fierce as the squadrons tried to outdo each other in all activities. Squadron drill teams went through the manual of arms and marches. The women's reserves were no less prominent with their display of expertise in the manual of arms—sufficient evidence of the training they had received. Swimming and track events consumed most of the afternoon. Even though VMF-452 won either first or second place in every event, it was Maj Bill Millington's VMF-124 that won the cup.

A barbecue topped the afternoon. And it was here that our fine friend old man Duntley, who owned the ranch in the Tehachapi Mountains, became a great benefactor, proudly showing his prowess in the art of barbecuing. He tantalized his listeners with tales of the old days when Mojave was considered the richest little town in America and perhaps the biggest gambling joint in the world.

"You see," he told us, "there are all kinds of gold mines around here, and miners go out and stake claims and pan for gold. Sometimes they strike it rich, but most of them are paupers."

That evening the tables were moved out of the mess hall at the officers' club and it was magically transformed into a gambling casino. Costumed cowboy pilots milled around the roulette, craps, chuck-a-luck, and blackjack tables. Money was cashed in for chips. Later in the evening, the profits of the house were totaled and raffled off as war bonds. As usual, I didn't make a nickel.

*   *   *

There were many Hollywood celebrities who came to Mojave to put on extravaganzas at the base theater. They were treated as the VIPs that they were. It was only natural for the officers' club to host anyone who happened to arrive early, perhaps for the purpose of imbibing a few drinks. Gregarious comedian Frank Morgan, the actor Ralph Bellamy, and many others did their part to help boost the welfare and morale of troops on the desert. Veronica Lake, she of the seductive blonde peekaboo hairstyle, was also a big one for helping out the boys. Everyone was crazy about Veronica. She played those angelic roles in the movies . . . a man couldn't help but love her.

One evening before a show, Veronica and her manager arrived early at the officers' club. She was already in fine spirits and had had, perhaps, just a few too many drinks at the club. The show had already started at the base theater when she appeared on the stage. Those beautiful tresses were quite disheveled and her speech was incoherent. The manager's coaching from the sidelines was to no avail, and soon the theater crowd sensed what was wrong. The inevitable happened: She was booed off the stage. The manager, with the help of a few Marines, took her to the sick bay for a little treatment. The show continued without the star, but the whole thing was a gigantic flop.

After the show the theater crowd dispersed—many of them going to the officers' club. Josie and I did likewise and joined up with a party that was getting mighty lively. Later in the evening Bob Graham, technical representative for Pratt & Whitney, went with us for a 14-mile road trip to the town of Rosamond for a nightcap. We walked into the dimly lit bar, and there on barstools were Veronica Lake and her manager. As there was no one else in the bar but the five of us and, since we were in gala spirits, some lively conversation ensued.

Veronica's vocabulary consisted mostly of four-letter words—directed primarily at her manager. The girls got into a conversation about clothes. Josie and Veronica discovered that they wore the same size shoes and went to the ladies' room to swap. The manager was getting more frantic—it was his duty to get Veronica back to Hollywood after the fiasco at the base theater—and he went into the ladies' room to pull her out. So we all departed and went our separate ways.

Alas, the image I had so cherished of that angelic creature had just flown out the window. Too bad.

*   *   *

Those intelligence bulletins Lt Olson was putting on my desk every morning seemed to be getting more interesting by the day. My curiosity was accelerating at the same rate.

Normally, ship movements or names of vessels were not mentioned—at least not in the confidential reports we received; however, one report in particular caught my eye. There was a new carrier assigned to Task Group 58.2: The USS *Franklin*, an Essex-class, fast carrier, had joined up with three veteran carriers already on station: *Wasp, Monterey,* and *Cabot.* The dispatch went on to say how, in support of the Marianas operations, these carriers had made strikes against Iwo Jima and the Bonin Islands—namely, Chichi Jima and Haha Jima. On July 5, 1944, the *Franklin* had then steamed southward to launch strikes against Rota and Guam for softening up prior to the amphibious landing there. It was all very interesting news. As far as the *Franklin* was concerned, that news was quickly forgotten—until a much later date.

As I said, each bulletin seemed more interesting than the one before. The one I read next concerned the amphibious landing on Tinian, July 24. The 2d and 4th Marine divisions were making the assault against nine thousand Japanese troops. Just 3 miles to the northeast lay Saipan, where mopping-up operations were taking place after the V Amphibious Corps had made its invasion there three weeks earlier.

What struck me as so special about the Tinian operation was a new element introduced in the way of ordnance: napalm—a concoction of diesel fuel, gasoline, and naphtha, which could be hung from the aircraft in belly tanks and dropped during low-level attacks. Because of its jellylike properties, it stuck to everything upon hitting the ground, burned fiercely, and devastated the camouflaged Japanese troops in the jungle. We too would soon be employing this new addition to the ordnance arsenal.

The outer ring of Japanese defenses in the Marshall Islands had pretty much been eliminated when Kwajalein and Eniwetok were taken. Now the inner Japanese defense ring in the Marianas, which included Saipan and Tinian, would shortly be U.S. supply and maintenance facilities. Shortly after that, Guam, 200 miles southwest of Tinian, would be added to the list.

*   *   *

It's odd that now, after all these years, we refer to certain routine training events as "incidents." *Incident* sounds so benign, yet at the time it happens, it stirs apprehension, and perhaps even fear in the adrenaline-packed hearts of some well-meaning pilots. Sometimes the accusations were justified, and the "boys will be boys" excuse just didn't hold water. On the other hand, sometimes there was a job to be done that was handled resolutely and with single-minded determination. Such was the case at Bicycle Lake.

An Army antiaircraft regiment was training at Bicycle Lake on the Mojave Desert. The commanding officer of the regiment phoned the Mojave base commander, requesting that a flight of Corsairs be sent at low level so that his soldiers could calibrate their radar. He also asked that they not be notified of the actual attack, saying it would be good "combat conditioning" for his troops.

VMF-452 was selected for this surprise attack. First Lieutenant Kenny Bennett, who by then had advanced to the position of a senior division leader, would coordinate the attack. He picked Lt Rocky Staples as his second-division leader. At the preflight briefing, it was decided to attack from out of the sun at 20,000 feet and continue the runs from lower altitudes until it was time to return to base.

Needless to say, the first run was a complete surprise. A few tents were blown down and some troops jumped off radar towers and groveled in the dirt. After about the third pass, the soldiers were getting angry and shaking their fists. The attack broke off and all planes returned to Mojave.

In the meantime, the Bicycle Lake base commander (not the regimental commander who had arranged the attack) phoned Mojave and described in no uncertain terms how careless, reckless, and life-threatening the Marine pilots were. Our immediate response was to place eight pilots in hack (confined to quarters), pending an investigation into a mission that had apparently gone awry.

At the time of the raid, an Army general was just entering the base at Bicycle Lake and was thoroughly impressed by the attack. It was exactly what the infantry would be going through in real combat, he said. He was so impressed, in fact, that a short time later he called Mojave to say that the demonstration was the best he had ever seen and that our squadron should always be called on for such duty. The squadron had done a good job after all. It had all been a big mistake; an hour later, all eight pilots were released from hack, exonerated for doing the job they had been told to do.

There were other incidents, like the time the squadron was supposed to lay down a smoke screen for an Army exercise near the Mojave/Bishop highway. The smoke screen was laid down according to plan, but it inadvertently drifted over the highway and smoked up a few automobiles. This caused paint corrosion on some of the cars, and some angry drivers called on the base commander. At first the squadron was thought to be at fault, but it was later exonerated. The drivers submitted claims and were eventually compensated.

On another occasion someone dropped a 500-pound bomb in the yard of a ranch between the house and the barn. The rancher, who was already a friend of Kenny Bennett, came to the base and asked that the crater be filled—nothing else. He had befriended many Marines. Kenny Bennett and other pilots would go out to his ranch to shoot the troublesome jackrabbits that ate his alfalfa.

All these so-called minor incidents added up to great big headaches for the commanding officer. It seemed that he was always being called on the carpet to answer for one thing or another. And just when he thought he had everything under control, *wham*—something else happened. Take Lt Norwood Hanson for instance. I was pretty confident in my knowledge that he had been toeing the line. It had been some time since the Muroc Dry Lake episode, and he was beginning to shape himself into a first class-fighter pilot. But, on another level, I knew it was contrary to Hanson's hyperactive drive not to put a Corsair in a most untenable position. Hanson had done himself proud with the squadron insignia he'd produced. And he handled the Corsair airplane like he handled his art—with perfection. But he was about to push this perfection a mite too far.

Major Bulgy Bryson was in the Operations office when his phone rang. When he recognized the voice on the line, his normally affable countenance turned angry.

"Sir, this is Bo Little. I'm calling from Merced Army Air Corps Base."

Bulgy interrupted him.

"What in hell are you doing there? You're supposed to be on a cross-country to San Francisco."

"Well, sir," Bo stammered, "we've run into a little trouble. You see, Norwood Hanson and I were flying along and, without my knowledge, I believe

Norwood had to land in a farmer's cornfield."

Bulgy was in a rage: "You stupid Okie, you had to be flathatting not to have seen him go down! Find out what you can about Hanson and then get your ass back here immediately and fill me in with all the details."

The receiver banged down on the cradle.

A crumpled Corsair did indeed lie in a cornfield, and Lt Hanson walked away from the accident. He pleaded engine failure. Mojave base transportation dispatched a flatbed truck to the scene to retrieve both plane and pilot.

Hanson was a tall, good-looking young man. He always had a smile on that boyish face of his. Whenever he came in for a confrontation with me, it was always with a hurt expression. Innocence was written all over his face. He was given to the arts. The culture-infused society in Philadelphia that groomed him had definitely enhanced his personality. He was a hard man to deal with, yet you couldn't help but love the kid.

Instrument flying was an important adjunct to a pilot's training, and in order to keep his "hand in," a periodic check was made with an under-the-hood flight—at least one per month. Most often the Mojave Air Station provided the personnel and a North American SNJ tandem-seat trainer to meet this requirement. The instrument pilot sat in the back cockpit with the canvas hood pulled completely over the inside of the cockpit. With no outside references, he was forced to rely on his instruments and follow instrument doctrine.

The Corsair also had an arrangement with a hood that was used on occasion, but this meant another Corsair chase plane had to be employed as a safety measure. Intermittent exchange of radio communications provided the safety feature through the eyes of the chase pilot. But this was a distraction to the instrument pilot, albeit a necessary one, and it tied up two Corsairs. This was not conducive to economy of effort, as the Corsairs could be used more effectively in gunnery or dive-bombing tactics.

We all earned a restricted "pink card" instrument rating, which allowed us to penetrate not much more than thick clouds.

It was at about this time that we had to contend with another fatal accident in the squadron. First Lieutenant Donald L. DeCelles was killed along with his instructor in an under-the-hood instrument flight one weekend. There was some speculation concerning the instrument instructor's competence.

Earlier that week 2dLt Jim Ormond had been on just such a flight with the same instructor, and he was especially concerned. Ormond had sat in the rear cockpit under the hood with the instructor in the front of the SNJ trainer.

"I was on a flight with this instructor," Ormond explained. "He told me that whenever I was under the hood and he shook the stick, I should release it because he was taking over. I was going through a procedure when he shook the stick from side to side, so I released control. He did not pop the hood. Soon, the airspeed was building, the altimeter reading decreasing, and we were in a turn. I popped the hood to see what was going on and, at about that time, he took over and brought the plane back to level flight at 1,500 feet. I asked him why he did not take over immediately after shaking the stick, and he said he was not taking over, that he was just checking to see if I had a positive grip on the stick. I understand that others had trouble with this pilot, also."

CHAPTER 14

Pursuit of Perfection

Training was always first and foremost in the minds of those trying to produce first-rate combat pilots. The methods used and the tools at hand were state-of-the-art for 1944. Some of the old pros in the area looked with skepticism at the way new pilots were trained. These combat veterans were very much aware of what was realistic in battle and shook their heads at some aspects of the training cycle. But there was really no alternative.

A real-life scenario of actual combat, with real pilots and real lives at stake, couldn't be duplicated and used for training purposes. Even attempts by Hollywood to produce simulation were flawed. And, as Maj "Trigger" Long expressed it, those of us who actually experienced aerial combat and survived will be the first to admit that the passenger in our cockpits was a lady named Luck.

Major Long then digressed a bit about combat preparedness, offering explanations. Combat for fighter pilots consists of a never-dull scenario. The objectives? To protect our own while destroying the enemy. This in turn translates to pilots of opposite sides trying to kill each other, because shootdowns are required to accomplish the assigned mission. It doesn't matter if forces involved are unevenly matched. The maneuvering, diving, turning, and gyrations, all to the tune of machine-gun fire, are difficult to teach those pilots preparing for combat.

It was the consensus of all those old pros, however, that a buildup of flight time in the fighter was a necessity. Constant, daily emphasis on section and division tactics, gunnery, dive-bombing practice, and navigation was essential. Our isolation out in the desert was probably an advantage in a sense; there really wasn't much of anything else to do but fly, and this we did by the hour, day in and day out. The importance of building time is evidenced by the dilemma the Japanese faced once they lost so many skilled pilots early in the war. The attrition at the Battle of Midway, the Solomons, and elsewhere led to the debacle in the Marianas, the Japanese force being reduced to relatively few airplanes manned by inexperienced aviators. We now pretty much had command of the skies in the Pacific.

We at the squadron level felt a real responsibility for maintaining that dominance. This meant doggedly pursuing every aspect of the training available, one of which was the art of self-preservation amidst the hazards of flying. It was a given that any emergencies originating in the combat zone would most often end in the water—be it evacuating by parachute or ditching an airplane at sea. Therefore, we figured aquatic training in the desert would support our objectives no matter where we ended up being based.

The huge indoor pool at Mojave would serve to facilitate this phase of training. Pilots wearing flight gear and other paraphernalia had to make laps back and forth across the pool for survival training. At the deep end, the yellow "Dilbert Dunker" poised high on its stanchions. With a pilot strapped in its cockpit, it slid down the ways to simulate an aircraft water landing, submerging the pilot. Once in the water, it tilted over on its back. The pilot learned to extricate himself from the sinking plane, then inflate his Mae West life preserver and life raft. All pilots had to qualify in this ditching procedure, wearing their cumbersome equipment. It was a mandatory part of the training syllabus and just one more in a long list of lifesaving procedures. I personally knew all too well the importance of this phase of training. Many of my Guadalcanal buddies owed their lives to the lessons learned during this part of the training process.

A weakness in dive-bombing tactics was another thing with which the squadron had to contend. The daily flight schedule reflected this plan, as well as a monopoly on dive-bombing targets in the area. At the same time, we were also trying to perfect our gunnery runs. Competition among the pilots helped spur accuracy in this regard. After a gunnery flight, the tow plane would drop its banner, and the pilots would gather around when it was brought in by the ordnance crew, to scrutinize for holes made by the color-coded .50-caliber rounds that pierced its coarse fabric. After a good hour of intermittent firing, it was expected that each pilot would score a dozen or so hits. The scores were tallied, and certain of the smug pilots accepted the wagers paid off by their less-skilled buddies.

The overhead gunnery runs we performed were another example of how unrealistic actual battle conditions can be during training. Here we had a target being towed in a set pattern, on a steady course, and holding to a fixed airspeed. There was no evasive action to contend with—no jinking, no twists, no turns, no defensive maneuvering at all. In actual combat there had been certain cases that were likened to a towed target, but they were pretty much the exception. The big, slow, lumbering Japanese Emily reconnaissance seaplanes were sometimes a case in point. There were specific occasions when Japanese bombers bent on an attack mission, without deviation and dictated by strict discipline, became sitting ducks. This would come under the heading of "by the book" gunnery tactics.

Our gunnery doctrine varied techniques as much as possible, however, within the parameters of safety. Overhead runs were first perfected with planes peeling off and making near vertical runs on the tow-target banner. But then we practiced high-side gunnery runs (not vertical) and developed techniques of moving in close and firing prior to the 90-degree angle. This amounted to a near head-on run shot. Low-level attacks were also developed but, again, without any perceptible evasive maneuvering on the part of the target.

Despite these irreconcilable differences in training, we plodded along unfettered. But, every once in a while, those little unexpected and unnerving incidents would pop up and create headaches we could have done without. Lieutenants Joe Warren and William R. Swenson were pretty typical of the clean-cut, classy kids in the squadron, but in one instance all attention was suddenly riveted on those two.

Second Lieutenant Joe Warren was on a high-altitude gunnery flight one day and was towing the target. A safety pilot always flew alongside the tow target going to and coming from the gunnery range; this assignment went to Lt Swenson. After completing the gunnery runs that day, as the flight was returning to base Swenson began doing acrobatics over the tow plane and target. At the top of a loop, Swenson's plane stalled out and went into an inverted spin, and he bailed out at about 10,000 feet. Joe cut the target loose and immediately followed him down. He radioed the other planes in the flight—they were almost back to Mojave—and asked them to report the accident. They called the tower. The Corsair that was in the spin righted itself and started flying all over the sky. At one point, it almost hit Swenson, who was still descending with a parachute. They both hit the desert at about the same time. The plane hit with a big explosion.

Swenson lay prone on the desert floor, and Joe circled him until low fuel dictated his return to the base.

Joe was the only person who knew where the unfortunate pilot was located. In those days search-and-rescue helicopters were unheard of. When Joe landed there was another Corsair waiting for him so he could return to circle the site. He buckled himself in while taxiing out. At the runway intersection, he decided to take off at this halfway point rather than use the whole runway. He applied full throttle, but when he got to the end of the runway he was still not airborne. He popped full flaps and retracted the landing gear simultaneously. He just barely skimmed the roofs and staggered over the town. This was cutting it pretty close, but a shaken Joe continued on the mission. Until dark, he

orbited Swenson, who was not moving. It was almost morning before the surface crews got to Swenson and found him alive but with broken bones.

* * *

Later there was an incident with the high-altitude gunnery flight I was leading. Second Lieutenant Walter M. Shirley was towing the banner and, after our
first pass, inadvertently dropped it. It was all over as far as gunnery was concerned, so on the radio I yelled, "Every man for himself. Return to base."

Johnny Cox's enthusiasm had not yet been vented, so he decided it would
be a good time to buzz the concrete plant east of the field. He pulled up to go
around just one more time. I was observing this illegal bit of chicanery and
immediately pulled up on his wing. Johnny was very surprised to see me and
proceeded meekly back to base.

Once on the ground, it wasn't long before the adjutant advised Johnny that
the CO wanted to see him.

"Why didn't you buzz the place again?" I asked him. "I was waiting for that
second buzz so you could keep Lt Carl L. Webber company. He's in hack for
ten days and you could've joined him."

Johnny had already decided that he didn't want to press his luck, so he was
very contrite. He became one of our best pilots from then on.

* * *

I was in the office one day when Maj Bulgy Bryson burst in to say the tower
had just called about an emergency on one of our planes. We ran outside and
saw a Corsair trailing smoke far off in the distance. All eyes were turned
upward as we prayed for a safe landing. It was Lt Jimbo Ormond in Number
16-A. His plane was losing oil, so engine seizure was imminent. Jimbo had
been on a practice run at a tow target when someone radioed that he was smoking badly. He saw no indication of a fire, but his oil pressure had dropped. He
made it back to Mojave field and, as soon as his wheels touched down, he cut
the engine. Inspection revealed that the oil reservoir was almost bone dry.

On August 1, we lost Maj Phil Crawford to another unit. For some inex-
plicable reason, he was suddenly transferred to MCAS El Toro. Admittedly, we
were a little top heavy in rank and experience, but at least we had the chance
to maintain the status quo for a long time. Major Bulgy Bryson was a natural to
fill the void as executive officer, so a smooth flow of squadron affairs continued during the transition.

As operations officer, Bulgy Bryson had done a phenomenal job with training; his subordinate, Capt Wally Wethe, was a strong adjunct to the team. This
was reflected in the status board, which was nearing completion as the *X*'s

filled the squares of the various syllabus phases. There were a few weak spots here and there in the training cycle, but for all practical purposes we were rapidly approaching the stage of training in which we could expect transfer orders for overseas assignment.

Navigation was one phase in our training that could stand a little more attention. So much, in fact, that when a request by some of our lieutenants came up for a cross-country to Cheyenne, Wyoming, it was granted without question. In a sense it was also kind of a reward for the pilots who had doggedly withstood the demands of the flight schedule, day in and day out, for weeks on end. It was no coincidence that Lt Dale Oakes's home was in Cheyenne and that there just happened to be an annual "Frontier Days" celebration going on that particular weekend in early August. Dale was born and raised there, and his brother owned a ranch in the area. This would be a gala affair for everyone involved. An arrangement had even been made with the townspeople for a low-level flight demonstration by the eight Corsairs participating in the cross-country.

Everything went off without a hitch on that flight to Cheyenne—kind of a testimonial to how professional our pilots were becoming. They were wined and dined by the citizenry and recognized as valiant warriors about to go off and do battle with the enemy. They were even given a footlocker full of booze with the stipulation that it be consumed at a squadron party at a remote overseas destination. This would eventually happen, but not without taking a very devious and calamitous route.

On that same weekend in early August, closer to home, other things were going on. This occasion was supposed to have been a fun thing, too, but it didn't work out that way for a couple of the boys. Mr. Duntley was having another one of his renowned picnics at his ranch in the Tehachapi Mountains. The motorcycle gang was having an especially good time during their foray into the hinterlands. They careened up and down the hills and along trails well off the beaten path. Second Lieutenant Frank Morrison had invited Jimbo Ormond to ride piggyback with him. The thrill of this motorcycle escapade was exhilarating, the barbecue and beer were just about as good, and the camaraderie among the other pilots and their wives who attended enhanced the whole affair. Lieutenant Wallace "Hose Nose" Mattsfield demonstrated his prowess as a beer bottle juggler. And there couldn't have been a better imitation of Col Joseph Adams, the base commander, giving hell to Lts John W. "Bill" Rogalski and Gerry Vetter than that performed by Lt Pete Schaefer. In between sessions, old man Duntley told more stories about the Wild West. Finally, it was time to bring a good afternoon to an end.

Frank and Jimbo were returning to the base when the accident happened.

They were within three blocks of the main gate when the car they were about to pass suddenly turned left. The motorcycle struck the car's left rear wheel and fender. Frank was pinned beneath the cycle. Jim was thrown clear and, despite his broken right foot, managed to drag himself over to the motorcycle and lift it so Frank, suffering from a broken collarbone, could get free. The car was driven by Lt Charles E. "Chuck" Hill, who was returning from the same party with his wife, Marcia.

Motorcycle accidents at Mojave could almost vie with aircraft accidents for the disruption they caused. Now we had two pilots out of commission for an indefinite period of time. It got to the point where I had to give a combination safety and reprimand lecture. I finalized it with, "Remember, if you have to have an accident, be sure to land on your head. That way you won't get hurt!"

Morrison kept his motorcycle for quite some time. In fact, he left it with his girlfriend, Jeanne Stirling, just before he went overseas. After his return he sold it to buy her an engagement ring. So there was something good to be said about motorcycles after all.

Doctor James Reames was the squadron flight surgeon, and incidents like the motorcycle accident kept him busy. Among his other varied duties, he looked after the health and well-being of our squadronmates. Bo Little, one of our senior lieutenants, had an arthritic problem with his legs; they just wouldn't operate as they should. He hid this little secret from almost everybody, for he knew what the consequences would be if he faced up to a stringent physical. But he did respect the judgment of our flight surgeon, although Doc Reames treated him without much success. The good doctor told Bo that if the ailment persisted, he would be professionally and morally obligated to separate him from flight status, if not the service of the Marine Corps. The pleading and tear-jerking arguments that Bo gave the doctor had their desired effect. Whenever he had an arthritic attack, Doc sent Bo to his room with pills. It was never put on his record. As it turned out, Lt Bo Little fulfilled his flying obligations resolutely and with valor, and no one else really ever knew the difference.

CHAPTER 15

An Expanded Flight Syllabus

One could tell that things were astir up in Headquarters, Marine Corps as dispatches, bulletins, and rumors filtered down to the lower echelons. It all concerned carrier aviation, in which at this point in time the Marine Corps had no part. Traditionally, Marine fliers had always operated from aircraft carriers, but now there was a real void and a sense of exclusion that was felt throughout the Corps. Since the beginning of the war, our operations in the South Pacific had been largely in rear areas and always land-based, as amphibious operations proceeded one island after the other—Guadalcanal, the Russells, the New Georgias including Vella Lavella, and Bougainville. Subsequent areas of amphibious invasions got spaced out and there was just no way Marine aircraft could support these landings by island hopping. Carriers were the answer, but at this point none was available to the Marine Corps. The Navy argued that this exclusion was justifiable.

The campaign for an air support role aboard escort carriers began during the Saipan invasion. Major General Ross E. Rowell, who commanded Marine Air Wings, Pacific, pointed out this deficiency, as well as the isolation of our Marine Air arm in areas to the rear. He had a strong argument and it went through channels; but it fell on Navy ears so wrapped up with their own carrier commitments that they were deaf to the proposition and barely considered it.

Immediately after the Saipan invasion, LtGen Holland Smith, commander of the V Amphibious Corps, also lent support to this campaign. Except for the small spotter observation planes involved, he said, it was more than obvious that Marine Corps aviation was completely left out of the whole Marianas picture. As things stood, their main mission of close air support could not be augmented in these crucial times. After the Saipan battle, Smith received a token commitment from Adm Chester Nimitz that four escort carriers would be assigned to the Marine Corps. But it would be months before any program could be fully implemented and in force by Marines once negotiations up at headquarters were set up. The lag time prevailed, and on this date in early August something was finally happening.

In view of the possibility of Marine tactical squadrons being assigned to escort aircraft carriers sometime in the future, we worked up a frenzy of effort to meet this commitment. We received directives from upper echelons to inject into the flight syllabus a rigorous phase of field carrier landing practice (FCLP). These directives applied to all five tactical squadrons operating from the Mojave base as well as any other tactical squadron located anywhere in the entire continental United States.

I could fully appreciate this turn of events in view of my situation exactly two years earlier. It was during the planning stages for the Guadalcanal invasion in the summer of 1942 when I was a pilot in VMO-251, a full-fledged Grumman Wildcat fighter squadron. Almost immediately, we were sent to Espiritu Santo from Noumea, New Caledonia, to become the buffer against the Japanese on Guadalcanal. It originally had been planned that once the Japanese airfield (later Henderson Field) had been rehabilitated by our forces after the landing, our squadron (VMO-251) and another (VMF-212) located at Efate, would then be the first to become operational and provide initial land-based defense at Guadalcanal. Rear Admiral Richmond Kelly Turner, commander of the amphibious force, however, upon advice from RAdm John S. McCain, commander of all land-based aircraft in the theater, belayed the orders because, as he put it, these two squadrons were not carrier-qualified and were weak on gunnery tactics. As a result we were bypassed in favor of Capt Bob Galer's VMF-224 and Capt John L. Smith's VMF-223 fighter squadrons. It had seemed an interminable wait before we actually saw combat at Guadalcanal.

So now, with this state of affairs before us, we had to be prepared. No squadron was sure that it would ever go aboard a carrier. After all, there were now a dozen or so tactical squadrons vying for the best slots, but how many escort carriers would the Navy turn loose to accommodate them? A good guess might be a half-dozen at best. A more reasonable figure might be the four that Adm Chester Nimitz proposed the previous June. Nevertheless, the status board now reflected an extension of blank squares, and they all came under the heading of FCLP.

Training in FCLP was paramount for achieving success at landing aboard the heaving, pitching deck of an aircraft carrier. Aboard ship the landing signal officer positioned himself on the aft port quarter platform of the flight deck. An aircraft at the proper altitude on its downwind leg would turn onto the base leg. The pilot would double-check procedures: wheels down, flaps down, tail-hook extended, prop full low pitch, canopy locked full open. He would then turn on the final approach, where the LSO picked him up with the paddles. From that point on, the pilot flew in accordance with the paddle signals—too high—too low—too slow—too fast. With outstretched paddles—just right. A pilot's natural instinct to fly his plane in for a landing had to be disregarded.

The LSO's directives were mandatory. The attitude of the plane was always in a gentle left turn up to the carrier ramp—nose high, power full on, hanging on the prop, just above stalling speed.

If the aircraft attitude and speed were correct, the LSO would signal with a "cut," the slash of a paddle across his face. The pilot would then cut the throttle and flare out to catch a wire. If his plane was not quite in the right position, he would get a "wave-off," a wigwagging of paddles above the LSO's head.

Anticipating a cut could be disastrous—even fatal. A good LSO could gauge the cut with precision and figure the timing of a pitching deck so that the tailhook would grapple one of the nine athwartship cables for a smooth though abrupt halt.

We acquired one such landing signal officer from the air group pool immediately. His name was Capt Gus Faulk and he would be part of our daily lives from then on.

Whether it were simulated carrier landings on a runway or actual landings aboard a carrier, the procedures were the same. No matter which it was, a pilot had to keep his wits about him constantly. On land a typical flight consisted of a four-plane division—they took off individually and spaced themselves at intervals to the left in the racetrack pattern. The control manipulations of landing gear, wing flaps, cowl flaps, and rpm, and constant vigil on temperature gauge and airspeed, took enough concentration, let alone flying the airplane at a hedge-hopping altitude before picking up the LSO positioned at the end of the runway. About eight to twelve landings were as much as a pilot and the Pratt & Whitney R2800 engine could stand at one time, and then it was back to the flight line for a shutdown and recoup period. Another similar flight could be expected by each pilot later in the day. It was obvious that all those unfortunate citizens who found themselves living beneath this noisy traffic pattern had to readjust their attitudes about personal comfort to conform to the deprivations of wartime conditions.

It was apparent that the schedule would be brutal with countless flights until the LSO felt a pilot was qualified to make his first landing aboard a carrier. We commenced this schedule immediately on the airfield at Mojave, as did the other four tactical squadrons, and suddenly the air traffic on the duty runway became unbearably hazardous.

Breathing room was needed for this new phase of air operations, so we set off to find a solution. About 160 miles up the line to the northwest was an abandoned airstrip belonging to the Army Air Corps. This airfield had a single concrete runway and would be perfect for our purposes. It was located beside the little town of Bishop, California.

A cursory investigation showed that it was under control of the Army Air Corps, Tonopah, Nevada, but overall jurisdiction belonged to an Army commanding general in San Francisco. I flew to Tonopah to get initial permission for use of the Bishop field. Upon landing there I was impressed by the isolation of the area and could appreciate the feelings of the people who had to live on this other desert. I began to think that Mojave was an oasis, however, comparatively speaking. The business session with the commanding officer at Tonopah was congenial and in the affirmative, so I departed with smiles and handshakes all around. Very shortly the whole thing was finalized among my boss, Col Dan Torrey, and the general in San Francisco.

CHAPTER 16
Hiatus in the High Sierras

On August 16, 1944, the squadron relocated to Bishop—lock, stock, and barrel. This move was no small thing, for it involved logistics and administration on a scale almost equal to an overseas transfer. The one major difference was that no embarkation plans involving shipboard loading were necessary. Basically, the move had a twofold purpose. The first and primary goal would be to accomplish the commitment of field carrier landing practice by our pilots; second, it would be a shakedown drill by the whole squadron for eventual deployment to some supposedly remote combat area opposing the Japanese.

The airfield at Bishop had remnants of some facilities left by the Army when they abandoned the site. The tower building would be our Operations center and would be manned for traffic control by the duty officer. We took over the existing wood barracks, where all personnel lived. The officers slept on canvas cots and lived out of suitcases and locker boxes. The cooks set up their expeditionary kitchens in one of the old mess halls.

This was a wonderful diversion. There were no "groupies" breathing down our backs every minute, but we did adhere to a rigid flight schedule of night flying, FCLP, and tactics—with no outside interference. Concentration was on FCLP, a priority, which commenced in earnest on August 23. The pilots as well as the airplanes took a daily pounding during this rigorous phase of training.

Bishop was located in the high Sierras in a valley between two north–south mountain ranges. The back door of Yosemite National Park was about 75 miles to the northwest and Mount Tom rose majestically to the west of the airfield. This part of the country seemed very isolated from the rest of the world. The town of Bishop was small, but the residents took to us immediately and very fine relationships developed. Gas rationing was in effect, but we seemed to have no trouble obtaining all the gas we needed. I was able to buy a complete set of tires, without coupons, for my 1940 Ford convertible.

The countryside was serene and pristine with lush vegetation. That's why I elected to set up a camp for Josie and me alongside a swift trout stream flowing down from the high peaks of Mount Tom. Although it was summer, snow melting from the mountaintop made the water so cold it was painful to wade in. Fishing was good, with trout abounding in the stream, so trout became the main item on our menu.

A couple of curious Native American boys were our constant companions. They looked wide-eyed at what they perceived as foreigners and their equipment. And, of course, there was an occasional beer party for which some of the officers drove the four miles up the slope from the airfield. This sojourn was delightful indeed.

We had many excursions during our time at Bishop. We enjoyed the trips to Yosemite National Park through its back door, where suddenly we were enveloped by the breathtaking, majestic redwoods. Then we went down the meandering canyon to behold the other wonders of nature.

I became acquainted with an official of the tungsten mine located on the peak of Mount Tom, and he offered me a tour. We proceeded by jeep up the nearly vertical rocky road, sometimes peeking down hundreds of feet of sheer precipice. Tunnels had been built under blankets of snow, and we walked through these to the mine operations—an impressive sight.

That summer of 1944, the Republic Film Studio was shooting *Tall in the Saddle* starring John Wayne and Ella Raines at Bishop. Our boys used to go into town every night during the filming. John Wayne became a gracious host and a great benefactor, throwing champagne parties for the Marines at the hotel and bar where he and Ella were staying. The boys carried many fond memories of this interlude.

An R4D based out of Mojave resupplied our mess with food. If it were suddenly out of commission, the squadron had to fend for itself—no real problem, as resources were locally available. The ingenuity of the pilots and enlisted people always went to work to rectify any lack of food.

On one occasion the guard at the gate shot a deer. The barber in town was also the game warden, so any hunting trips that sallied forth provided more venison. Another time he took several pilots, including 1stLt Dale Oakes and Lt Pete Schaefer, on a fishing trip to Kilo Hot Springs. They came back with gunnysacks full of trout. There was never any shortage of food at the mess hall.

The pilots used to go down to the Owens River right after securing the flight line from the bridge to go skinny dipping. Pete Schaefer told how they'd string a line about 200 feet down the fast-flowing river. They'd dive in and catch hold of the far end of the line to haul themselves back in. No one could swim against the current except Lt Charlie Weitzel, who had swum on the University of Oregon swimming team. Pete recalls an incident one day when a herd of cattle was being driven down the road to the bridge by a couple of cowpokes. As they drew closer, someone noticed that they weren't cowpokes at all—they were cowgirls. The pilots jumped bare-assed into the river, waiting for them to pass by. But the cowgirls didn't seem to be in any hurry. Meanwhile, the boys were freezing to death. Finally, the stark naked, mortified Marines were forced to climb out. The girls just laughed and slowly herded the cattle across the bridge.

Bishop had its annual rodeo-roundup in early September. It was a phenomenal affair that could vie in scope with the one in Pendleton, Oregon. Cowboys came from miles around to exhibit their prowess as bronco busters and calf ropers and to show off their beautiful horses and wagons.

Josie and I attended the rodeo, then later in the afternoon headed to the Longhorn restaurant for dinner. We met up with WO Clayton Smith along the way. Smitty was with his girlfriend, who had come up from Los Angeles for the weekend. Her personality was very compatible with Smitty's, and they made an interesting couple. Smitty, the old Marine mustang in the outfit, must have been pushing forty. His years in the Marine Corps reflected the ingrained respect he had for his superiors, in turn a product of the training he had received. I, of course, was often the recipient of this courtesy, whether it be a business matter on the flight line or a social passing at the club. But there was a mutual respect between us, and this was symbolic, in a sense, of what made the squadron tick. The effect rippled down through the ranks. The odd thing about the whole situation was that I, being the commanding officer, was universally considered the "Old Man." I had just turned twenty-six and was already a combat veteran. It was a constant threat among some of the NCOs and their junior enlisted people: "You do it my way or we'll go in and see the Old Man." But threats aside, generally everything was "copasetic," a familiar term used by Smitty, which meant "just fine."

Two other couples joined us for drinks at the Longhorn lounge area. Before long, Kelly, the mess chef at camp, walked in, recognized us, and sat down. Kelly was something of an alcoholic, but a very good cook.

To strike up conversation, Smitty said, "What are you having at mess tonight, Kelly?"

Kelly casually replied, "Same old horse cock."

The men chuckled; the girls looked up at the ceiling. And Kelly moved on to get another drink.

Either a Douglas SBD Dauntless dive-bomber or an SNJ two-seat trainer was used for mail or sick-call runs to Mojave. It was also essential that the payroll be met while we were on temporary duty at Bishop. That meant flying down to Mohave, picking it up, and bringing it back on schedule. Second Lieutenant Alex Dutkin was just the pilot to take administrative SSgt Ted Gore with him to do the job. You could always depend on Alex. As it turned out, Gore deserved most of the credit. He rarely had the opportunity to fly, and this was a good chance.

On one occasion the payroll was picked up and the two-seater took off for the flight back to Bishop. Ten minutes of straight and level flight can get boring in a maneuverable airplane, so Alex descended to the desert floor. The two canopies were open, and Dutkin inverted the plane, just above the terrain. Gore was more intent on saving the money than his own life, so he staunchly secured the money bag to the floorboards with his feet while flying upside down. He wasn't about to let that money fall out! The payroll was delivered as per schedule and nobody knew the difference.

There were a lot of things the Old Man wasn't supposed to know about—like the payroll incident. Years later during get-togethers, and usually over a few beers, it all came out. Confessions came to the fore and it became a laughing matter. But most times when it happened, it was dead-serious business. I was beginning to wonder if there were any pilots who did not indulge in the hedge-hopping trips to and from Mojave. Jimbo Ormond told how Norwood Hanson gave him thrills galore on a mail run in an SNJ. Of course, I could expect that out of Hanson.

Things were going along very peacefully during our stay at Bishop—almost too peacefully. The first punctuation to this peace came when Paul Maginnis flew through Bishop's power lines and knocked out the town's electricity for a while. He had been engaged in field carrier landing practice. On the final approach to the runway, he dragged the Corsair in too low and through the power lines. The sparks flew but he was not injured. The plane suffered dents to the propeller and landing gear. Other than that, everything was rosy at Bishop for a short period of time.

But another event was about to occur for which we were totally unprepared. We should have surmised something was happening when we observed an Army crew stringing phone lines up the mountain for field telephones.

After a flight late one afternoon, I secured a little early and drove the jeep up to the camp with one purpose in mind: to dip a line in that fast-flowing stream in order to complement the dinner that night with some nice trout. Everything was in good hands back at the airfield with the people on duty, and I was looking forward to a little R & R.

First Lieutenant Pete Schaefer was the duty officer and he was making the usual rounds when he noticed the B-25 land. This was not unusual and he was not too concerned, for every so often an Army plane might set down on a cross-country and remain overnight.

An Army sergeant in residence maintained the field on caretaker status; he was the one who normally picked up visitors and provided for their care. This time he brought the pilot, an Army colonel, to our headquarters in the tower building. In Pete's absence, the colonel explained his visit to one of our junior officers who had just happened to enter the building minutes before.

"In the morning General Hap Arnold and General George Marshall are to fly in real early. They need to get away from the anxieties of business at the Pentagon for a few days to do a little hunting and fishing at Kilo Hot Springs. However, there is to be no publicity whatsoever."

Our intrepid young officer was sworn to secrecy and promised not to mention this to a soul. He kept his word. He didn't even tell me—the Old Man!

The next morning was a tranquil one—a typical Bishop summer day. At 0400 no one was stirring on the airfield. No one except Kelly. He was busy in the scullery, preparing the breakfast. The VIPs landed in their B-25, and the colonel drove the generals to the mess for a cup of coffee and possibly breakfast. The colonel tried to explain to Kelly who he was and whom he had out in the jeep. Kelly was unimpressed by his story.

"If you want a cup of coffee," Kelly said, "you'll have to go four miles up the mountain and get Major Weiland's permission. We don't serve coffee to anyone in the Army around here—PFCs or generals!"

The colonel demanded to see the duty officer.

Lieutenant Pete Schaefer, the duty officer, had been sleeping up in the tower but had already awakened when he was notified that a B-25 had landed with a colonel in uniform and three civilians. Pete, in his skivvies, strapped on his duty belt and pistol and came out to see what was going on.

"The mess sergeant says we can't have coffee or breakfast because all the food was flown in and he didn't have enough to spare," the colonel complained. "He says we'll have to go into town to eat!"

The visitors also needed transportation for the crew and baggage. Pete told them none was available. This was adding insult to injury. Reluctantly, Pete scrounged up an old carryall.

At this point, he was obviously unaware that the civilians were Gen Henry H. "Hap" Arnold, Gen George Marshall, and another flag officer.

I was faced with this dilemma when I got to work early that morning. I was astonished by the repercussions I visualized. I could see it now—Marine Fleet Air West Coast Headquarters in San Francisco restricting everyone to the base. And then the investigation!

As it turned out, however, cooler heads prevailed, and everyone with good sense figured out there was no way anyone could have guessed who the visitors were.

This incident could not be hidden for long. Shortly *The Stars and Stripes*

newspaper reported the event under the headline "MESS SERGEANT TELLS GEN-
ERALS TO SHOVE OFF!" A month or so later in the *Naval Aviation News* magazine, there was an item that led off with: "There is a certain Marine Squadron
based at Bishop, California, that is awaiting lightning to strike . . ." and it went
on to tell the rest of the story.

The young lieutenant who was first advised about the impending visit of Gens
Arnold and Marshall must not have known how extraordinary those VIPs were at the
time. This attitude changed abruptly, however, and the lieutenant will never forget
it. It was only a matter of time before the prestige of the visiting dignitaries was permanently engraved on his brain. It wasn't necessarily a volunteer arrangement on
the part of the lieutenant, but it was acquired. His superiors saw to that....

Our tranquil interlude was interrupted again a few days later. The Army Air
Corps base at Tonopah, Nevada, was also training young pilots. On weekends some
of their lieutenants came to Bishop to date old girlfriends. The inevitable happened:
Our Marines had taken over all the girls in town. This erupted into fistfights and hurt
feelings. The Army lieutenants flew back to Tonopah to file charges against those
bad Marines.

Unbeknownst to me, this news filtered back to the Army headquarters in San
Francisco. The commanding general there fired a letter to my air-group commander
for removal of the Marine squadron.

Colonel Dan Torrey phoned me for an immediate conference. The first action I
took was to restrict all hands to base. The boys had been warned, "We have a good
thing going here so don't abuse it."

It didn't take long for the townspeople to find out about the controversy—and
they did something about it. Although I had become acquainted with the mayor, I
was not sure whether he was instrumental in working up the petition or not. Many
of the citizens signed this document which, in effect, said, "We believe the Marines
of VMF-452 to be the best military outfit we have ever known. There has been no
disruption of our social or civic affairs, and, further, we prefer them to any other
branch of the service."

This was useful evidence in the confrontation I had with Col Torrey. As it ended
up, the situation was alleviated and we continued our stay to complete training as
scheduled.

The diversion at Bishop was an interesting one and memories of it would be forever cherished. But now it was all about to end. It hadn't been all fun and games;
the grueling schedule of FCLP had been accomplished, and we had finished everything else that we had set out to do in Bishop, including a quota of night-flying
hours to meet requirements. We could now return to Mojave and await the
orders that would commit us to duty overseas.

CHAPTER 17

Combat Ready and No Place to Go

The squadron returned to Mojave lock, stock, and barrel on September 16, 1944. We could now assume a more or less relaxed mode. On the following weekend, it was pretty much liberty for all hands.

The Roosevelt Hotel in Los Angeles became a sort of headquarters for many of the lieutenants. That is because Rocky Staples knew the assistant manager there. The others were given a suite of rooms on the fifth floor, replete with a full buffet and bar. One might say this was a contribution to the war effort by the people who ran the hotel. It opened a whole new field of adventure in the department of carousing and woman-chasing. John E. Farley, Tom Pace, Pete Schaefer, Joe Warren, and Wallace Mattsfield took full advantage of the situation.

In the meantime, Lt Jimbo Ormond had just met up with the boys in Los Angeles. He had come off an early leave period but had not yet logged in with the duty officer at Mojave. His intention of doing so was countered by a mis-understanding among the boys.

"Major Weiland said the return could be delayed and you could have the weekend off," they told Jimbo.

He believed them and did what all Marine lieutenants do when loose on the town for a big weekend. He joined them.

By midnight on Saturday, Lt Jimbo Ormond had been declared AWOL. On Monday morning Jimbo knew he had been a fool. He was called in by the CO. All explanations fell short and were without foundation.

"You know you can be court-martialed for this, don't you?"

A lot of waffling and wavering produced a weak "Yes, sir."

"Well, we'll let it go this time. Spend a couple weeks confined to the base. Dismissed."

Two days after our return from Bishop, our spirits were suddenly aroused by the news that two other Mojave-based tactical squadrons were on the move. VMF-124 under Maj Bill Millington and VMF-213 under Maj David E. Marshall were transferred to San Diego to board the USS *Ticonderoga*, which would transport them to Hawaii to await further deployment. The speculation that we would be next was foremost in all of our minds.

In view of impending overseas orders, leave was given to many squadron members for that last trip home to see the folks.

Meanwhile, an assessment of each individual pilot's ability and the collective teamwork accomplished over the months was satisfying and evoked smiles and optimism. The chance to pause and think about it all was refreshing. All the requirements of the syllabus had been met. Some pilots, such as Norwood Hanson and Blimpo Fletcher, had logged upward of three hundred hours in the F4U Corsair.

Over the months it was amazing to watch the new lieutenants become a cohesive unit. You could see them gradually meshing together—like a "well-oiled machine." Much of the training was premium because we were together day in and day out. Every little facet of flying was argued, discussed, and planned—in the ready room, over a beer at the club, and at the BOQ. Because we flew together so much, the boys came to know what the leader would do under any circumstance and were ready to react.

We had now accomplished the minimums necessary to face the enemy in combat. This was true of the proficiency of all enlisted ranks as well. Each individual with enhanced skills now fit with the others like pieces of a jigsaw puzzle. The day would soon come when this precision machine would be put to the test in combat with the enemy. Yet the relentless pursuit of even more refinement continued.

The days were fleeting as we awaited deployment orders. Rumors were the only thing keeping our psyches pumped up; but, of course, they were all unfounded and couldn't replace the cold hard facts. But we kept flying—day and night.

At this stage of the war, things were looking up. We were gaining air superiority in the Pacific and, at the same time, the Vought engineers were making the Corsair into a real juggernaut.

Immediately, a question arose among the more sophisticated pilots: "Why do we need specialist aircraft any longer?" Since rocketry had entered the picture, the fighters could do just as much damage as the bombers and, in view of accuracy, probably could do it much better. Why not write them off as obsolete?

The squadron daily flight schedule now reflected an intense concentration on rocket practice. Dummy runs began on September 24, with each flight composed of two eight-plane divisions. Various attack altitudes were tried and perfected with each plane peeling off, one after another, in a spacing commensurate with safety. The pilot would set up his dive angle—probably in the vicinity of 50 degrees—gunsight on the target with a release point between 3,500 and 3,000 feet. The pullout would then begin at about 1,500 feet. These hops averaged about an hour and a half.

October 9, 1944, saw us firing live rockets out on the range. These actually were 2.5-inch practice rockets, but their effectiveness was very real. Still later the 5-inch HVAR (high-velocity aerial rocket) was a matter of fact. Each plane in the two-division flight carried eight rockets, and that translated into sixty-four potential missiles of destruction. This destructive power was awesome and matched, in a sense, the might of the pilot. Once on the target, the pilot would let go the rockets. The trigger on the side of the stick would pickle off rockets in a sequence of individual, ripple, or salvo—all according to how he set the control on the instrument panel. The pilot's run would be a little steeper than when strafing, but the pullout would be a little earlier. It was easy to delay the pullout, because of the element of the eye-fix on the target. Watching the white streaks of rocket propellant converging on the target was an understandable fascination.

Warrant Officer Carl Omasta was a real asset to the squadron as ordnance officers go. He always seemed to be one step ahead in the latest weapons technology. Of course we sent him to the schools to update his knowledge, and he had just returned from the last one with some fascinating information. It concerned the "Tiny Tim" rocket, which scientists in California had been working on to counter the German V-2 rockets and their launchpads in Europe. At a pilots' meeting in the ready room, Carl described this awesome weapon of destruction. It measured 11.75 inches at the head, which contained 2,000 pounds of TNT. Even though the rocket itself had been pretty much perfected that summer, it would take the rest of the year to fine-tune the delivery system and the accelerated production methods. What perked up our ears was the fact that the Tiny Tims would be adaptable to the Corsair—but not the Hellcat.

We pilots in VMF-452 did not have the opportunity to practice-fire these rockets at this point. It was felt, however, that proficiency in the use of the 5-inch HVAR rockets would dispel any handicap once—if ever—the Tiny Tim was received.

The month of October was wearing on and although all our pilots had amassed the necessary flying hours as dictated by the training curriculum, there was never a gap in the daily flight schedule. It was always business as usual, and every pilot flew at least once a day. That meant the same airplane might be up in the air three or four times a day—a real challenge to the engineering crews who had to provide the maintenance checks and abide by the safety regulations. It meant working overtime almost every day of the week.

I felt especially proud of our division leaders. They were now naturals and they proved it during air-group forays on simulated targets in close air support missions. Some group exercises involved squadrons of dive-bomber and torpedo planes out of Santa Barbara. Our squadron of Corsairs would rendezvous at a predetermined point and then proceed with them as protective air cover during a simulated strike on a target out in the desert. The division leaders demonstrated exactly what they had been taught. They maneuvered the Thach Weave while keeping pace with the slower-moving strike planes. And of course the flight sections and wingmen reacted accordingly. Nobody got out of hand. I now had a smug feeling that we were ready to venture into the Pacific and blow Japanese airplanes out of the sky!

* * *

As the twentieth day of October approached, my thoughts turned to the pheasant-hunting season in South Dakota. I had missed very few hunts in my life. At this stage of the training cycle, I was satisfied that we at the top rung in the squadron had done just about everything possible to turn what had started out as a bunch of high-spirited renegade Marines into a first-class group of combat-ready fighters. With this in mind, I told myself that a few days hunting pheasants in South Dakota would be a reward justly earned.

I seized upon the opportunity to be flown there in a Douglas SBD dive-bomber. There was a Navy lieutenant (jg) who was a member of station personnel, and a pilot who needed flight time. I don't remember his name but, after that day, he was forever known as "Shaky."

We took off late one afternoon from Mojave with a refueling stop in Salt Lake City. The next leg of the flight was over Rock Hill, Wyoming, and through its high pass of the Rocky Mountains. I was tracking the route on the chart I held in my lap. Darkness fell and, over the intercom, Shaky asked if he could borrow my chart. I was puzzled about this but slipped it to him over the headrest. Shortly, when he gave it back, it slipped between the two canopies and blew away into thin air. I could not believe that Shaky had no chart of his own! I could see some of the navigation lights on the ground—lights that helped pilots track a course through the pass.

Some time went by and then, over the intercom, Shaky announced that we had lost radio communication. I could just barely see the silhouettes of the mountains on either side. Later he said, "We've got fifteen minutes' fuel remaining."

It got to be a panic situation. The terrain was leveling out. Shortly, he said, "We have five minutes' fuel remaining."

I seized the mike and transmitted an emergency.

"We're a lost plane running out of fuel. We're in the vicinity of eastern

Wyoming or western Nebraska. Anyone hearing this, turn on your runway lights or any facility lights."

I happened to be looking down over the port side of the plane when I saw lights come on at an unidentified airfield. I shook the stick and at the same time Shaky saw the lights. In a half-turn and a severe dive, Shaky made the approach—too high and too fast. It was too risky to go around again. The gas tank was almost empty, so he practically dove the plane into the grass runway. We hit the ground and the jolt was shattering. The plane skidded for several yards and finally came to a stop. The dust cleared and I shook myself to see if I was okay.

"Shaky, you all right?"

It took a moment before he answered, "Yes, I think so."

Two minutes later a car pulled up and its bright headlights illuminated the broken remains of the airplane.

A young, good-looking blonde woman jumped up on the wing and exclaimed, "You all right?" She was so beautiful that I thought we must have died and gone to heaven. We drove back to the Operations hut in her sedan.

We had set down on a Northwest Airlines emergency landing field. The little town of Sidney, Nebraska, was not too far away. At the Operations hut, I phoned Mojave Operations to report the accident. I told them I would take pictures with my camera in the morning and get them to Mojave to be included in the accident report.

The beautiful woman then drove us into town. She found a restaurant, where we all had a couple of good, stiff drinks followed by dinner.

The next morning she picked us up at the motel and returned us to the airfield. I surveyed the wreckage: The engine was hanging off its mounts, and I located the right landing-gear wheel beyond the confines of the airfield itself. There was more communication with Mojave in which Shaky was ordered to stay with the plane. I had done all I could possibly do for the time being and, since I was on leave, notified them that I would continue my trip to South Dakota by rail.

Eventually, the Douglas SBD Dauntless dive-bomber was loaded aboard a rail flatcar and returned to Mojave. Fortunately, neither Shaky nor I had to pay for the plane.

During November 1944 the squadron continued to sharpen its skills in rocket, gunnery, and dive-bombing practice. The program in dive-bombing was especially noteworthy. We discovered that the habit we had earlier in the summer of turning into the dive was just not the right way to do it. It made it more difficult to level the wings, and this in turn resulted in a slight skid, which threw the bombs off target. It took a little arguing and a lot of blackboard dia-gramming that led to experiments in the air in order to perfect the dive. We learned that a 270-degree dive-bombing entry run seemed to ensure the dive with its wings level. Accuracy was further developed by increasing the angle of dive beyond 60 degrees. We would strive for a 70-degree angle, which made all the difference in the world.

November 1944 flew by and we were now well into December. Our sister squadron, VMF-451 on the sand lot next door, was also in a quandary for lack of anything firm concerning transfer orders. We were both ready to go and we wanted to get the war over! Of course we were all very much aware of the bureaucratic way in which the service sometimes runs at the higher echelons. Our only recourse to our frustration with the slow-moving wheels of progress was to grin and bear it—and maintain the grueling flight schedule. In off-duty hours, however, there was another recourse that was more appealing and relax-ing. Since it was wintertime, intramural basketball prevailed.

VMF-452 had a very good basketball team at Mojave, mostly due to Lt Alex Dutkin's excellent coaching skills. The team was a mixed bag of officers and enlisted men, with SSgt Ted Gore one the mainstays. The squadron won a big tournament one evening and, of course, this called for a victory party.

Even though the BOQ where Dutkin lived was considered officer country, Gore was prodded into joining the party. The booze was flowing and everybody was having a good time. Suddenly, word came that Col Adams, the base com-mander, was on his way over. For a minute it was a panic situation—getting the window open, shoving Gore out, and stashing him up on the roof. Gore whiled away the time, shivering in the cold wind. Finally Col Adams left the BOQ. Once back on earth, Gore hightailed it back to his own barracks, vowing never to attend another party at the officers' quarters.

"There was that other war going on in Europe," some of the boys jested. Somehow, closer vigilance to the news coming out of the Southwest and Central Pacific seemed to be more important. That's where the Marines were. That's where our buddies were! Whether it was East or West, however, every news report was important. There was real concern when we heard of the setback caused by the Battle of the Bulge, beginning on December 13, 1944, in Europe. There again, Gabriel Heatter was the first to apprise me of this bad news.

In this month of December 1944, we were about to make our own news on the Mojave Desert as events began to accelerate beyond our expectations.

PART IV
The Sea

VOUGHT F4U CORSAIR

CHAPTER 18

Workup

It was Christmas Day 1944. Staff Sergeant Theodore K. Gore was on duty in the squadron office. It had been a boring, listless day so far, as most nonessential personnel were enjoying the holiday. But then the phone rang.

"VMF-452, Staff Sergeant Gore speaking."

"Let me speak to the commanding officer."

"Major Weiland is not present, sir."

"Well, then, let me speak to the executive officer."

"He's not here either, sir."

"This is the commanding general of the Marine Fleet Headquarters in San Francisco."

Gore snapped to rigid attention, exemplifying the demeanor of a proper Marine.

"Give me your name and rank again, Sergeant. I want you to pass on a message."

"Yes, sir!" Gore said at his smartest.

"Tell Major Weiland the squadron is to stand by immediately for a move to Santa Rosa, California, to join Navy Air Group 5 and then go aboard the carrier USS *Franklin*."

"Yes, sir, General!"

The receiver slammed down at the other end.

Gore passed the message to 2dLt Emmons Maloney, the squadron duty officer on that Christmas Day. The explosive impact of the news was enough to unseat every member of the squadron instantaneously. It rippled through the barracks and mess hall. Within ten minutes the people in Tehachapi were on their way to the squadron office to garner details. By this time the air group had also received the news and it seemed the whole station was abuzz with activity.

This was it! This was beyond anything we had remotely imagined. We were going aboard an aircraft carrier—not just an escort carrier, but one of the fast carriers—the USS *Benjamin Franklin* (CV-13), of the Essex class. It was phenomenal!

Christmas was a minor consideration for the rest of the day. The exhilaration brought on by this new twist of events and the implications were mind-boggling. The rest of its day was sheer turmoil—we were allotted only seventy-two hours to prepare for the move to Santa Rosa!

Uprooting a squadron that had been firmly ensconced in the desert for so long was a formidable task. The logistics involved were gargantuan; the packing, crating, administration, and family arrangements all had to be handled in the short space of three days. It demanded the attention and energies of every hand, around-the-clock.

At this point there was no time to analyze events that precipitated this sudden extraordinary venue in Marine aviation activity. The serious business of moving to Santa Rosa was first and foremost on our minds. The implications of being a carrier-based squadron would hit us later. And the impact of this revelation would be startling.

At the end of the second day after Christmas, all hands knew pretty much what actions to take to achieve our collective goal. This upheaval did not prevent the party spirit from spilling over into the work regimen, however. Lieutenant Don Phillips and his wife, Gerre, lived in town in the old house with a potbellied stove. It was kind of late when some of the boys arrived for "salty dogs." Jimbo Ormond was there and so was Wally Mattsfield, plus a few more happy-go-lucky pilots. Maybe it was just one salty dog too many, but somebody bumped into the potbellied stove and down came the smokestack, scattering soot and smoke all over the place. It took two days to clean up the mess. But back then that was women's work; the boys had much better things to do on the base. The chuckles derived from that episode made the workload a little easier the next day.

It was a rainy day on December 28, 1944, when the Corsairs sat down on the slick runways of Naval Air Station Santa Rosa. In another day or so, the rear elements would arrive. VMF-214 (the Black Sheep squadron), out of Santa Barbara, California, had already arrived. Major Stan Bailey was commander and an old friend from when we were instructors at Pensacola just before the war. His squadron was also to join Navy Air Group 5. We both had been directed to fly in with only eighteen Corsairs.

Santa Rosa, on the Russian River, was located about 60 miles north of San Francisco. No quarters were available for the three married pilots who had brought their wives. I eventually found a bungalow in Kenwood, in the Valley of the Moon, for Josie and me. The Valley of the Moon was the home of the famous author Jack London. I was quick to learn why he loved it so. The commute to Santa Rosa was not too bad, so I was able to come home almost every night.

Protocol dictated that I make my presence known immediately to the Air Group 5 commanding officer. I did so in his office located in the squat, gray wood building next to the hangar on the ramp. Commander E. B. Parker seemed gentle enough at first. He was of medium build, a little above average in height, thin faced, and slightly balding. His reputation was quite well known, as his carrier experience went back to the Battle of Santa Cruz of October 1942, when he was commanding officer of VT-6 off the USS *Hornet* (CV-8). The *Hornet* was sunk October 26, 1942.

My thoughts were pretty much wrapped up in the Navy indoctrination period we were about to face. But, in the back of my mind, I was also trying to analyze the events that had suddenly shifted our destiny from land-based to carrier. Commander Parker seemed as nonplussed about this turn of events as we were. As a matter of fact, the change came as a big surprise to the whole air group. The nebulous business of reorganization immediately came to the fore when we were notified to revamp the whole squadron. It had to be streamlined in order to make it compatible with carrier operations.

Why this reorganization was necessary would soon become obvious. Lack of knowledge of carrier operations was evident on my part, and I was caught cold. Operations had to be tuned to the confined space aboard ship and adhere to the tried-and-true routine of an aircraft carrier. At the moment, this was disaster, and I was faced with a very distasteful task. It meant eliminating many important billets, a process of sweeping through the whole departmental spectrum, and had to be coordinated with Maj Bailey in VMF-214. The two Marine squadrons would have to integrate with one another. Which engineering sections would stay and which would go? What about the ordnance and materiel sections? What would be the mix between the two squadrons? And what about the pilots? Who would stay and who would go? This hitch upset the whole table of organization.

Now we understood why the commanding general of AirFMFPac (Aircraft, Fleet Marine Force, Pacific) had ordered us to fly to Santa Rosa with only 18 of our 24 Corsairs. The total of 36 Corsairs between the two Marine squadrons would match the 36 Corsairs that complemented VF-5, the Navy squadron in Air Group 5. And this total of 72 fighters, along with bombers and torpedo planes, was considered optimum aboard an Essex-class fast carrier. We also understood what, at this late date, had caused the delay in our having the squadron carrier-oriented.

The extreme kamikaze problem out in the Pacific was the root of this evil, what precipitated the sudden placement of Marines on the fast carriers. Ever since this insidious weapon got its start off the Philippines in October 1944, the menace had grown by alarming proportions, and now fleet commanders had become perplexed by its success. By November 1944 this peril had reached the critical stage. The only way to eliminate the kamikaze hazard was to employ more fighters aboard carriers. Due to the rapid changes in wartime tactics, the Navy now had a disproportionate number of fighter pilots to bomber pilots. Marines, now well trained in Corsair fighters, were instantly available. The Navy had a real need, and until more Navy pilots were trained in fighters, the Marines would become a temporary salvation to fill the gap. The availability of the F6F Hellcat was being stretched to the limit as well; and even though some Navy squadrons were being complemented with Corsairs, the Marines were instantly available and raring to go. So, unlike earlier in the war, the Navy now demanded that Marine pilots be placed aboard the fast carriers.

It was now obvious to us that this had been a snap decision by the powers-that-be on the extreme top level in Washington. Of course, the influence and pressure of Adm Marc Mitscher were without question and welcomed by the Marine Corps. This had all been taking place in early December. Events were slow to catch up with reality, so by the time the classified information filtered down through channels, along with decisions on what squadron was to go where, it was Christmas Day before we in VMF-452 became aware of our immediate future.

VMF-452 had developed into a close-knit group over the months. We had focused on team effort with only one objective in mind—combat with the enemy. It was understandable then that there would be hurt feelings. To be rejected was demeaning. It lowered the morale all who had worked so hard and diligently for the common cause. I felt personally that all pilots—and the enlisted men, without reservation—were well qualified to do the job. This aggravating dilemma was eventually resolved. The personnel of the squadron who were not included for shipboard duty aboard the *Franklin* formed the rear echelon of VMF-452. They returned to our old base at Mojave.

The forward echelon of VMF-452, now ordered on temporary duty with Navy Air Group 5, consisted of a complement of thirty two officers and sixty enlisted. Twenty-nine of these officers were pilots, including two majors, one captain, twelve first lieutenants, and fourteen second lieutenants.

We were now well into our first week at NAS Santa Rosa. Most of the social proprieties had been performed, and integration of key officers into the system had been accomplished. An acquaintance of all Navy counterparts had been established. The presence of peacetime protocol was now something of the past; gone were the days of parade and review. The formal presentation of a new squadron was now nothing more than a handshake between squadron commanders at a very informal air-group conference.

Flying commenced almost immediately, with the operations officers coordinating the flight schedules. There had to be a lot of cooperation and there was a lot to learn. This would be the beginning of Marines and Navy flying together. A lot of compatibility would have to be tried and tested. The work would mainly reflect Group exercises in the air, and exhaustively on FCLP. The latter was especially emphasized, because there had been too many operational accidents aboard carriers by new pilots. This began immediately, but we never saw the sun: The low-hanging clouds and fog rarely got above 300 to 500 feet, but that was an adequate altitude for the practice. When group exercises could be scheduled, we showed our prowess in performing escort tactics by covering the bombers and torpedo planes.

In one sense, we had an advantage over the Navy pilots in Corsair experience. Lieutenant Commander Macgregor Kilpatrick was skipper of VF-5, the Navy Corsair fighter squadron. They had trained for months at Fallon, Nevada, flying Grumman F6F Hellcats. It had been only within the last six or seven weeks that a transfer to Santa Rosa was made. Not only was the weather terrible, but to make matters worse, they were told to switch to Vought F4U Corsairs. Every pilot in the squadron balked at this change. To them, the Hellcat was a perfect aircraft around carriers and the most comfortable to fly. Now they would have to contend with that long nose with its poor visibility and resort to wheels instead of the more comfortable three-point landing. But the Corsair had the advantage in speed and climb and the critical factor of deck clearance to accommodate the Tiny Tim 11.75-inch rocket. The Hellcat did not.

The USS *Ranger* (CV-4) was cruising off the west coast of California in January 1945. She was the fleet's fourth carrier, the first ship to be built as an aircraft carrier from the keel up. She was commissioned July 4, 1934. Her speed wasn't comparable to the present-day fast task forces and she had only one elevator, so in early 1944 she was designated a training carrier. During flight operations her three smokestacks on either side of the after third of the deck were laid from vertical to horizontal to eliminate the obstacles imposed during flight operations. Her presence off the coast was for qualification in carrier operations for many Navy and Marine squadrons.

The *Ranger* berthed at Alameda Naval Air Station in San Francisco Bay to pick up Navy Air Group 5 and its planes. We had flown the planes onto the airfield there and then they were loaded aboard the carrier. By January 16, 1945, the *Ranger* was well out to sea, weighted down by an air group full of wary pilots anticipating the serious business of carrier qualification. We Marines were especially concerned and we were now confronted with a new dimension of flight. The exposure to the new discipline and custom of shipboard routine was constant. It was absorbed almost by osmosis—and we learned rapidly.

On the first day of operations, the Navy said they would qualify to show the Marines how it was done. Lieutenant Danny Winters was Navy Air Group 5's landing signal officer. Sometimes they called him "Crash," for the many times he had to bail into the safety net from his station on the port stern platform of the ship. It was not unusual for this to happen when an errant plane was trying to land. One time Danny broke an assistant's leg when he fell on top of him, hence his nickname.

On that first morning out, several of us were on the island, observing the landings. Our air-group commander, E. B. Parker, was the first to come aboard. It was a perfect landing, and the LSO, Danny, said over the bullhorn, "Just like shooting ducks in a barrel!"

The second plane, however, flew into the island where we were standing. Second Lieutenant Johnny Cox calculated that there were many major crashes before it was time for the Marines to fly. Finally, the first flight of Navy fliers landed and, after refueling and respotting, the Marines could take their turn. It was interesting to watch the ballet performance of the deck crew on the flight deck. Whenever a plane landed, a member of the tailhook crew would detach the tailhook from the cable and give the pilot the signal to retract it. The various spotters, handlers, refuelers, chockers, and catapulters all wore identifying colored jerseys. In their silent communication and animated body contortions, they moved planes about, passing a taxiing plane from one handler to another. It was also a hazardous occupation, considering the windswept deck and propeller stripstreams that could blow an unbalanced crewman into the whirling blades of the next plane aft.

Now it was our turn. I was about to face up to this dreaded but otherwise fascinating challenge. To personally qualify aboard a carrier was something of no light concern. It would be a real test not only of skill but also of honor. What were my chances of doing it right? I rationalized it this way: Assuming the engine and structural integrity of the airplane stood up, my chances were pretty good. After all, it was safe to assume that the majority of pilots would eventually qualify; perhaps some with difficulty, but qualify nevertheless. But then there was that annoying 5 percent who would not make it. I would rather be flogged at the stake than fall into that category. As a matter of fact, any kind of mishap in plain view of your peers would be an unacceptable degradation.

As my time grew near, I found myself with a nervousness and apprehension that wouldn't quit. At the same time, I was trying hard to exhibit a little bit of bravado and nonchalance expected of a squadron commander. So for all outward appearances, I went about it in stride, but I don't think I was fooling anybody. Every one of those pilots about to qualify was as human as I was.

The plan of the day reflected a 1000 launch for Marine carrier qualification. The first several aircraft spotted forward would be catapult shots; the other aft, flyaways. I was in one of the first planes to be catapulted. At least this was a drill in which I had experience. I recalled the catapult shot I had off the auxiliary carrier *Long Island* in Segond Channel, Espiritu Santo, in September 1942. Only that time it was in a Grumman Wildcat and the carrier was at anchor!

While each plane was individually hooked up to the catapult by the catapult crew, I, like the pilots following me, went through the check-off list: flaps, rpm, mixture, throttle lock, then headrest position. Once assured by signals to the pilot that the plane was ready, the catapult officer would almost launch himself off the bow of the flight deck as he thrust his whole being forward with a pointing gesture: "Go!" The hydraulic catapult was like a slingshot, and flying speed was almost instantaneous. I retracted the wheels immediately and seconds later retracted the flaps. As a result, there was a slight sinking sensation as the Corsair settled somewhat to compensate for the change in aerodynamics. I made a climbing turn to the left to effect rendezvous with the rest of my two-division flight. We were orbiting the carrier at 10,000 feet, awaiting the prep-Charlie signal.

Thirty minutes went by—an interminable wait—and then came the signal. We descended in a wide orbit and then, in a strung-out formation, passed over the *Ranger* to fore from aft at 1,000 feet. At a point about 2,000 yards ahead of the carrier, we broke off individually and took up elongated intervals. I had now turned downwind and was on a reciprocal course parallel to the carrier on the port side. While letting down to 200 feet, I reviewed the check-off list: stall warning light—on; tail wheel—unlocked; mixture—rich; prop—2300 rpm; wheels—down; flaps—30 degrees; hook—down. Just to be sure, I reviewed it again. When I came abreast of the carrier ramp, I began an easy turn to the left. Now I was on the 90-degree leg. I could see the small khaki figure with the bright-colored paddles. As I turned onto the base leg, I picked up the outstretched paddles. I was hanging on the prop, just above stalling speed, with almost full power on. But I was also glancing back and forth between my instruments and the flight deck. That was the "Roger" signal the LSO had given me; so far so good. The LSO's signals were mandatory from now on. As the ramp was coming up, I was letting down. Then I got the "fast" signal. Ease back on the throttle. The ramp was now right in front of me, and I saw the motions of a cut as the LSO slashed the paddles across his face. The Corsair slammed into the deck and caught a wire. The inertia pressed me against the shoulder harness hard for an instant, and then it was over. I had made it the first time. Or at least I had made it for the moment. But there was no time to dwell on that. The tailhook crew had already given me the signal to retract the hook, then it was a tapping of the brakes for alignment with the flight deck and an immediate takeoff. The plane following me was already on the base leg for the next landing.

My takeoff was a flyaway from the carrier, and I joined the racetrack pattern for another landing attempt. Concentration on the LSO seemed harder this time. As I drew closer to the ramp, I saw him kick out his right foot—a skid—then suddenly wave the paddles above his head. It was a mandatory wave-off, and I pushed the throttle hard forward for a go-around. I finally did make three more successful carrier landings. In the morning there would be another CarQual flight to complete the qualification.

The *Ranger* flight deck was slippery from aircraft oil and grease. Braking had little effect. Lieutenants Staples, Cox, Schaefer, Maloney, and Bennett all complained quite vocally. Lieutenant Kenny Bennett went up to the bridge to observe landing operations prior to his flight. When the ship turned sharply into the wind, one aircraft slid on the oily deck and went over the side, landing on its back in the water. Fortunately, the pilot surfaced and the escort destroyer picked him up. Bennett finally took his turn to qualify. Whether it was the traumatic event just witnessed that caused the bad day, he admits to the twenty-six wave-offs it took to get him aboard the first time. Danny, the LSO, came down to the ready room and cursed him for several minutes. Major Stan Bailey happened to come into the ready room and overheard this heated chastising. He told Danny to get out and never come into the Marine ready room again without the CO's permission.

Lieutenant Jimbo Ormond remembered the very first landing he made aboard the *Ranger* and the trouble he had with Danny Winters. After several wave-offs Jimbo was approaching the ramp and getting satisfactory signals, but before he got the cut signal, the leading edge of the port wing obscured the LSO. While advancing the throttle to go around, the LSO came back in view and Jimbo could see the final motions of having received a cut. He cut the throttle and caught one of the last wires on the flight deck. A short while later Danny caught Jimbo and gave him a haranguing that was tantamount to slander.

Lieutenant Pete Schaefer was warming up his engine along with the rest of the flight on the aft end of the *Ranger*. The crew removed the chocks after they untied the plane. The captain turned the ship rather sharply, and Pete's plane skidded into another plane alongside it. Braking had no effect. The two planes' propellers chewed each other up, eliminating two brand-new Corsairs. Pete cut the switches, but the prop of the other plane came within six inches of Pete's right leg.

There was another hitch that developed during our qualifications aboard the *Ranger*. Bo Little was one of those unfortunate souls prone to seasickness. He stayed in his bunk most of the time, hoping he would die. Finally, I went to his stateroom and told him it was simply a matter of getting up there in that airplane or being transferred to a land-based outfit. Bo exhorted himself into meeting my demands. The minute he took off from the carrier, he was a new man. It was a great feeling and the best medicine he ever had. I was waiting for him on the flight deck after four successful carrier landings that day. I shook his hand and congratulated him. Much later, Bo said he didn't know whether Major Weiland was going to kiss him or pin a medal on him!

That constant field carrier landing practice had paid off. Eventually, all pilots qualified with eight successful carrier landings each. Now sights could be set on something bigger.

Something bigger? That vision had been widening ever since Christmas Day, when we learned that we would be going aboard the USS *Franklin*. Curiosity and speculation had been gathering steam ever since.

The USS *Franklin* AVT-8 (CV-13) fit in the fast carrier category. She was one of the ten original Essex-class carriers built. It had been only a year and a half that she was launched at Newport News Shipbuilding and Drydock Company on October 14, 1943. Her keel had been laid on Pearl Harbor Day. We also learned about her vital statistics: displacement, 27,000 tons; overall length, 872 feet; beam, 93 feet; extreme width of flight deck, 147 feet 6 inches; speed, 33 knots. (We had learned already how these dimensions shrink dramatically when actually landing aboard a carrier!)

The USS *Franklin* had joined Task Force 58 at Eniwetok June 22, 1944, and then supported amphibious operations in the Marianas, Peleliu, the Palaus, and the Philippines. This support also extended with long-range strikes against fortresses in Formosa and the Ryukyus.

In October 1944 the kamikazes began playing havoc with the U.S. fleet. Japanese RAdm Masasumi Arima, in the interest of promoting the program of supreme sacrifice to emperor and homeland, was to set a dramatic example. Earlier in the war, as a Navy captain, Arima commanded the *Shikoku* and was one of Adm Isoroku Yamamoto's most trusted commanders. He distinguished himself during the southern Solomons campaign and the Battle of Santa Cruz. There was no doubt that he was a talented carrier commander and pilot. On October 13, 1944, in a torpedo plane, he flew in low over the water, dropped a torpedo, and then aimed for the port side of the *Franklin*. All antiaircraft poured concentrated fire on his plane and, at the last instant, scored a direct hit. The Japanese plane, out of control, sideswiped the flight deck, fell into the sea on the opposite side, and then exploded. One seaman was killed and five were injured as the plane skipped across the deck.

Only minor damage was sustained by the *Franklin;* however, the flight deck was gouged in several places by the propeller of the enemy plane as it bounced across the deck. The torpedo passed harmlessly under the fantail. It can only be assumed that RAdm Masasumi Arima found his way to heaven.

Time and time again, the *Franklin* fended off kamikaze attacks with massive walls of antiaircraft fire. There were many near misses.

Two days later, in support of the Leyte landings east of Luzon, the *Franklin* came under attack by several kamikazes. It was a bomb, however, that hit the afterboard corner of the deck edge elevator and exploded. Three planes were damaged, and a small gasoline fire erupted in the hangar. This resulted in twenty-five casualties including three dead.

There was a rapid succession of battle actions in the Philippines later in October. The *Franklin* turned to meet and help devastate units of the Japanese fleet in the Sibuyan Sea. Then, when our fleet turned to decimate VAdm Saburo Ozawa's forces in the Leyte Gulf, Air Group 13 further distinguished itself. But, on October 30 , about 100 miles east of Samar, the task group was attacked by six kamikazes, three of which made bombing and suicide runs on the *Franklin.*

The first plane missed by 20 feet to port and crashed into the sea. The second struck the flight deck at a 20-degree angle and went crashing through the gallery deck and into the hangar, where its bombs detonated. The third plane dropped its bomb—a near miss on the starboard side—then continued on to crash into the carrier *Belleau Wood* (CVL-24). As a result of this holocaust, fifty-six men lost their lives and sixty were wounded aboard the *Franklin.*

Raging fires immediately enveloped planes located on both the flight and hangar decks. Dense smoke and heat required immediate evacuation of the casualties. This fire was considered the most serious conflagration any USS vessel had survived up to that date. The kamikaze hit at 1426, and the fires were finally extinguished at 1635.

The kamikaze's impact created a gaping hole 12 feet by 35 feet on the flight deck. Other spaces were wrecked by the blast, and the elevator was left in the canted position.

Several other carriers had been attacked by kamikazes at the same time, leaving fleet commanders terrified of this devastating weapon. It was deadly accurate.

Navy Air Group 13 had established a compelling record aboard the *Franklin* in the five months of June through October 1944: 87 1/2 Japanese planes had been shot down; 148,500 tons of warships had been sunk; and 275,000 tons of merchant ships had also slipped into Davy Jones's locker as a result of aggressive Air Group 13 actions.

The battle damage to the *Franklin* was so great that it was beyond the repair capabilities of the forward areas, including Pearl Harbor. She returned to Bremerton, Washington, and for two months she underwent extensive repairs at the Puget Sound Navy Yard. On January 26, 1945, she was ready to return to service. Her estimated time of arrival at San Francisco Bay's Alameda pier was February 2.

It seemed that intercepting the *Franklin* off the coast of California would be a good test of Navy Air Group 5's ability to make a mock attack. Everything was well planned, but the situation turned into a fiasco. The air-group commander decided we didn't need loaded belly tanks. The weather was bad and the *Franklin* could not be located as early as planned. Second Lieutenant Jimbo Ormond's was one of four air group planes that experienced fuel starvation en route back to Santa Rosa. Lieutenant Robert L. "Bob" Harrington was aware of Jimbo's plight and was calling it pretty close with the fuel he had remaining. Jimbo headed for the nearest landfall, which was Point Arena, California. Just as they approached the beach, about a mile or so from the lighthouse, Jimbo's engine quit. Luckily, it was low tide and he had enough room between the water and the driftwood to set the plane down, wheels up, on the beach. He signaled to Bob Harrington that he was all right, so Bob proceeded to Santa Rosa and landed on fumes. Jimbo went to a lonely house about a half mile inland to use a telephone. While there he was told that he was the third pilot to put an airplane down on that beach since the war began. Jimbo spent the night at a Coast Guard station.

The USS *Franklin* arrived at Alameda, ready to pick up Navy Air Group 5 for its tour of combat. Our destiny lay in that big, formidable hulk.

Then came the orders to go aboard ship.

Josie and I spent the last two days in San Francisco before I was to go aboard. It was our first time in that rambling city and I was impressed. San Francisco was a fascinating place, a bustling city with tall skyscrapers and steep hills. We had difficulty finding a hotel room, but we finally got one in Oakland, across the Bay Bridge. I thought the 7-mile Bay Bridge more magnificent than the Golden Gate. Though its lines weren't as clean or as beautiful, it somehow seemed more mighty and dynamic. The Bay Bridge linked Oakland to San Francisco, with Treasure Island in the middle. Out in the bay sat a rock named Alcatraz, which looked as foreboding as the name has come to sound.

Navy Air Group 5, in the interest of maintaining morale at some time in the distant future, gave us permission to purchase a store of liquor to be consumed ashore by the air group. All hands chipped in a contribution to the cause. Our squadron already had a cache of booze in the footlocker that had been given to us by the good citizens of Cheyenne, Wyoming, when some of the pilots had put on an air show for the Frontier Days celebration. Since Navy regulations stipulated that no alcohol could be consumed aboard ship, tight security of the booze had to be maintained. The day it was delivered to the ship, the captain broke out the Marine ship's company and followed the last case to the storage locker. The door was locked and the key pocketed. The booze was eventually consumed at a much later date, by way of a very hazardous and devious route.

These were the last days to celebrate stateside, and celebrate we did! It was a kaleidoscope of squadronmates, favorite places, and excess wining and dining. We had dinner at Fisherman's Wharf amid the famous restaurants and smelly fishing boats. Then there was the Top of the Mark, with its rotating bar and restaurant. From the glass-enclosed room on that usually clear night, the city was breathtaking—a broad, sweeping panorama of glittering lights.

Trying to navigate the angled, curving streets was a challenge, even for a bunch of fighter pilots! It was an accident that we stumbled across Chinatown, so unlike the rest of America, with its bright neon signs and Asian architecture and residents.

This was a real break in routine. It would be the last celebration for weeks to come. For many of the boys, it would be the last celebration ever. I was inclined to want to spend that final evening at home in the hotel.

VMF-452 Corsairs and pilots after landing at Naval Air Station Santa Rosa, California. December 28, 1944.

An aerial from above the port bow view of USS *Benjamin Franklin* (CV-13)
as she departs Norfolk, Virginia. February 21, 1944.

The "Big Ben" underway in her camouflage paint. August 1, 1944.

The Landing Signal Officer directing Corsairs aboard the *Franklin*.

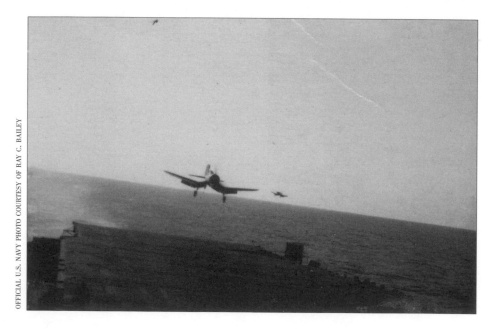

A Marine Corsair snags the first arresting wire with its tailhook.

A Corsair at the moment its forward momentum
is stopped by the *Franklin*'s arresting wire.

This Corsair's belly tank became unshackled,
went through propeller, and exploded in a ball of fire.

The *Franklin*'s fantail filled with Marine Corsairs.

CHAPTER 19

TransPac

The special sea detail manned their stations as the USS *Franklin* slipped its moorings and the ship moved away from the dock. Most hands were topside and as the band played "Anchors Aweigh," they waved to the people on the dock below, bidding San Francisco a fond good-bye. There was one exception: 1stLt Bo Little was bent over the rail, already seasick . . . again.

The omnipresent fog and gloom pervaded the air as the USS *Franklin* wound its way through the Golden Gate and out to sea. Looking back on it all, it didn't seem that long a respite stateside. As the land disappeared in the midst, I pondered the future. The date was February 7, 1945.

Our immediate destination was Pearl Harbor, Hawaii. During that five-day voyage, the pilots flew combat air patrols and became acquainted with their Navy counterparts aboard. A complement of 3,300 souls composed the manpower of this complicated floating city.

I had personally been acquiring knowledge of nautical etiquette and naval routine in travels since early 1942. Now other members of the squadron were adjusting and acclimating themselves to shipboard routine. Back in port they had already learned the proper decorum of saluting the colors whenever boarding or leaving the ship. The ensign was flown from the staff on the ship's stern. The boarding ladder led from the dock to the quarterdeck, which was the station of the officer of the day. Upon boarding, proper etiquette dictated that the individual face aft, salute the colors, then advance to salute the officer of the day and obtain boarding permission. Once our Marines got aboard, it was pretty much "Do as the Romans do"—and they learned fast.

Going aboard the USS *Franklin* at NAS Alameda was unceremonious, to say the least. There was a sign at the quarterdeck that said simply, "Welcome aboard"—and that was it. Captain Leslie Gehres, the ship's skipper, went a little further in the way of reception by inviting all the squadron commanders for dinner. This was a nice gesture, but when he insisted on having pilots stand watch on the way out, he was fiercely resisted. Pilots had to focus on their jobs, not on his watches.

The formality of shipboard protocol had changed since the war began. In peacetime, during meals in the officers' wardroom, the ship's executive officer sat at the head of the table nearest the pantry and was surrounded by his department heads. The other officers were then assigned seats in accordance with rank. Squadron commanders would normally be entitled to sit at the other, lower end of the wardroom. But now under wartime conditions, the seating arrangement was less formal. Squadron commanders generally sat with their own pilots at one of the other tables in no particular order.

The personalities aboard the *Franklin* were many and varied. Captain Leslie Gehres was in command. He was considered a hard charger, very demanding, with a temper to match. He had received his commission as ensign at the Naval Academy in 1918, then his wings at Pensacola in 1927. He had flown off all the U.S. aircraft carriers built at that time, including the *Langley*, *Lexington, Saratoga, Ranger, and Yorktown.*

His indoctrination into a theater of war began early and it came from an unexpected quarter. His assignment to the Aleutians was in a zone of frustration because of the weather. Right after the Japanese carrier raid on Dutch Harbor and the occupation of Attu and Kiska, he received orders to lead a patrol wing of PBY Catalina flying boats to be based on tender *Gillis* at Atka. He and his group would reinforce other naval elements, as well as Army and Army Air Forces, with the mission of countering any offensive operations the Japanese ventured to entertain in that sector. Because of the perpetual fog, mist, and snow, operational accidents were alarmingly high. During the bombing offensive of June 11–12, Capt Gehres lost three PBYs. He eventually received his just reward when ordered to assume command of the USS *Franklin* at Ulithi Harbor on November 7, 1944.

Commander Joe Taylor was the ship's executive officer. He had already distinguished himself in battle immediately after Pearl Harbor; he had then participated in the Battle of the Coral Sea and the Battle of Midway and been awarded two Navy Crosses.

Lieutenant Commander Bob Downes was already familiar to me. He was first lieutenant of ship's company and the damage control officer. Among his other varied duties, he directed the special sea details to effect departure and docking maneuvers. Bob was a very good friend of my family in Coral Gables, Florida. I had also known him well as a student at the University of Miami, where he was one of the professors.

Don Russell was the only civilian aboard. Almost every Marine knew Don well as the Vought technical representative for the Corsair. He wore glasses, had a studious look, and was a very likable sort of fellow. Don, along with the engineering personnel, was dedicated to keeping the Corsairs flying from the deck of the *Franklin*.

The Navy squadron commanders were notable. Lieutenant Commander Macgregor "Mac" Kilpatrick was commander of Navy Fighter Squadron VF-5, consisting of fifty-four pilots and thirty-six Corsairs. It was the equivalent in scope and size of the two onboard Marine squadrons combined. Mac was an Annapolis graduate and was highly respected among his peers. Initially, I had a feeling that he saw us as intruders upon his territory, that he was the bull of the carrier woods and we were usurping his prerogatives in the fighter domain. Granted, his experience aboard ship as a veteran carrier pilot deserved respect, but I didn't feel it gave him license to wield a superior hand in command relations. The more I got to know Mac, however, the more I began to realize that he had a strong sense of vision. He fostered a doctrine of an all-fighter carrier. With the advent of the latest weaponry, the Corsair could do anything a bomber could do—and probably do it better. The addition of the Marine fighter squadron aboard fell right in line with Kilpatrick's thinking. I agreed with him 100 percent.

I quite often had an opportunity to talk to Macgregor Kilpatrick and compare notes on the pilot training we conducted back in the States. He was very positive in his thinking and direction and he considered himself strict but very accessible. As a consequence, he had very few disciplinary problems, perhaps more with experienced jg's than with the young ensigns who were busy "keeping up." Most of his problems involved flathatting out of Santa Rosa over boats and beaches. A pilot of his named Dick Jester came back one day with a section of clothesline stuck in the air intake. His explanation was "field carrier landings." This evoked a chuckle from me as I recalled very similar incidents back at Mojave.

Mac explained how he lost four pilots in training accidents: One didn't pull out of a gunnery run off Alameda; one didn't pull out of gunnery run at Pyramid Lake; one hit another plane with which he was doing a formation gunnery run; and one bailed out of an SNJ, was hit by the tail assembly, and didn't pull his chute.

Mac Kilpatrick originally qualified in Grumman Wildcats aboard the carrier USS *Enterprise* off Hawaii in September 1942. Shortly thereafter, the *Enterprise* left for Espiritu Santo with Kilpatrick aboard as skipper of Navy Squadron VF-10. They joined up with the carrier *Hornet* in time for the Battle of Santa Cruz on October 26, 1942. During this battle, Mac attacked a Japanese Kate torpedo plane. It was hit and smoked, but disappeared into a cloud. That's all he could claim. He had another encounter with a torpedo plane flying low on the water parallel to the carrier. Mac was about 500 feet above, making a high-side run on the Kate. Its tail gunner was shooting back.

Suddenly, another U.S. fighter came along and flew right up his tail, and the Japanese plane exploded. "That's how you do it!" he learned.

In November 1942 Mac was credited with shooting down a Japanese patrol plane. The Kawanishi was a huge four-engine patrol seaplane. She was scouting the *Enterprise* task group and was the only plane there. Radar picked her up on the horizon about 18 miles to the west. Mac and his wingman were catapulted to make the attack. They made high-side firing runs on the big plane, which took no evasive action at all. They could see the explosions in the blisters of the plane; the whole top wing blew off in one piece, which fluttered down like a leaf. The crew on the *Enterprise* was watching the scene, and when the cloud of smoke went up, the ship cheered. Macgregor Kilpatrick had certainly made a name for himself already in this great war.

Japanese twin-engine Betty bombers were land-based on Rennell Island about 100 miles southwest of Guadalcanal. By the end of January 1943, the *Enterprise* was part of the task force dispatched by Adm William Halsey to the south of Guadalcanal to protect a fleet of four transports carrying U.S. Army units to Guadalcanal. On the evening of January 29, the Japanese conducted a very successful night torpedo attack against the task force. Several U.S. warships were damaged, including the heavy cruiser *Chicago*. The *Chicago* had been damaged earlier, right after the invasion of Guadalcanal, during the battle of Savo Island. She was now under tow by the USS *Louisville*.

In the late afternoon of January 30, 1943, Mac was flying combat air patrol and encountered a flight of twelve Bettys making bombing runs on the *Chicago*. Mac received credit for shooting down two Bettys and sharing in another. The hapless *Chicago,* however, received another torpedo hit. This one proved fatal, and she sank.

In one of our conversations, Mac digressed on the mission of a fighter airplane and its limited but significant usefulness. This line of thought was indeed provocative, and I decided to search it out.

In the traditional sense, a fighter airplane was designed to shoot down an adversary in aerial combat. To actually measure the ultimate effectiveness of this highly touted weapon would be to measure the time from when the pilot pulled the trigger until the rounds of ammunition reached the mark on target. Imagine, just a few seconds to fire off those few hundred rounds of ammunition. But what was the genesis of this short-lived scene of action? Where did it begin? How long did it take? What were the complications involved leading up to this moment of truth—the final act?

To take a backward glance in the case of the Corsair, we can trace the sequence of events from the time it spits out its deadly rounds of .50 caliber at a Japanese airplane back to the time when the Corsair is only a gleam in the aeronautical eye of the designer. In the fever of war, the mobilization of men and materiel take place in monstrous proportions. Suddenly, this fine piece of machinery in the form of a Corsair becomes a reality and is carted across the sea aboard a complicated ship. It may take weeks or months, but the hardware and the systems come into play together. A particular Corsair is now on the line, and for just a few seconds is satisfying its ultimate purpose—firing its machine guns at an enemy aircraft. This goal represents the culmination of the coordination of tens of thousands of facets in a gigantic plan. Imagine the time, money, brainpower, and supreme effort that it took to meet this momentary demand. And this is just one infinitesimal piece of the whole system involving the war effort. It is almost incomprehensible.

* * *

Lieutenant Commander Jack Sheridan was skipper of VB-5, flying the Curtis SB2C Helldivers. He was experienced, wise, cynical, and a very stable officer. Lieutenant Commander Allen C. Edmans was commander of VT-5, flying Grumman TBF Avengers. All of these squadron commanders were what I considered the epitome of the ideal pilot and leader.

Another memorable personality aboard was Lt Bob Black. His claim to fame was the accident he had had aboard the USS *Yorktown*. In the movie *Fighting Lady,* a sequence showed an F6F Hellcat landing on the *Yorktown.* It was a bad landing; the Hellcat hit the island hard and broke completely apart just aft of the cockpit. Bob was not hurt and the movie shot was spectacular.

One particular friendship developed between Navy chaplain Edward J. Harken and our Lt Norwood Hanson. Hanson was a gung-ho Marine and loved flying. He was a likable sort, always grinning, with a countenance that was almost boyish. It came to light sometime later just how much Father Harken admired Hanson. In the memoirs he wrote about the *Franklin,* the chaplain said:

> Second Lieutenant Hanson, USMC, was a fighter pilot of Air Group 5. He played the little organ and organized a choir for me for Mass and Benediction. He was from Philadelphia, a convert to the Catholic Church. Reason? He liked to paint and as a non-Catholic enjoyed coming into Catholic churches and sitting down and drawing and painting: statues, crucifixes, shadows, colors, windows, religious expressions, sacramentals, and sentiments of the faith. Soon he liked it and had the faith himself.
>
> He was a most interesting, active lad of about twenty-three or twenty-four years old. The day, March 3, 1945, I was packing to be trans-

ferred from the *Franklin* at Pearl Harbor, I told him I was leaving. He said he would paint a memento for me from him. I said, "Paint a picture of the crucifix and put it in my room." It took him about thirty or forty-five minutes to do it. I found it in my room. Later that day I met him and said he should have written his name on the picture. He said he would. Later, I returned to my room; he had by then written his name on a piece of paper instead of the picture.

The air officer aboard the *Franklin* was Cdr Henry Hale. He was the third-ranking officer of ship's company and managed and controlled the facility that allowed Navy Air Group 5 to operate from the carrier. In other words, the *Franklin* and its ship's company were host to the air group.

There seemed to be a continuing personality clash between Cdr Hale and Navy Lt Danny Winters, the LSO. This adverse relationship could have been construed as insubordination on the part of Winters. Danny had a temperamental streak that eventually led to a head-on collision with the air officer.

The day before the *Franklin* docked at Pearl Harbor, the entire air group was airborne. Danny was manning his LSO station on the port stern platform. The air officer was on the bridge, overseeing operations. He became irritated with the way the LSO was carrying out procedures, and said as much over the bullhorn, directing it all at Danny. Danny shook the paddles at the bridge then threw them overboard. He then went to the ready room to drink coffee while they kept piping for him to report to the bridge. Finally, Cdr Joe Taylor, ship's executive officer, came down to the wardroom and ordered Danny to return to his post and recover the rest of the air group.

As the last division of aircraft was making its break, the Marine Guard, part of the ship's company, was making its way down the catwalk. After the last plane was safely aboard, the lieutenant in charge of the Marine Guard placed Danny under arrest. As they marched him forward up the flight deck, all the enlisted men cheered him along the way.

Upon arrival at Pearl Harbor, Danny was immediately transferred out of the air group. When the *Franklin* departed about ten days later, Danny Winters was on the dock below, smashed to the gills. He gave the finger to the bridge and shouted, "Good luck! And I hope they get the air officer!" Later he was reassigned to Ferry Command at Floyd Bennett Field, New York.

The USS *Franklin* had docked at Ford Island's carrier pier at Pearl Harbor on February 12, 1945. Planes and pilots were off-loaded for a seven-day hiatus at Ewa on Barber's Point, Hawaii.

It was Captain Gehres's intention to have all pilots night-carrier qualified. So at Ewa we began intensive night FCLP, which proved a rather harrowing experience. Flying low among the stacks of sugar refineries, pass after pass, and encountering intermittent rain showers at night made it very hazardous duty indeed.

The *Franklin* moved out to sea for night CarQual. Most of our squadron pilots were aboard to observe the Navy qualify first. The ship was taking spray over the bow, the darkness was total, and there was an occasional rain shower. One Navy plane landed with his hook up and crashed into planes spotted forward on the flight deck. Almost every plane that landed either suffered a wrinkled fuselage or experienced a barrier crash. Perhaps twenty-three planes fell into this category. This bad luck ended Captain Gehres's plan to have all pilots night-carrier landing qualified. The decision was made before the Marines had a chance to qualify, so we were all very much relieved.

Back at Ewa, it was an otherwise pleasant interlude. The officers' club had an outdoor, palm frond bar, and the tropical atmosphere was delightful. It was a crossroads where many old Navy and Marine acquaintances met—some returning from battle and others on their way out. The beer and the stories flowed freely.

The newspaper in Hawaii kept us up-to-date on the progress of General Douglas MacArthur and his drive into the Philippines. The liberation of the Bataan Peninsula was imminent. Then it would be a drive to eliminate Japanese forces blocking Manila Bay. Elements of an Army airborne infantry division had landed on Corregidor, the island fortress in Manila Bay captured by the Japanese in May 1942.

On the late afternoon of February 19, 1945, I was having a beer on the patio of the Ewa officers' club. A newspaper stand stood at the edge of the patio, and a native boy was stuffing a stack of the latest edition into it. My eyes shifted to the newsstand and I was suddenly aware of a small yellow tabloid staring back at me with a bold black headline—almost half the page—that proclaimed the landing of U.S. Marines on Iwo Jima. There was a collective rush for the newsstand. Details were rather sketchy but they did indicate a terrible loss of life to the Marines.

We had already heard that two of our Marine squadrons—the first Marines to go aboard the fast carriers—had participated in strikes over Japan in the Tokyo area. VMF-124 (Maj William A. Millington) and VMF-213 (Maj David E. Marshall) had gone aboard the USS *Essex* only two months earlier. We now realized that this strike over Japan was in support of the Iwo Jima operation. It was a deterrent to prevent Japanese forces from reinforcing Iwo. We found out later that sixteen fast carriers in Task Force 58 had made strikes against Iwo Jima prior to the landing and would continue to make strikes well after D day.

The frantic call less than three months earlier for Marines to board the fast carriers was now complete. Eight of the ten squadrons assigned had participated in the Iwo operation. Besides the *Essex,* there were now two squadrons each aboard the *Bennington, Wasp,* and *Bunker Hill.* The last two squadrons to complete the assignment were of course VMF-214 and VMF-452, now aboard the *Franklin.*

To become part of this fast carrier task force was considered a unique opportunity for the ten Marine squadrons involved. All the more so when one reflects on the accelerated buildup of Marine Corps aviation. By the summer of 1944, there were five Marine aircraft wings comprising twenty-eight Marine air groups. This in turn translated into 126 Marine Corps squadrons. The number of pilots necessary to satisfy these billets was 10,407—and they were now available. Yes, the small niche the ten squadrons played in the overall plan was quite unique.

*   *   *

The next big operation would be the air group's shakedown, with the *Franklin* cruising off the Hawaiian Islands to the south. It would last only a few days but would involve a mock battle with all aircraft simulating bombing, rocket, and torpedo attacks against the ship. The Navy fliers would be the defending force, and the Marines would be the attackers. We put out to sea and early the next morning the exercises commenced. Major Stan Bailey was leading a flight of sixteen Corsairs, and I followed with my flight. It was to be a vertical dive-bombing run directly on the *Franklin.* We climbed to 18,000 feet and then were given the order to attack. Each plane peeled off in a vertical dive. There were flimsy cloud layers between us and the sea. As the last section of Stan Bailey's flight flipped over for the run, I began the same maneuver followed by my flight of planes. I went through a wisp of clouds just in time to see the last two planes in Stan's flight come together in a midair collision and plummet into the sea. They both hit the water straddling the bow of the *Franklin,* and she steamed through the wreckage. This happened right before my eyes and it was over in seconds. Lieutenants Clare R. Beeler and Herbert D. Scramuzza lost their lives. The exercise continued as though under wartime conditions.

On the evening of the accident, I returned to the stateroom that Stan and I shared. I found him staring blankly at the desk with his head buried in his hands, distraught at the loss of two of his pilots.

"Pat, I feel like an old, old man," Stan said softly. I knew the feeling but there was nothing much I could say to console him.

Actually, at twenty-six, Stan and I were about the same age. Major Stan Bailey and I went a long way back. He was that pesky little Vermonter who'd instructed with me at Pensacola way before Pearl Harbor, he in primary trainers and I in instruments. We had even shared a house in East Pensacola with two other lieutenants during that tenure of duty. Later we'd shared a tent at Espiritu Santo in the South Pacific. Our friendship had endured a lot.

The day after the fatal midair collision, Stan called the replacement pool for two more pilots. Later that afternoon one of his squadron pilots, Lt Ralph W. Husted, flew out to the *Franklin* from Ewa, carrying a fully loaded belly tank. The LSO brought him in and he caught a wire, but the belly tank came loose and the prop split it, causing a fire that enveloped the plane. Husted died in the fire. Stan was forced to call the replacement pool again and expressed extreme anguish for having to do so.

The *Franklin* returned to Pearl Harbor to be refitted and brought up to strength with men and materiel. This time it would be for self-containment for an indefinite period of time. We received our last mail call—the last for a long time, anyway. I, in turn, posted letters that I had written aboard ship. I mentioned that I had met Father Harken, the Catholic chaplain. He had been aboard the *Franklin* during the Battle of Leyte Gulf. He was now being relieved by a new chaplain, Father Joseph O'Callahan, whom I hadn't yet met.

Father O'Callahan was well acquainted with carrier-based duty after serving aboard the old *Ranger* (CV-4). He associated with the enlisted men as much as with the officers, maybe more so; he always had at least one meal per day down in the enlisted men's mess. During combat, simulated or otherwise, he wore a helmet with a large white cross emblazoned across the front. Later in TransPac (crossing the Pacific Ocean) a choir was assembled and we practiced the Gregorian Mass in preparation for Easter Sunday.

The *Franklin*, with Navy Air Group 5, departed the Hawaiian Islands on March 3, 1945. It headed westerly across the Pacific with its complement of thirty-three hundred officers and men aboard. Its course was altered somewhat toward Johnson Island for the purpose of conducting a search for a downed plane.

Lieutenant General Millard F. Harmon, commander of all Pacific air forces, was aboard a converted B-24 carrying him from the Marianas Islands to Honolulu. The plane disappeared between the Marshall Islands and Wake Island. Search planes were already scouring the area. We participated, too, running search patterns for several hundred square miles. The one I flew revealed absolutely nothing. Lieutenant Jimbo Ormond was on another search flight. Halfway on the cross leg of the search pattern, something happened to the flaps on his plane; they dropped and he could not get them retracted. The increased drag made it a close call on returning to the carrier with sufficient fuel. When he made it aboard, the fuel gauge registered *E*.

The mystery of General Harmon's disappearance was never solved.

* * *

There was a special "op division" (not part of ship's company) that also embarked aboard the *Franklin* at San Francisco. It was a five-man team that the Navy referred to as the "Tiny Tim Evaluation Group." The Tiny Tim was the 11.75-inch rocket with the explosive equivalent of 2,000 pounds of TNT. This would be the first deployment of this rocket in combat. Lieutenant (jg) Fredrick Smith headed up the team. Fred had only recently been recalled to active duty. In civilian life he had been a film editor for MGM in Hollywood. The Navy was quick on the uptake in applying his expertise to the production of training films. The team's mission included both still and motion photography in chronicling the process and progress of the Tiny Tim deployment. This would include a debriefing of the pilots who used them as well as the tabulation of success or problems encountered.

Lieutenant Smith's right-hand man was another lieutenant (jg), Edward Monsour, who acted as photo intelligence officer. One of the photographers, who would become noteworthy later aboard the *Franklin*, was Photographer's Mate 1st class, Willard E. Vary. Some of his photos would become historic.

During the sail westward from Pearl Harbor, we were flying antisubmarine patrols from dawn to dusk with three F4Us and three TBF torpedo bombers. There were also daily combat air patrols.

Captain Gehres was always berating the pilots for not doing their jobs well. He could be very intimidating and reminded me of the gruff Wallace Beery of film fame. One day, when a six-plane antisubmarine flight broke down for a landing, the ship was still sailing downwind and it took thirty minutes to get the six planes aboard. Gehres threatened to boot the whole air group off the carrier. Commander E. B. Parker, the air group commander, came down to our Marine ready room to read a dispatch from Gehres. The dispatch pointed out what miserable aviators we all were. One of the penalties was a mandatory tour by all squadron commanders of the ship's machinery spaces, engine rooms, and bilges.

Second Lieutenant Joe Warren was included in a four-hour training flight one day. This meant carrying the 200-gallon auxiliary belly tank. After takeoff he discovered that the pump wouldn't siphon fuel from the belly tank. He was told to circle and that he would be recovered as soon as the last plane took off. On the downwind leg, he was instructed to jettison the belly tank and thought that he had received an affirmative that it had dropped. But it had not and as a result he overshot the groove coming up to the carrier ramp. He received a wave-off three times. On the fourth try, Joe turned real short, and the aerodynamics of the plane drifted him over to the proper position for a landing. As he taxied up the deck, the bullhorn blared, "Pilot of aircraft Number ten, report to the bridge." Joe was confronted by Gehres, who, of course, dressed him down for the inordinate length of time it had taken him to land.

Late one afternoon Capt Wallace Wethe came into my stateroom. In his own inimitable way, Wally always had a grin on that thin countenance of his, even if the matter at hand were serious. This time it was really serious.

"Guess what?" Wally asked, still grinning. "The Ox just flew into the ocean!"

"What?" I jumped to my feet.

"Yeah, he's blind, you know," Wally said jokingly. "He was on his downwind leg coming in for a landing and he just flew into the ocean. He's okay, though."

I relaxed. I had expected the worst. Obviously, a distraction in the cockpit had caused Bruce "The Ox" Guetzloe to concentrate more on it than on flying the airplane. The escort destroyer picked him up just as the plane sank. Shortly, Ox, his head bandaged, was transferred back to the *Franklin* by breeches bouy.

Then there was the Lt Kenneth Linder affair. Ken was a member of VMF-214. In this case, the carrier was heading west and the wind was always in the east. This meant turning the ship 180 degrees in order to recover aircraft. The task group was almost out of sight before Ken finally got aboard with his flight. He was leading the flight and so thoroughly messed up a landing break that the captain threatened to beach him. Gehres intimated that all Marine pilots were stupid and he never wanted another Marine squadron aboard his ship again. Ken's skipper, Maj Stan Bailey, pleaded his case in front of the captain, who reluctantly decided to give Linder another chance.

Of course the degrading news of the Marine fiasco spread throughout the ship. Marine pride was restored shortly after the Linder episode, however. The next flight was about to break for a landing and all hands were in the catwalks, gawking at those clumsy Marines. The breakup was perfect and the ship was still fishing for the wind line when the first aircraft hit the deck. All Corsairs landed in record time, and the *Franklin* didn't even lose position in the fleet. A cheer went up from the gallery, not unlike that at a football game, and the Marines were exonerated.

Lieutenant Jimbo Ormond had another close call on the TransPac. The seas were rough and the carrier was pitching wildly. The Corsair he was flying already had a few creases ahead of the cockpit from previous rough landings. He came up the approach for a landing and got the cut just as the stern was coming up. He caught a wire, and the nose came down with a good jolt. Jim turned the plane over to the deck crew and thought nothing more about it. Just before sundown he saw that the plane had been stripped and they were pushing it over the side.

The activities and business of a single squadron were not exclusive aboard an aircraft carrier, but we pretty much maintained our identity and kept to ourselves. The squadron did not fly as an entity unto itself. Many flights were a mix of Navy and Marine. Schedules were coordinated, for the most part, through the air-group commander, but we made our own pilot assignments. In flights involving multiple divisions, each four-plane division would be composed of either Marine or Navy pilots. This practice had begun at Santa Rosa and so now was well accepted by all hands.

Landfall was made at Ulithi Atoll on March 13, 1945. It was a breathtaking experience, absorbing the sight of this huge warship-filled lagoon. One beheld the various types of aircraft carriers, battleships cruisers, and destroyers—all straining on their moorings and facing the direction of the prevailing wind. It was the consensus of all hands aboard the *Franklin* that in all our lives, we had never seen such a gathering of so many ships.

The earlier invasion of Ulithi had taken place September 21, 1944, against very little enemy opposition. This largest of all anchorages in the western Pacific was now being utilized to the fullest by U.S. naval forces. It struck me immediately that this congestion of ships now present seemed ripe for kamikaze attacks, even though the nearest kamikaze threat was about 1,300 miles away at Kyushu. And then we learned that two days before our arrival, a kamikaze had hit the carrier *Randolph* anchored in the lagoon.

We had heard earlier about a little island in the Ulithi group called Mogmog. It was supposed to be some kind of recreational retreat where sailors could try their land legs and sip a beer. It was a tantalizing thought, but we weren't surprised when we were informed that there would be no liberty as there was no more room on that tiny atoll.

The USS *Franklin* anchored next to the USS *Bunker Hill* in the lagoon. The *Bunker Hill* was a welcome sight, because we knew the Marine squadron aboard her. VMF-451 had been our sister squadron at Mojave. Major Hank Ellis and Maj Herbert "Trigger" Long were still running the squadron. They had gone aboard the *Bunker Hill* in late January and had already been involved in strikes on Tokyo in support of the Iwo Jima invasion. The other Marine squadron aboard was VMF-221, with Maj Edwin Roberts at the helm and Capt James Swett as executive officer. The day after our arrival, Trigger Long took a launch and visited our ship in order to apprise us of problems with the .50-caliber guns installed in the Corsairs. In essence, he said that all oil had to be wiped from the machine guns because the gun heaters had been removed. At high altitudes the oil would freeze and the guns would not fire.

Warrant Officer Carl Omasta was especially concerned about this phenomenon. He was our ordnance officer, an old mustang who had come up through the ranks. He kept tabs on every aspect of his section and he groomed and trained his ordnancemen regularly until they were well honed. They all looked up to him. His section matched the aircraft maintenance and structural sections in trust and confidence, producing the reliability that was so necessary in combat. All this worked together to support the struggle a pilot might have in a life-or-death situation.

Carl Omasta was determined to come up with a solution to the problem of the well-oiled .50-caliber guns freezing up at high altitude. One of his right-hand men in the ordnance section was MTSgt William T. Eckert, the NOCIC (noncommissioned officer-in-charge). Another was Sgt Robert Eggleston. It was Eggleston's initial contention that you couldn't have one without the other. In other words, the oiled guns were as important as were the heaters. Eventually, however, they would come up with the best solution possible.

It was inconceivable that the Bureau of Ordnance had not already come up with a fix to the problem. But it was Carl Omasta's considered opinion that the Bureau of Ordnance, in its own bureaucratic sort of way, was simply too slow to come up with solutions. At one time, naval ordnance at the Naval Gun Factory had come up with gun heaters, but they were declared inefficient, so the project was dropped.

Warrant Officer Omasta and his ordnance section delved into the problem immediately. They experimented with a solution of wing and prop deicing fluid mixed with sperm whale oil and applied this to the guns. The concoction was an improvement but not a permanent fix.

Over the years Carl had been exposed to so many-called unsolvable problems in ordnance. They were just things one had to live with while tenaciously trying to find a satisfactory solution.

Carl reminisced about the problems he had had during his days at Guadalcanal. In the fall of 1942, he'd come out with Col Al Cooley's Marine Air Group 14 as a tail gunner in an SBD dive-bomber squadron. By late September 1942, BriGen Roy Geiger had set up his headquarters (ComAirCactus) in the wood Pagoda next to the Henderson Field runway. At that time, he put Al Cooley in charge of all bombers on Guadalcanal. Colonel Cooley, in turn, was quick to recognize the talent that Sgt Carl Omasta had with ordnance, and he put Carl in that section full-time.

One major problem at that time was the accidental misfiring of a .50-caliber bullet through the propeller blade of an SBD Douglas dive-bomber. In aircraft such as the SBD, the machine guns were synchronized by a camshaft to fire between the blades of the propeller. But sometimes things went wrong and the bullet round went into the prop blade instead. This meant replacing the whole propeller and, in those days, parts were hard to come by in forward areas.

At that time Carl had a sergeant working for him who had once been a cowboy in Montana. The ex-cowboy repaired the hole in the prop with lead, counterbalanced the prop, and reinstalled it on the airplane, which then flew perfectly well. This promptly resulted in the restoration of one more airplane to the much-needed inventory of combat-ready aircraft.

The procedure violated BuOrd's technical bulletins, of course. The hierarchy in Washington sent out a couple of Navy captains and technical representatives to curtail this bit of chicanery. Colonel Al Cooley had the best suggestion of all. He addressed the visitors with a simple solution. "Gentlemen," he announced, "I recommend that you all get back on the next plane and return to Washington!"

CHAPTER 20

Beans, Bullets, Bandages

Finally, one morning at early dawn, the ships began to leave the Ulithi lagoon one by one, forming into four task groups. Soon these groups would rendezvous and become Task Force 58. It was a formidable force with 16 aircraft carriers, 8 battleships, 16 cruisers, and 63 destroyers—a total of 103 warships. Its length and breadth stretched close to 100 miles. With this giant armada now assembled, it took up a heading a little west of north on a course headed straight for Japan proper.

The *Franklin* was assigned to Task Group Two (58.2), which was the flagship of RAdm Ralph Davison. Within our own task group were the carriers *Hancock, Bataan, San Jacinto,* and *Franklin.* Battleships were the *North Carolina* and *Washington;* cruisers were the *Baltimore, Pittsburgh,* and *Santa Fe.* Seventeen destroyers composed the screening force.

Ship movement was top secret and security was paramount—even the mail was censored. Still, the night Task Force 58 departed Ulithi, Tokyo Rose came on the radio and out over the ship's PA system: "To all men aboard the USS *Franklin,* welcome to the Far East."

Vice Admiral Marc A. Mitscher, USN, was in command of Task Force 58. Already a legend in his own right, his reputation as a trail-brazer had preceded him to Tokyo.

His feats had begun as skipper of the carrier *Hornet* when it was fully commissioned on October 20, 1941. Six months later, as rear admiral, he launched LtCol James H. "Jimmy" Doolittle's B-25s from the deck of the *Hornet* for the famous raid on Tokyo on April 18, 1942.

Mitscher was always a friend of the Marine Corps, and he had showed it over the years. His activities and commands seemed irrevocably entwined with Marine Corps affairs. After General Geiger's valiant and heroic efforts with the Cactus Air Force at Guadalcanal, the central Solomons were the next scene of activity. All aircraft control had now been reorganized into Aircraft, Solomon Islands (AirSols). This in turn was divided into the Fighter Command and the Bomber Command. It comprised not only Marine aircraft, but Navy and Army Air Forces as well. By the spring of 1943, Adm Mitscher was in command of this organization for a few weeks. He had placed Marine Col Ed Pew in charge of the Fighter Command. His operations officer was recently promoted LtCol John Condon.

Mitscher distinguished himself again when he directed Col Pew, and in turn LtCol Condon, to make assignment of aircraft to intercept and effect the demise of Adm Isoroku Yamamoto during the South Rabaul, Kahili visit. Admiral Yamamoto took off with two twin-engine Bettys and a cover of Zero fighters. John Condon had selected P-38s, the fighters with the longest legs, to do the job. The interception was accomplished at the appointed time and Yamamoto was killed in the crash. This event occurred on April 18, 1943—exactly one year to the day after the Doolittle raid on Japan.

By February 1944 Marc Mitscher was in command of TF-58 and had sunk more than 200,000 tons of shipping and obliterated 325 Japanese planes at the so-called impregnable island fortress of Truk. It was also this force that figured in the Marianas "turkey shoot" in June 1944, in which 383 Japanese planes were destroyed.

It was Mitscher's relief of the fast carrier task force in late November 1944, and an appointment in Washington, D.C., to discuss the alarming kamikaze situation, that led to the placement of Marine aviators aboard the fast carriers. Once again, our friend voiced words that were gospel, and they were no sooner spoken than done. Suddenly, ten Marine Corsair squadrons found themselves aboard the fast carriers.

Early February 1945 found VAdm Mitscher with eight Marine Corsair squadrons among his carrier forces. Stepped-up activity led him to trounce Tokyo with this force prior to the Iwo Jima operation that occurred February 19. Then it was time to pound Iwo and support the invasion. The Marine air support left much to be desired on the beaches of Iwo, but at least Marines were making an attempt to help their own.

Vice Admiral Marc A. Mitscher was to continue as a figure of undaunting courage and aggressiveness. We in VMF-452 were about to help him do it.

While the task force moved relentlessly on toward Japan, the planning for the Okinawa invasion more than sparked our interest. I sat in on RAdm Ralph Davison's briefings, and they gave me some inkling of what our job was cut out to be. The invasion was to commence in two weeks, and it was made crystal clear that the kamikaze threat had to be contained first. It was emphasized that this was the most effective and dangerous weapon that the Japanese had to offer. And once again the briefings gave a rundown on damage assessments.

Vice Admiral Takejiro Onishi was the mastermind and architect of the devastating weapon, that he called "The Divine Wind"—or, in the vernacular of the Japanese, the kamikaze. This threat was much more deadly than most commands realized. It had already sunk or damaged many carriers and other U.S. Fleet units, and this damage would total about 40 percent of the fleet units in the Pacific campaign. The record would show that 1,228 Japanese aircraft were used for kamikaze attacks, during which thirty-four U.S. ships would be sunk. It was a critical problem, and one that had to be solved prior to the Okinawa invasion.

It was St. Patrick's Day 1945. Task Force 58 had been on a northerly heading for quite some time. The mood in the air was sinister as night fell. Early in the morning, we would make our first strike on the empire's homeland. Suddenly came the *bong-bong-bong* of general quarters. We were moving swiftly into Japanese home waters, and enemy snoopers had us spotted. Torpedo defense was in effect. The alarm rang most of the night, reminding us in no uncertain terms of the gravity of the situation.

The next day was Sunday, and it crept upon us with as much foreboding as the proverbial imperial dragon. Naturally, there was tension and speculation but, in reality, the experience turned out to be surprisingly routine. Task Force 58 was a dynamic machine. Because of this formidable force, we felt secure against anything the Japanese could contrive to counter.

The USS *Franklin* was really just a small element of the whole task force. Her firepower consisted of twelve 5-inch, .38-caliber antiaircraft guns; twelve quadruple 40mm; and fifty-seven single 20mm AA guns. But combine this armament with one hundred warplanes aboard, armed with a complex system of weaponry, and all at once the *Franklin* became a formidable force in her own right.

It became even more spectacular as one moved up the table of organization. This firepower multiplied in direct proportion when one considered the other three carriers in the task group. Plus there were the supporting ships: the destroyers, the cruisers, and the battleships. Four such task groups composed Task Force 58. The offensive and defensive capabilities were awesome. This juggernaut was enough to boggle the mind.

At dawn on March 18, 1945, each carrier in the four task groups launched its planes for the beginning of a well-planned assault on the homeland. Timing and precision were paramount for takeoffs, rendezvous, and eventual fighter sweeps and strikes against the empire. The various targets consisted of the largest military bases and installations on the southernmost island of Japan: Kyushu. With preassigned targets, each group struck a telling blow at Kagoshima, Szumi, Uso, and others. The fighter sweeps and strike groups were followed by photo-reconnaissance planes with fighter escorts.

On that same morning of March 18 the air-group commander, E. B. Parker, made his predawn takeoff with a sixteen-plane flight. His mission was to clear the skies of enemy fighters over Kyushu. This sweep would pave the unfettered way for the main strike group to take off later from the *Franklin* in order to bomb shipyards and airfields over Kyushu. Our own Lt Frank Morrison was flying wing on Parker, and Capt Wally Wethe would lead a four-plane division. Lieutenant John Lawrence would be Wally's wingman, and the second section would be composed of Lts Mal Maloney and Norwood Hanson. The other planes in the flight were all Navy.

They climbed to about 20,000 feet en route to the target area. Their armament included not only the 2,400 rounds of .50-caliber ammunition for each Corsair, but eight 5-inch HVAR rockets as well. An extension of time in the air was provided by the external fuel tank that each plane carried.

Over Kyushu someone sighted enemy aircraft approaching. The air-group commander ordered all fighters to drop their belly tanks and get rid of the 5-inch rockets. They fired the rockets at the ground. There were antiaircraft rounds exploding all around the flight, but none of the planes was hit. The flight gave chase to the enemy planes but none was shot down. They flew around looking for more enemy but found none. The wisdom of getting rid of the 5-inch rockets was later questioned—otherwise they could have gone on their secondary mission of attacking an assigned airfield. But out in combat, one doesn't normally question his superior officer!

When low fuel dictated a return to the *Franklin*, Parker's flight headed back. En route they passed over the escort destroyer that visually monitored all aircraft approaching the task force to clear the flight into the approach lanes. At this time of day, they orbited the destroyer to the right as per instructions. The destroyer could see if any enemy planes were following the flight.

Many of our pilots were assigned combat air patrol (CAP) that day. I was assigned to a northwest sector with my flight. We were instructed to stay within 15 miles of the task force at an altitude of 30,000 feet. Captain Wethe and Lts Maloney, Cox, and Lawrence flew in another CAP sector. In relative terms they were uneventful missions, yet over the fleet the sight was awesome and spectacular as kamikazes made their attacks to the death. The USS *Hancock*, part of our task group, came under kamikaze attack but was able to stave off the onslaught with only near misses. The antiaircraft fire filled the skies with thousands of black bursts.

Two other divisions of our pilots were assigned as escort cover for a Navy F6F Hellcat photo mission over Kyushu. On one mission 1stLt Dale Oakes led a flight that included Lts Kenny Bennett, Walt Hurst, and Chuck Hill. As Kenny recalled, the strike target had been changed and, as a result, the photo planes had no reason to go in to take pictures. At any rate the photo planes aborted the assignment, rolled over, and were gone. Relieved of escort responsibility, the flight cruised at 20,000 feet and saw several Zeros chasing tail at about 5,000 feet. The Corsairs peeled off to attack. Their speed was so great that they overshot the Zeros but then winged over to continue the chase. The problem we were warned about at Ulithi came to the fore. Because there were no gun heaters and the oil had frozen on the rounds, the .50-caliber machine guns would fire only intermittently—one round at a time. The dogfight broke off and the Corsairs continued on. They saw another dogfight in the distance, but the time they arrived at the scene, they saw two aircraft crashing and several parachutes drifting down—all colored, so they knew it was the enemy.

The other photo-reconnaissance mission that day of March 18 was to Nagasaki. Major John Stack and his flight were to fly protective cover over the two F6F Hellcat photo planes. At the preflight briefing that morning, it had been emphasized, *"Do not engage the enemy in any fights, for the photos are needed back as soon as possible."* Lieutenant Tom Pace flew on Stack's wing, with Lts Bo Little and Rocky Staples composing the rest of the division. They were well on their way when Pace's engine developed a malfunction and he had to return to the carrier. Squadron doctrine in such situations dictated that another plane accompany the crippled plane back home. Nevertheless, Pace radioed that he was turning back and left unaccompanied. Bo Little filled the void as Stack's wingman.

The flight continued its mission until suddenly, as Bo explained, "There were meatballs all around us." Stack broke and was able to shoot down two Japanese airplanes. Bo's guns would not fire so he stuck to Stack's wing like a leech.

In the meantime, Pace was returning alone to the task force. There were certain procedures to follow before flying over the outer destroyer screening force. Friendly aircraft had to execute a radical turn one way or another for identification. This signal changed from day to day, and pilots were briefed before every flight. It is only conjecture that Pace had forgotten this procedure, or that perhaps the malfunctioning plane prevented the identification maneuver. And it was only natural for tensed-up sailors to assume a lone plane would be a kamikaze, so the gunners on the destroyers opened fire on his plane. Lieutenant Tom Pace was shot down and lost at sea.

The photo planes and our three escorts accomplished their mission and landed safely aboard the *Franklin*. Stack was jubilant over his victories—two Japanese planes shot down. Bo confirmed the kills. With two kills acquired at Guadalcanal, Stack's score was now up to four. The prospect of becoming an ace looked good; all he needed was a fifth, which he might very likely secure in the immediate future.

It was a kind of Pyrrhic victory, however. The euphoria that overwhelmed Stack did not extend to other members of the squadron; the loss of Tom Pace was hard for his squadronmates to comprehend. Pace and Pete Schaefer had been especially good friends. Schaefer had a confrontation with Stack about his lack of wisdom—not to mention his downright violation of orders—in sending back the troubled plane unescorted. This would be a growing bone of contention between the two for months.

* * *

When thirty-three hundred souls aboard a ship like the *Franklin* exercise their sworn duty in time of crisis, they function as a unit, like a piece of well-greased machinery. That's the way the big picture looks, anyhow. But then you remember that each soul has his own unique personality, and that's what makes history books so interesting.

Seaman 1st Class Tom Leo was a case in point. Tom Leo manned the 5-inch twin .38 gun mount on the port side aft. Of course he was part of ship's company, but his personal concerns extended to the air group as well and he appointed himself guardian of a particular plane and pilot. Tom "adopted" Corsair Number 22 and Marine pilot, Lt John E. Lawrence. It was through sheer willpower that he continued to see Number 22 or Lt Lawrence safely through missions and back home again. Others in ship's company did the same and, in a sense, it was a game. In another sense though, it was this attitude of competition that kept up the motivation and the fighting spirit.

Seaman 1st Class Leo's vigilance had been successful up to this point. On the other hand, Leo's buddy, who had adopted another plane—and another Marine pilot named Tom Pace—was not so fortunate. Even though the relationship between a seaman and a pilot was usually little more than friendly recognition in passing, the impact of any loss was overpowering. In the heat of battle, feelings are fragile—and, yes, grown men do cry.

In the middle of the afternoon, I landed and was debriefed. The debriefing officers were busy people during this period of intense mission activity. The intelligence officers, including our own Lt Fred Olson, set up their station in the wardroom. In their preplanned and very efficient routine, they ran the gamut, debriefing each division and section leader and any individual who could report any special activity. Once a pilot had landed back aboard the carrier, he took his turn at this exposé. These bits and pieces of information were evaluated and classified and forwarded to a higher authority. This formed the basis for decisions about future operations.

The ship's staff, in coordination with other fleet units, designated the objectives of a day's flight operations. This included the number of aircraft to be employed on a certain fighter sweep, or a certain air strike, on a certain target in a certain area. The squadron commander and his operation officers would do their own scheduling.

On this day of March 18, 1945, LtCdr Mac Kilpatrick seemed to have the edge on mission priority. At 0600 he took off and led a twenty-four-plane fighter sweep into Kagoshima, the huge seaport on the east side of the island of Kyushu. The purpose of this mission was basically to rid the area of kamikazes. Many Japanese planes were lying in wait to reclaim their airspace from these intruders. The flight had hardly overflown the land area when Mac ordered all planes to drop belly tanks and prepare for combat. Kilpatrick and his wingman promptly shot down what appeared to be a Mitsubishi Ki-67 twin-engine bomber. In the melee, he spotted a single-engine Japanese airplane and made a head-on run. The airplane blew up right in front of him, and he flew through the wreckage. Mac could smell the oleo and odor of the Japanese plane as he did so. This plane was believed to have been a Nakajima Ki-43, code-named Oscar.

This flight wasn't finished yet. The planes regrouped and executed their secondary mission: They successfully attacked a spindle factory on the waterfront and then a train that was coming into Kagoshima through the mountains. But all this was not without casualties.

Two pilots were shot down on that flight. Ensign Paul A. Cassbeer was never picked up and was presumed lost. Lieutenant Robert J. "Dapper" Nelson landed right in Kagoshima Bay. He was able to inflate his life raft but was drifting toward the shore. Even though stimulated by the small-arms fire from the beach, no amount of rowing seaward seem to help. A cruiser-based Vought OS2U Kingfisher scout plane on floats observed the plight of Lieutenant Nelson and set down for the rescue. The Kingfisher taxied up to him, and then Nelson hung on to the pontoon while the plane taxied away. The crew of a torpedo bomber from another carrier had also set down in the bay. The Kingfisher picked up that crew as well and kept taxiing to seaward to rendezvous with an American submarine on station for just such a rescue operation.

I did not have much to offer during my debriefing except to mention small-boat shipping movements off the coast that I had observed from altitude. Back in the ready room, I updated myself on our own squadron activity and it was then that I learned about the loss of Lt Tom Pace. The tension of the day had taken its toll and I was very weary. I felt compelled to steal away to a place of refuge, a place where I could meditate and think. But there was no such place and nothing to do but stand and face a disagreeable situation. I exchanged my flight helmet for a steel one and went up to the catwalk at flight deck level. This was not much help. All I could see was the horrendous vision of kamikazes zooming in to attack ships, antiaircraft flak blackening the skies, and planes splashing into the sea.

Over the loudspeaker came reports as though from a commentator at a football game.

"A Zeke is seen about 30 miles off our port bow . . . now the *Bunker Hill* is firing on him . . . and there he crashes in flames about 50 yards off her starboard bow . . . our patrol has just splashed two more Oscars . . . our strike flight should be nearing the target at Kagoshima . . . will keep you informed in a couple more minutes . . ."

The skies were filled with antiaircraft bursts and zooming planes. It was unbelievable.

It was almost dusk and the strike groups were returning to their carriers. To the west of the *Franklin*, the *Hancock* had just turned into the wind, ready to receive aircraft. A Corsair, shot up and with one landing gear dangling, was given a wave-off. He was ordered to orbit until the other planes had landed, because time was of the essence and it was getting dark. The poor fellow was extremely low on fuel. Finally, he got the order to land. He turned onto the final and into the groove, and the LSO directed him to the deck. Within 100 feet of the ramp, his engine quit, obviously from fuel starvation, and the plane hit the water and quickly sank. A few more seconds of power on that Corsair would probably have saved his life. The escort destroyer searched the area to no avail. It was only a cursory search, as torpedo attacks were imminent and the fleet had to move on. I had watched this heartrending scene and was very distressed over the loss of this young man's life.

From other fleet carriers, search planes returned from their missions and reported finding part of the Japanese fleet near Kobe Harbor in the Inland Sea. For this reason some of the next day's strike flight operations against Kyushu targets were diverted to seek out and destroy this remaining part of the Japanese fleet.

Since the devastating blow at the Battle of Leyte Gulf, the Japanese had ample time to repair and reequip the remainder of their fleet to a more or less threatening degree. To keep pounding and hacking at her fleet was to nullify any threat that she might venture to entertain. Any one of our four task groups could engage to inflict devastation on the enemy's remaining naval power. So on Sunday night, Task Force 58 moved north to poise for a stab against the enemy fleet with a second stab against the main island of Honshu.

* * *

March 19, 1945: At 0400 pilots were in the ready room, jotting down last bits of information. I stressed again the particulars of coordination with the Navy on order of takeoff and positions in formation. We had already been advised the night before about our primary mission, and that aspect of the briefing had pretty much been covered. It pointed out that a large section of Air Group 5 aircraft would participate with other fleet units in a fighter sweep over the island of Honshu as far north as the city of Nagoya. Our secondary Marine mission was to bypass the huge Japanese airfield of Itami and attack the biggest aircraft engine plant of the empire: the Kawanishi factory on the Inland Sea, just west of Osaka. We would attack with rockets as well as strafe.

Up on the flight deck, my flight of planes was positioned near the first third of the pack of about 45 Corsairs. Our takeoff would be a catapult shot. The Navy would lead off with two divisions of eight, followed by the Marines. The balance of fighters on another mission would be a mix of Navy and Marine pilots in a fighter sweep over Kyushu. Once all forty-five fighters had taken off, the flight deck would immediately be respotted for the main strike group of bombers and torpedo planes and their fighter cover. The mission of this strike group would be part of the fleet's attack force on the Japanese ships discovered the day before in Kobe Harbor.

Our own briefings were pretty well completed. While we were waiting for the "Pilots, man your planes" signal over the bullhorn, Lt Fred Olson filled us in on last bits of intelligence information concerning Japanese aircraft sightings and concentrations. During the process, it wasn't unusual to see a pilot or two repair to the head from time to time for a nervous pee. This waiting time was when tensions reached their peak and the adrenaline pumped hard. Once in the cockpit, there seemed to be a calming effect. A pilot had something to do. He was busy from then on.

"Pilots, man your planes." From the various ready rooms, the pilots ran through the hatches onto the catwalks, and up to the flight deck to their planes. The plane captains were waiting to assist each respective pilot onto the wing and into the cockpit, then help strap him in. It was a routine long practiced, including a subtle exchange of greetings. Then it was "Pilots, start engines" and, simultaneously, forty-five Corsairs began winding up.

The night was still very dark, but thin gray streaks in the east gave indications of a fast-approaching dawn. The deck crews with their illuminated batons led each plane, one by one, to the port side of the deck. The crews quickly attached the catapult rings and rigs. In the meantime, the pilot was going through his checklist: full flaps, full low pitch, full rich mixture, and all the rest. Then upon signal from the twirling baton, he pushed the throttle full forward, placed his head firmly back against the headrest, and awaited impact of the thrust. A few seconds later, he felt himself flung off the bow and into the black night. Now he was on his own.

With rendezvous completed and course set, we climbed slowly through the clouds to gain altitude. It seemed as though every plane in the fast carrier task force was flying that day. The armada of formations stretched as far as the eye could see. It became a splendid day as the cloud layers rapidly dissipated and the sun climbed above the horizon. The weather was all we could have asked for. Several minutes later the clouds completely disappeared, and soon we saw the southern point of Shikoku Island looming before us.The panorama was almost unreal.

Any minute now we could expect the Japanese Zeros to close in. But this was what we had trained for. This was the moment of truth. It was the culmination of the drudgery, the heartfelt losses, the aches and pains endured out on the desert. And for a moment I reflected on the ones we had lost. This is all for you, friends, I thought. We'll make it up to you, Hal Trenchard. And you, Don Boyd, and you, Don DeCelles, and you, Tom Pace. All those months of hard work were about to pay off.

The Thach Weave was working. My wingman, Gerry Vetter, was tucked in just right. The second section, with Blimpo Fletcher and John Lawrence, was processing the turns with the right undulations at the right time. To the far right, Dale Oakes, leading the second division, was playing it true to course. We had come a long way and we knew what we were doing.

On the other side of the island of Shikoku, the Inland Sea weaved southwestward. From 30,000 feet the island of Honshu suddenly lay before us. It was hard to believe that this was real. Its mountains and valleys were covered with snow. For a second I interrupted the automatic habit of keeping a swivel head—looking for enemy planes. My gaze rested briefly on the placid scene of mountains in the wintertime. Subconsciously, I suppose I was expecting to see a red or orange Japan leaping angrily from the sea. But there it lay, peaceful and picturesque; it might have been Utah or Colorado in the winter. There just wasn't anything grotesque about it. My thoughts languished on this scene for only a few more seconds, then I began searching the skies for Japanese interceptors or heavy antiaircraft flak.

We must have cruised for an hour right down the center of the mainland, waiting for an attack. There was none. Scores of Japanese planes had been expected to come screaming down upon us, but far to my right I caught sight of only three Oscars, which were being attacked by a Navy Corsair squadron.

A while later I saw one lone Zeke dive for his life with four Corsairs on his tail.

A radio transmission to the air group flight as a whole directed that we execute our secondary mission immediately. The Navy was to attack the heavily defended Itami airfield, and we Marines the Kawanishi aircraft engine plant on the Inland Sea. Just before our attack, we crossed the Itami airfield and there we met our first heavy flak, at around 18,000 feet.

If one were to fly at a given altitude, in a certain direction, in time amounting to one second for every 1,000 feet of altitude, by radically changing his direction or altitude or both, a pilot would most probably be able to avoid the flak. For instance, we were flying at 18,000 feet in the same direction for 18 seconds. By suddenly making a radical turn, one could usually avoid the big black burst right in line with the former direction of flight, and right at that altitude. It was concluded that the better the AA fire, the more predictable it was, and the safer the pilot would be. It took only a few moments for the AA gunners to make the proper fuse settings after they determined the altitude of an aircraft by radar, hence the predictability of the bursts. The experience our pilots had the day before on Kyushu confirmed this. Those guys on the ground knew what they were doing, but they couldn't defeat that time lapse. There's no way the gunner could outguess the pilot.

From 18,000 feet we approached the target area. Atmospheric conditions were reasonably good and the air was quite stable. The demarcation line between the Inland Sea and the shoreline was well defined. The most important interruption to that shoreline was the industrial sprawl of the Kawanishi aircraft engine plant that rambled along the Inland Sea. At the briefing the night before, we had studied the aerial photographs of the engine plant and could now pinpoint its entire location with accuracy. The sprawl lent itself to a large target area.

I think we were doing things right. We approached the initial attack area in what could be assumed under the circumstances as a slow, methodical manner. But it really was excruciatingly slow and methodical. Full throttle was already set, and the big black bursts of antiaircraft fire were a compelling force to push the throttle even beyond its stops. All this put an induced edge of superalertness in each pilot of the formation. But we were doing things the way we had planned it the night before. Our approach had been from the northeast to the southwest. Just before we commenced the run, we turned left on an easterly heading. Timing was critical at this point, and I gauged the peeling-off point with what I considered precision. The peeling-off process was staggered, as each plane in succession entered a 270-degree turn when commencing the dive.

The Corsairs in each division had now spread out. The sprawl of the engine plant would give each of us a target of opportunity. We were all now in a 50-degree dive. The HVAR rocket control on the instrument panel had been set on salvo, and the engine plant was now looming large before us as we screamed down upon it. But now we had to contend with the automatic-weapons fire. From the whole perimeter of the engine plant, nests of sparks were crackling in every direction. First it was the 40mm and then the 20mm automatic weapons. You could see it coming up at you—like a softball on fire. There was not a damn thing you could do about it.

I took a quick glance at the other planes in the formation and they seemed to be in good position behind me. The altimeter was unwinding rapidly and as it went through the 4,000-foot level, my eye was on the gunsight and I was ready to pickle off the salvo at 3,500 feet. Just for an instant, I watched the rocket contrails converge on an imposing part of the engine plant. I eased the stick back slightly in a veer, and the other aircraft did likewise in their slight right turn. The warehouses in the dock area were the objective of the strafing run. The automatic-weapons fire was still intense but seconds later we pulled out at about 700 feet above the docks and warehouses. We applied war emergency power, and our Pratt & Whitney engines responded.

The recovery was supposed to have been over the waterway in a southerly direction—a vector to take us out of harm's way—seaward and eventually to the fleet. Seaward, however, I was surprised to see parts of the Japanese fleet. Rather than fly through their horrendous firepower, I elected to turn inland, across the outskirts of Osaka. I hugged the earth for several minutes, still bombarded with AA and small-arms fire. We curved around the city and gained altitude. In every direction the big black puffs burst close about our formation. I had the throttle bent forward, but it seemed as though I was suspended in midair; we couldn't seem to go fast enough. We were tucked in so close together that I felt I could reach out and touch anybody in the formation. I really don't think the AA or automatic-weapons fire was the formidable deterrent intended. The fear factor was missing in the attack, because each pilot was concentrating intently on flying the airplane and accomplishing the mission. Besides, it was amazing how ineffective that ground fire ended up being against our rocket and strafing attack. None of us got shot down, but we all had holes in our airplanes.

We continued to gain altitude, and soon our southerly heading took us down the blunt peninsula of Kii Haneo. We deviated to avoid another city to the east, then paralleled the coast of Shikoku Island until we came to open sea, then to our task group.

We maneuvered past the destroyer screening force and homed in on the *Franklin*. At this point I observed a cloud of smoke on the horizon; some ship must have been hit. Suddenly, a sense of desolation overwhelmed me.

CHAPTER 21

In the Heart of the Disaster

Warrant Officer Carl Omasta was at his battle station at the foot of the island on that morning of March 19. He had been there since 0400, overseeing the hanging of the 5-inch HVAR rockets to the eight racks under the wings of each Corsair. He also had to ensure that four hundred .50-caliber rounds of ammunition were in each of the six ammunition pans in the Corsair wing and that they were filled and feeding properly.

The aircraft for the predawn fighter sweep had already taken off and now the aircraft for this first strike of the day were spotted on the flight deck, fully armed and awaiting the signal for pilots to man planes. Carl had seen to it personally that the ordnance crews had each plane armed properly and ready to go.

As a rule, bombs, rockets, and ammo were armed to the planes on the flight deck. Captain Leslie Gehres had a phobia about arming planes in the hangar deck, visualizing an inadvertently fumbled bomb rolling around with deadly consequences. Therefore all armament was elevated up to the hangar deck from the ordnance magazine three decks below, then trundled to the deck-edge elevator for assembly above. Only on rare occasions were both hangar and flight deck used for arming purposes. This was one of those times when it was considered prudent to arm on both decks.

The phone talker, not far from where Carl was standing, had direct contact with the bridge and kept the captain apprised of the situation on the flight deck—information like readiness of personnel who had just launched planes, and who could now recover or launch another group. It was 0630 when the phone talker informed the skipper that the strike group was ready. The launch had been scheduled for 0700 in coordination with other fleet units.

Captain Gehres couldn't believe that this flight was ready to go so soon. He told the phone talker to hold WO Omasta on the spot so they could come down and see for themselves. He and Cdr Joe Taylor, ship's executive officer, came down to the flight deck to check it out. Captain Gehres was very pleased with WO Omasta's efficiency. He asked Carl if he'd had breakfast. The answer was no, so the captain said, "Young man, I want you to drop everything right now and go down and get breakfast." He turned to Cdr Taylor, "Joe, tell Chief Jones to take Omasta's place until after breakfast."

Carl walked down the catwalk and stopped off momentarily below to talk to the men in the ordnance compartment. He wanted to share his enthusiasm and the congratulations received from the captain. Master Technical Sergeant William T. Eckert and Sgt Bob Eggleston broke out in large grins. The rest of the crew were just as happy. It was a big boost to morale, especially since we had worked so hard achieving it. There were perhaps ten of our Marines in this compartment at the time, and they represented the ordnance starboard section on duty. The port section, now off duty, was down below having breakfast.

Carl went down into the warrant officers' mess, where he always had his meals. It was separate from the regular officers' mess in the wardroom. A messman brought his first cup of coffee. As Carl lifted it to his lips to take the first sip, an explosion rocked the ship.

*   *   *

The battle cruiser USS *Alaska* (CB-1) was in the next task group over (TF-58.4). She was one of the only two battle cruisers built. The other was the USS *Guam*. They were close to being the size of a battleship; for instance, the battleship *Missouri* was 880 feet long; the battle cruisers were 808 feet long and their firepower was formidable. Condition One had been in effect with her as well as the whole fleet that early morning of March 19. Marine Gunnery Sergeant John Smith had taken up his battle station as mount captain for the twin 5-inch .38 mount on the port side of the battle cruiser.

"Gunny" Smith was not new to the Marine Corps. In fact, back at the Marine Corps Sea School at Portsmouth, Virginia, he had been chief instructor when the war broke out. He had also helped make up the detachment lists for Marines going aboard naval ships, including carriers like the new *Yorktown*, and, eventually, the *Franklin*. He had been doing this since the beginning of the war. After having spent some time at this job, he decided it was time to "fleet up." When the USS *Alaska* was commissioned at the Philadelphia Navy Yard in early 1944, he had a very good friend aboard, Capt Earnest T. Savianno, the Marine Detachment commander. So Gunny Smith worked a deal with Headquarters Marine Corps, and they let him go aboard. Now he was one of the eighty Marines who formed the detachment aboard the *Alaska*.

As captain of the 5-inch gun mount crew, big John cut a mean profile with his large but well-proportioned frame sticking halfway out of the turret. The USS *Alaska* had been at General Quarters since 0510 that morning. John, wearing his steel helmet and earphones, was all business. Down in the handling room, a crew of seven supported the gun mount above: two men each on powder hoist, projectile, and passers, and the single captain in charge. In the gun mount itself were also two trainers, projectiles, powders, and hot casemen. These crewmen, for the most part, were very muscular. They had to be, considering the 50-pound weight of the shells they threw into place. The training and coordination of this sixteen-man crew was, of course, under the purview of Gunny Smith. Now, in the thick of battle, it functioned like a well-oiled machine. From the vantage point of the gun mount, John could see everything that was going on, and he received additional data over the earphones from Sky One.

Sky One was the radar controller for the bow and two side-mounted 5-inch gun mounts. Sky Two controller did the same for the three aft gun mounts. By casual voice communications, the mount captains were alerted and advised of bogeys entering the airspace. The radar controllers also gave automatic input as to fuse settings in relation to altitude, speed, and course of the intruder— and the command to fire if and when the time was right.

It was barely after 0700 when Sky One came on the phones to say a twin-engine Betty was making a run on a carrier off on the horizon. Gunny Smith picked up this action immediately and then saw a huge explosion in the distance. He stared in disbelief at the gigantic fireball. He stood there transfixed, watching one explosion after another. Some ship just kept blowing up and blowing up. He could hear the explosions over the phone. He muttered aloud, "God, she'll never last!"

*   *   *

On that early morning of March 19, the flights of planes on the fighter sweep had completed their takeoffs by 0557. This meant forty-five planes aloft. Fifty-three remained aboard, with thirty-one poised on the flight deck, their propellers winding up in preparation for takeoff. These planes constituted the first heavy strike of the day and were fully loaded with bombs, 5-inch HVAR rockets, and .50-caliber ammunition. Twelve Corsairs carried the new Tiny Tim rockets, which were being used for the first time in combat. These had the explosive power of 2,000 pounds of TNT. The Corsair fighters, escorts for the strike group, were spotted on the deck forward. They were followed by the Curtis Helldivers and then, farther aft, the Grumman torpedo bombers.

At 0649 the *Franklin* had picked up speed and was brought into the wind to launch aircraft. By 0659 the launch had commenced with Cdr E. B. Parker's catapult. Within five minutes, four other Corsairs were in the air and following Parker. This included Lt Kenneth Linder of the VMF-214 Blacksheep squadron. The sky was overcast with occasional breaks in the low, scattered

The USS *Franklin* engulfed in smoke. March 19, 1945.

OFFICIAL U.S. NAVY PHOTO COURTESY OF RAY C. BAILEY

This starboard-side view shows the "Big Ben" with a 13-degree listas she lies dead
in the water only 52 miles off Shikoku.

As the light cruiser USS *Santa Fe* assists in fighting fires aft of island
on the starboard side, the destroyer USS *Hickox* approaches
from astern to remove wounded sailors and Marines.

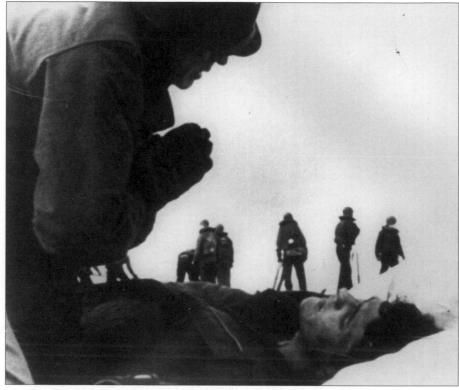

Father Joseph O'Callahan administers last rites to crewman Robert Blanchard. (Official U.S. Navy photo courtesy of Ray C. Bailey)

This starboard-side, bow-to-stern view of the
USS *Franklin* was taken from the USS *Santa Fe*.

Casualties are transferred to the USS *Santa Fe* (right foreground) over the *Franklin*'s broken antennae. The heavy cruiser USS *Pittsburgh* is off the carrier's bow, preparing to two the disabled ship. (Official U.S. Navy photo courtesy of Ray C. Bailey)

The USS *Franklin* under tow by the USS *Pittsburgh*. The *Franklin*'s list is now to port due to intentional counterflooding.

The burned, twisted remains of Air Group 5 aircraft on the
Franklin's flight deck.

clouds. The radar screen reported no bogeys; the USS *Hancock*, however, reported that her lookouts had sighted an enemy plane closing in on the *Franklin*.

Photographer's Mate 1st Class Willard E. Vary had all his photography equipment on the flight deck that morning. He was a member of the Tiny Tim Evaluation Group, the five-man team that was recording the deployment of the new 11.75-inch rocket. The predawn fighters had been launched and now the strike group was preparing for takeoff. Willard Vary, his camera at the ready, was recording the arming of this new deadly weapon on the twelve Corsairs by the ordnance crews. Everything was going according to plan.

* * *

Lieutenant Commander Macgregor Kilpatrick was not assigned to a mission this day. He had done himself proud the day before, having led a very successful flight over Kyushu and personally shooting down two Japanese airplanes. He would fly a combat-air-patrol mission later in the day. Just before 0700 that morning, he was on the flight deck and then up on the wing of a Corsair, talking to Commander Parker, who was leading the strike group that was about to take off. A few minutes later, he was standing astride the deck-edge elevator. He admits to it being a rather stupid thing to do as, the elevator suddenly started down and, of course, the recessed railing started coming up—right between his legs. So Mac jumped on the elevator as it was going down. When it got to the hangar deck, he walked across and up to the island. As soon as he got to the bridge, he saw the airplane flying low and fast from dead ahead of the ship—right over the flight deck. He did a double take at the sight of a red meatball on the fuselage and wings of the plane.

* * *

Lieutenant Pete Schaefer had been in the ready room with three other Marine pilots for briefing of the second strike of the day. This flight was a mix of Navy and Marines and was scheduled for takeoff at 1000, right after recovery of the planes that had been on the predawn fighter sweep. With the briefing over, Pete left the ready room and walked up to the catwalk to watch the present strike group commence takeoffs.

Pete noticed a single plane swoop by from fore to aft and thought, Some damn fool is making a message drop right in the middle of a launch. Then he too saw the red meatballs.

* * *

Lieutenant (jg) Wally L. Young was sitting in his VT-5 TBM torpedo bomber awaiting his turn to launch. Like the others, he was involved in the Kobe strike and was carrying four 500-pound armor-piercing bombs aboard his TBM.

As Wally Young sat there waiting, he could see the multitude of aircraft which had already taken off from the other three carriers in the task group. At one point, he swiveled further to the left and became entranced with the sight of a single-engined airplane flying low on the water about a mile away. It was converging slightly on the *Franklin*. As this strange plane approached, Wally noticed that it did not have the big white diamond on the vertical tail that identified all planes from the *Franklin*. He further observed that the plane was flying at reduced throttle and that the cockpit hatch was open. The explanation was simple: We had been trained with a technique of a low, slow approach, bisecting the flight deck with hatch open to drop a leaded pouch on the deck under conditions of absolute radio silence. This plane was obviously from another carrier, making a message drop.

By this time, Wally observed the plane approaching abeam from only about 200 feet. It had a radial engine and an elongated cockpit—and he truly believed the pilot with the tear-shaped goggles was looking directly at him. The pilot had straightened his approach and was now paralleling the *Franklin's* course. When he was about 100 feet ahead, he depressed the nose of his aircraft and went below the level of the flight deck. Then several things occurred almost simultaneously, including Wally Young's horrible realization as to what was happening.

The pilot yanked the aircraft into a nearly vertical position as he shoved the throttle all the way forward, then kicked hard right rudder to execute a vertical reverse, or a very rapid wing-over. A big burst of black smoke from all the exhausts on either side of the engine was visible, and then the big red balls on the wings became apparent as the aircraft climbed. The pilot completed this maneuver in a few seconds and ended up in a position slightly ahead of the *Franklin's* island at about seventy-five feet above the carrier deck. He was at maximum power and accelerating rapidly in his shallow dive angle from bow to stern.

In those few moments, Wally Young's eyes grew wide as he half rose from his cockpit seat and uttered a long drawn-out "No-o-o." When the Japanese plane was only 30 to 40 feet above the flight deck, the bomb that was visible on the left wing detached and glided downward.

* * *

At precisely 0708, a lone twin-engine Japanese plane dove out of the clouds and, flying at mast-top level along the *Franklin's* flight deck fore to aft, dropped two small bombs. One bomb went through the flight deck just aft of the forward elevator; the second exploded almost simultaneously farther aft on the flight deck. The direct damage by the two bombs was relatively minor compared to the tremendous damage caused by the eruptions of the ordnance attached our own aircraft. It was only a minute or two before a chain reaction of fires and explosions began a five-hour holocaust. On the hangar deck below, twenty-two planes were being readied for the midmorning strike. Each plane was being refueled with 300 gallons of high-octane gasoline. They were also being armed with rockets and bombs, including Tiny Tim rockets slung to the brackets of five Corsairs. The high-octane fuel immediately caught fire and exploded. With hurricane force, sheets of flame swept the entire length of the hangar deck. Then the bombs and rockets exploded. Two thousand pounds of TNT erupted from each of the Tiny Tims, which compounded the disaster. No one in the hangar deck survived.

Radio communication failed. Interior communications and general announcing systems were lost.

Then the fires enveloped the planes on the flight deck above, and the ordnance started exploding, hurling planes, pilots, and deck personnel overboard. Flames and explosions reached the bowels of the ship, blowing up ammunition magazines, setting fire to fuel storage tanks, and trapping many people in locked-down compartments.

* * *

When the lone Japanese plane dropped its bombs, Lts Wallace Mattsfield, Jimbo Ormond, and Joe Warren were in the squadron ready room. The first explosions knocked them down. Almost simultaneously, the lights went out. The dazed pilots were groping around in the dark as smoke rapidly filled the compartment. Explosions rocked the ship every few seconds.

Ormond tried to get up from the ready room deck but was unable to walk on his left foot, the concussion having fractured his heel and ankle. In the dark he made it around by crawling or hopping on his right foot. He and the others tried to make it to the flight deck, but were met with flames when the hatch was opened. They tried the doors to the VMF-214 ready room as well as the gang-way door to the hanger deck, but those too were enveloped in flames. Once again, they went back to the flight-deck hatch where, for an instant, the flames had subsided. Jimbo made his escape. He crawled across the flight deck to the gun turret forward of the island. On the way he was met by a flight surgeon, who gave him a shot of morphine. First Lieutenant John "Bill" Rogalski was already at the gun turret, so they hunkered down there until a seaman told them to vacate immediately because the turret was about to explode. Jim crawled across the deck to the port side, burning his hand on the hot steel tie-down channels. He stayed on the forward part of the catwalk near the bow for about two hours, buffeted by the incessant explosions. A lieutenant (jg) pilot of

VF-5 administered some first aid and provided blankets to Jimbo and other injured personnel in the group. The lieutenant then advised them to make it to the turret located just below the flight deck on the bow.

Lieutenant Joe Warren was in pretty bad shape, too, although not as badly injured as Jimbo Ormond. He finally found his way through the maze of smoke and darkness to a hatch and then out to the catwalk at flight-deck level. The explosions around him hurled him off the ship and into the water below. He floundered about without any kind of flotation device. Nearby he saw another swimmer and moved wearily toward him. Joe was elated to see a lieutenant (jg) with a life preserver. Joe clung to the young Navy pilot and they both immediately set their hopes on an imminent rescue.

Lieutenant Wallace Mattsfield was killed. It is only speculation that he may have suffered severe injuries, lost consciousness, and then died as the result of smoke inhalation. His body was found in the ready room.

*   *   *

Lieutenant Pete Schaefer witnessed the release of the two bombs from the Japanese plane. The first bomb penetrated the deck just a few feet from where he was standing. The flash fire melted the synthetic material of Pete's flight suit, and his face was burned. He instantaneously decided that the best thing for him to do was go over the side.

In Pete's precipitous departure from the ship, he apparently hit the water just right when he made his dive headfirst from the flight deck of the *Franklin*. Diving was strictly against procedures recommended for jumping from heights. The ship was turning and he could feel the vibrations of the screws in the water. He kicked off his boondockers so he could swim better and frantically headed outward.

Lieutenant Bo Little had just finished his breakfast and had returned to his bunkroom in the forward section of the *Franklin* when the bombs hit. He had been scheduled for a flight later that afternoon. When the bombs shook the ship, he remembered the instructions: *When off duty and in event of an emergency, assemble in the wardroom.* This he did immediately and found himself trapped with many others. The hatches were locked down, the lights had been extinguished by bomb blasts, and smoke was pouring into the compartment. Pandemonium took over, with people clawing, screaming, and hammering at the hatches. A panic situation prevailed as explosions around the wardroom rocked the ship every few seconds.

Lieutenant Fred Olson, the squadron intelligence officer, was also trapped there. Fred had been a cop in civilian life and had been in dire situations before. He was aware of the possible consequences but remained calm. He took hold of Bo and told him to get under the table, dip his handkerchief in the water pitcher, and hold it over his nose to breathe. It wasn't a suggestion—it was a command. Olson's look of determination was persuasion enough. Suddenly, his sense of calm was transmitted to Bo and he submitted. It seemed an eternity down in that hellhole, but only hours later they were rescued.

* * *

Lieutenant John "Bill" Rogalski was to have taken off on a flight early that morning. He was called out of the ready room just before the flight by TSgt LaVerne Nelson, who apologized for his failure to detect shrapnel damage to the plane the afternoon before. The damage was in the vicinity of the wing locking pin and very difficult to see with the wing in the folded position. FlyOne had noticed the damage and downed the aircraft just prior to Bill's takeoff that morning.

Bill was standing on the catwalk outside the ready room when he was engulfed by a tremendous explosion and flames that swept over the port elevator side of the carrier. He tried to enter the ready room to no avail, so he proceeded onto the flight deck and then over to the deck-edge elevator. There he saw CWO Clayton Smith lying on the deck. Bill bent over to ask about his injuries, and Smitty pointed to his ankles. Apparently, the concussions had shattered them. For a moment the explosions and smoke obliterated the scene. When Bill looked back down, Smitty was gone. He had crawled over the side of the deck-edge elevator and dropped into the water 100 or so feet below.

Technical Sergeant LaVerne Nelson found Bill and offered him a cartridge-type life belt, which was a spare, as Nelson was also wearing a kapok life jacket. In Bill's haste to put on the belt, he triggered the cartridge, which now made it more of a hindrance than a help. He knew that abandoning ship with the belt on, in this fashion, was out of the question. He made his way to the starboard side of the ship and ran into the injured Jimbo Ormond. They made their way to the fo'c'sle deck to get away from the flames.

Lieutenant Rocky Staples was in his bunk near the bow on the starboard side of the ship when the Japanese bombs dropped. Fortunately, he was not hurt. He found his way to the flight deck and then readily helped man a hose to fight fires.

* * *

Lieutenant (jg) Wally Young, who was awaiting takeoff in his VT-5 TBM, witnessed the whole sequence of events leading to the *Franklin* bombing. Fortunately for him, the bomb that hit the flight deck near him had a slight delayed-action fuse and went through the flight deck to explode in the hangar deck below. As Wally ducked down into the cockpit, the shock of the huge explosion beneath the flight deck was taken up by the hydraulic struts of the

TBM's landing gear. The result was some bounces. Black, oily smoke engulfed the whole ship. The TBM ahead of Wally's had disappeared. Its pilot and crew were lost. Wally jumped from his plane and ran under the tail. Instinct told him to drop flat to the deck, just under the whirling propeller of the plane behind his. He then crawled all the way to the fantail of the ship.

Wally Young ended up with other pilots at the extreme end of the flight deck. Finally, he was able to grab a line in the vicinity of the quad-40mm gun mount and lowered himself to the the water below. Partway down, a horrendous explosion jerked the rope away from him, and he fell into the ocean. The explosion came from the nearby high-pressure cylinders in the oxygen shop.

*   *   *

Down in the warrant officers' mess, Carl Omasta never had a chance for a second sip of coffee. The first explosion gave him a flash burn. As he hurriedly started toward the passageway door, it opened and a sailor stumbled in, clutching his stomach. His whole midsection was torn open and he fell into Omasta's arms. He lay there and, almost inaudibly, asked Carl to take the ring off his finger to give to his mother. In the next instant, this young sailor was dead. Carl could not tarry.

The lights suddenly went out, and in this labyrinth of passageways, compartments, ladders, and hatches, Carl became disoriented in his frantic search for an opening above. In one compartment, the deck was covered with ankle-deep aviation fuel and diesel oil—and it was rising rapidly. He almost collided with a man who had just opened a hatch. This Navy man was badly hurt and could only point in the direction of possible escape.

*   *   *

Our Navy comrades suffered the same indignities in their struggle for survival as did the Marines—maybe more so because there were so many more of them. Electrician's Mate 2d Class Robert St. Peters was a case in point. He had been at a battle station from 2000 the night before until sunup. When relieved, he was so tired that instead of going to Mass in the library or to breakfast, he lay down on the bunk fully dressed and went to sleep. When the bombs hit, the ship shuddered and it sounded like violent thunder. He immediately reported to his battle station down in the Number 4 fireroom. The fireroom soon filled with smoke as explosions continued in the decks above. The heat reached 120 degrees, and Bob had to resort to using his rubber gas mask and a one-cell flashlight. All communications were lost, and twelve men were trapped in this locked-down compartment just above the bilges. The only thing that saved them was a little 1-inch vent line that ran down into the bilge area. The twelve of them lay on their bellies, taking turns sucking fresh air out of this single tube.

* * *

Just before the bombs exploded, battle conditions had been secured. Flight operations had been under way since 0500. Most hatches were open and most hands were in a more or less relaxed mode. It was breakfasttime, and the chow line was so long that it stretched across the hangar deck and wound down through the Marine compartment and into the third-deck mess hall. All those hundreds of men in the hangar deck were killed instantly.

Photographer's Mate 1st Class Willard Vary's mission of recording the Tiny Tim rockets was cut short. He was just far enough forward on the flight deck to escape serious injury from the first bomb blasts. Once he recovered from the initial shock, he set out to record scenes alien to his original intentions. He moved in closer to the scene of disaster. He spied a steel-helmeted figure bending over a young man lying prone on the flight deck. The figure had his hands clasped in prayer. Willard noticed the large white cross emblazoned on the front of his helmet. It was Father Joseph O'Callahan giving last rites to a dying sailor. It only took a second to shoot a picture—and then take cover from the other bomb that shook the ship.

The chaplains bent over prone young boys, administering last rites. Over and over Father O'Callahan repeated the Act of Contrition, praying and trying to soothe the souls of the dying. All this time the bombs and rockets convulsed the ship, exploding one after another. Father O'Callahan, like many others, demonstrated complete disregard for his own safety and life. He manned firehoses, dumped hot bombs overboard, and assisted in saving the ship under the most trying circumstances.

* * *

All hands—officers and enlisted men alike—fought the raging fires, manned firehoses when there was water pressure, and rolled hot bombs and rounds of ammunition overboard before they exploded. The blasts were incessant. The powerful 11.75-inch Tiny Tim rockets exploded one after the other—and the carnage mounted.

From a distance of fewer than 3 miles, the observers on the *Alaska* watched as the explosions continued. Sky One informed the 5-inch twin mounts that it was the carrier *Benjamin Franklin*. At times it was impossible to see the ship for the smoke. When the blinding smoke and explosions cleared intermittently, it was possible to see, from all angles, people jumping over the side—from the flight deck, from the hangar deck, from the fantail! Other ships were firing on kamikazes at the same time. It was a cataclysmic event. The fires raged and the explosions continued for what seemed like hours. The *Franklin* had been making way, but shortly she would be dead in the water.

The cruisers *Alaska, Guam, Santa Fe, Pittsburgh,* and several destroyers were ordered to stay with the *Franklin* and assist in rescue and salvage operations. Once detached from their respective task groups, they moved in to protect her. The main task group force moved on to conduct the battle plan of the day against the enemy.

Gunny John Smith, aboard the *Alaska,* watched the ghastly sight and it was forever engraved on his mind. He observed more people jumping over the side from the midst of the explosions. Now destroyers were racing around, trying to pick up survivors.

It was now obvious that RAdm Ralph Davison aboard the *Franklin* had no control over the other ships in his task group, including the carriers *Bunker Hill, San Jacinto,* and the *Hancock.* It was propitious for him and his staff to evacuate as soon as possible. By 0900, while the *Franklin* was still able to maintain a reasonably steady course, the destroyer *Miller* maneuvered alongside for a temporary tie-up. Many members of the staff had already been killed, but the survivors made a frantic transfer to the destroyer by breeches buoy (mostly mailbag breeches). In the meantime explosions aboard the *Franklin* were creating casualties aboard the *Miller,* so the transfer was swift, the lines were cast off, and the hazardous area was vacated.

The *Franklin* was still under way, trying to seek a windward direction in order to facilitate firefighting from the forward positions of the ship. She was moving at 8 knots. At 0930 the *Santa Fe* took station 100 feet off the starboard bow and started to transfer wounded by trolley. At 1015 she had to cut loose when steerage of the *Franklin* was lost and the ship veered out of control. It was a dismal sight to the would-be survivors aboard the fiery ship to see that last ray of hope for rescue move slowly away.

The hangar deck of the *Franklin* was still burning. The ordnance compartment in the gallery deck just aft of the island was destroyed. The Marines who had been located there met an instantaneous death. This included MTSgt William Eckert and Sgt Robert Eggleston. Navy Chief Jones, Carl Omasta's temporary relief earlier, also perished.

There were many other casualties of the ordnance section in compartments way belowdecks. One ordnance man was later found dead with his head inside the toilet bowl—he had been trying to gasp for that last breath of oxygen.

In the meantime, Carl Omasta was groping his way upward and forward in the darkness of the ship's compartments. The *Franklin* had taken on a starboard list that threatened to capsize her and spell her doom. Carl was certain the ship was sinking. Of course the continuous explosions numbed the senses, but the will to live kept him groping forward along his intended path. It took him two hours to find an exit just beyond the ship's fo'c'sle. The breath of fresh air—and the relief at still being alive—were transfusing. Through bleary eyes he saw in the distance the bow of another ship moving very slowly toward him and, very shortly, below him.

* * *

The conflagration aboard the *Franklin* was catastrophic. She was now dead in the water and slowly drifting toward Japan—only 50 miles away. Lieutenant Commander Bob Downes, my former University of Miami professor, was the ship's first lieutenant, and damage control was under his purview. But, he thought, how can one control anything if the control itself has been inexplicably destroyed? The initial damage done by the two small Japanese bombs was minor, but the damage caused by the chain reaction of our own rockets and bombs was extensive. And the lack of damage control was exacerbated by the fact that most of the firefighting equipment had been put out of commission by the explosions. All power was cut off. Communications systems, both topsides and on decks, and in compartments below, were down. Main propulsion power was lost—mostly due to explosions of ammunition magazines and fuel reservoirs. Its attendant heat and dense black smoke flowed through the ducts, forcing personnel to vacate their stations.

Lieutenant Commander Bob Downes had to contend with this holocaust with only a few able-bodied men at first. In the confusion it was a matter of delegating authority and duty in a more demanding than judicious way. Most firehoses did not have water pressure. The violent and frequent explosions prevented any control of the major catastrophe centers in the midsection and aftermost portion of the ship. The sprinkler systems in the hangar and other compartments were inoperable because the control stations had been damaged and their staffs killed. Bob Downes and his surviving crews concentrated their efforts as close as possible amidships but, initially, the extreme forward end of the ship was about as close as they could get.

* * *

Just aft of the island of the *Franklin*, burning fuel blazed from the hangar deck like a waterfall of fire pouring over the side into the ocean. As this cauldron of fire produced many more casualties, the doctors and corpsmen who were not incapacitated rendered first aid and turned bunkrooms into hospitals in the forward section of the ship. They administered anesthetics, operated, and tendered first aid with only hand-held light illumination. This makeshift facility was a primitive arrangement, but it was the only one available.

Don Russell, our civilian Vought Corsair technical representative, was one of the undaunted ones. His valor and unflagging determination to render first aid with total disregard for his own personal safety were inspiring. As a stretcher bearer, he assisted a detail of able-bodied men in carrying the wounded to the makeshift hospital in the forward section of the ship. In this bunkroom hospital he held a flashlight and helped administer anesthetics. It was hard to keep his senses, but he noticed how Dr. Sam Sherman kept his concentration while operating on a patient despite the distractions of smothering smoke and the bombs and rockets that exploded every minute. The adverse environment did not deter the doctor's necessary skill and precision. Later, Don manned firefighting hoses. He was, indeed, one of the hundreds of heroes trying to save this ship in trouble.

*   *   *

From the time LCdr Mac Kilpatrick reached the bridge that early morning of March 19 and saw the lone Japanese plane drop its bombs, he was busy carrying out the rash of orders from Capt Leslie Gehres and the ship's executive officer, Joe Taylor. At one point he caught a glance of firefighting crews going back up the deck. When they got to a certain point within 200 feet of the bow, they split to go around something. That something was a 500-pound bomb sitting there melting. Fires were burning in the gallery underneath the flight deck. The bomb was on a kind of griddle, and the TNT was melting, running out of both the fuse and the tail end.

How do we get rid of this thing? was the question on everyone's lips.

Two seamen came along with a bomb truck, rolled the bomb into it, trundled it to the edge of the flight deck, and dumped it overboard. This was in the midst of violent explosions everywhere.

Below the bridge, Number 2 turret was heating fast—almost to the state of inevitable explosion. Mac organized a party to pass ammunition over the side. He went in the gun mount with a gunner's mate and emptied the ammunition out of the turret. This was the same turret where Jimbo Ormond and Bill Rogalski had been hunkering down when a seaman rushed over and told them to get away before it exploded.

*   *   *

The *Franklin* steadied on course momentarily, and the *Santa Fe* saw the opportunity to be of more help. It was a determined drive when she came from off the starboard quarter of the disabled ship and aimed for a snub under the starboard bow of the badly listing *Franklin*. It was almost like a ram of one ship against another, but the *Santa Fe* clung there upon contact and wouldn't let loose. Now all the wounded could be evacuated. The time was 1050.

Captain Gehres ordered all wounded to be transferred over to the rescue ship. It was almost a panic sort of exercise, for time was of the essence.

Kamikazes and Japanese submarines were all over the place. For two hours every rig available was enlisted to aid in the transfer. Whether it be makeshift, jury, or standard, if it worked, it was used. Jimbo Ormond, with fractured ankle and foot, went across in a breeches buoy made of mailbags. He needed a lot of help, and this was provided by Rocky Staples.

Staff Sergeant Ted Gore, of squadron administration, was wounded when trapped for more than three hours on the third deck. He somehow found his way to the flight-deck catwalk on the starboard side. The ship's antennas had been laid horizontal, and they stretched over the *Santa Fe* beneath. Ted crawled out hand over hand on one of those antennas and then dropped to the steel deck of the cruiser. The gravely injured SSgt Gore was quickly provided medical attention.

* * *

The seeming apparition that Carl Omasta had witnessed earlier, once he extricated himself from entrapment in the blacked-out compartments below, was the *Santa Fe* seeking to snub to the *Franklin* underneath the catwalk where he was standing. Once he came to his senses, he realized this was his salvation. Carl wasted no time getting in position for vacating the ship. He swung over to the *Santa Fe* on a line and struck a stanchion. Bill Rogalski was awaiting his turn for transfer and watched the injured Carl fall to the deck. He knew he would have to render assistance once he got across himself, but before that happened, Carl was carried off on a stretcher.

Captain Gehres had also issued orders for transfer of all air group personnel. Mac Kilpatrick would be the senior officer and assume charge of this contingent. Dr. Sam Sherman, the flight surgeon for the air group, refused to leave the *Franklin*. He was one of the two doctors not killed, and he felt his services usurped authority. Capt Gehres later commended him for that decision.

In the meantime, the *Santa Fe* was performing another critical function. All the firefighting equipment available was being used to the fullest in battling blazes amidships as well as aft on the *Franklin*. The fiery waterfall of aviation and diesel fuel spilling over the side was being quelled. And even though the continuous explosions of bombs and rockets were starting blazes anew, they were being taken in stride one at a time. But this was not without casualties of their own aboard the *Santa Fe*.

After two hours in the water, flash-burned Pete Schaefer lost track of time. He was now adrift far astern of the smoking, boiling *Franklin* and was certain in his distressed state of mind that he could see other heads bobbing in the water at quite some distance around him. Then, off in a southerly direction, still another object appeared before his blurry eyes, only this one was growing bigger and bolder.

The USS *Hickox* had been detached from its screening duties and ordered to assume rescue and salvage operations. A lookout from this ship spotted Pete and drew up for a rescue. Pete was hauled aboard and provided with the medical and hospitable attention that was his due. A doctor attended him immediately. He peeled all the burned skin off Pete's face, sprayed it with an atomizer filled with a solution of sulfa crystals, and wrapped him in Vaseline-soaked gauze. The skipper of the destroyer was Capt Joe Wesson, of the Smith & Wesson small-arms family. He invited Pete up to the bridge for a cup of coffee. Peering out of peepholes in the bandages, Pete luxuriated in a simple little pleasure that surprised him.

The *Hickox* continued to search and pick up survivors, then she moved in closer astern of the stricken *Franklin*, where she could see an urgent rescue need on the fantail. The *Hickox* moved her bow under the *Franklin*'s stern, where about a dozen men were trapped in the quad .40s. The men jumped off the fantail onto the deck of the destroyer. Some broke their ankles when they hit the steel deck, but at least they were safe. The *Hickox* reversed engines and, a few minutes later, the compartment where these men had been marooned blew up with a terrific explosion.

The *Hickox* had a normal complement of about 178 personnel. By the time it had finished picking up survivors, the population of the destroyer had doubled.

In another search sector, the destroyer *Marshall* was undergoing an almost identical rescue operation. She plucked one survivor after another from the sea. Two of the more jubilant were Lt Joe Warren and the Navy lieutenant (jg) with whom he had been sharing a life preserver. They had definitely become soulmates.

In still another search sector, the destroyer *Hunt*, under command of Cdr Halfo Knoetzer, picked up hundreds of survivors, including Lt (jg) Wally Young, the torpedo-bomber pilot.

* * *

The mission of many destroyers in the vicinity of the stricken *Franklin* was search and rescue. In some cases, the sea yielded only lifeless forms or victims so severely wounded that the emergency medical attention came too late. In one case, a destroyer came along on the starboard side of the cruiser *Alaska* and threw a lone line across for a breeches buoy. They had a wounded man in a basket, strapped, and ready to pull across. This particular man was so severely injured that the destroyer's medical facilities could not adequately treat him. The *Alaska* was chosen because its accommodations were far superior in surgeons and equipment.

The breeches buoy was rigged and the transfer began. When the wounded man was suspended over the water between the two ships, a kamikaze was making a run. Firepower erupted from the *Alaska,* and it looked like the man in the buoy was doomed. Under normal conditions, when two ships are together like that—refueling or otherwise—they'll break away when in peril. This time, though, they stuck with it and got the man aboard and down into sick bay. The patient was a Marine lieutenant.

The cruiser *Santa Fe* cleared the side of the *Franklin* at 1225. This rescue ship was now laden with the seriously wounded and the remaining able-bodied personnel of Air Group 5, or at least those who were not involved in flying the predawn mission that day. The *Santa Fe* would now take up the role of protective escort.

For five long hours, heavy explosions from aircraft bombs kept blasting away aboard the *Franklin.* The major explosions ceased at 1300 on that fateful day of March 19, but the fires continued. These fires were mainly in the gallery spaces, the commanding officers' country, and the fantail.

In the meantime, the Japanese were determined to finish the *Franklin* off. At 1254 a twin-engine plane was making a run on her but was exploded by antiaircraft fire just 200 yards shy of the starboard bow. Less than an hour later, our combat air patrol splashed another Japanese plane making the same kind of run.

The *Franklin* lay dead in the water for four hours, slowly drifting toward Japan. The damaged ship now had a list of 10 degrees and it was mounting at the rate of 1 degree per hour. When she was within 45 miles of the Japanese mainland, the cruiser *Pittsburgh* took her under tow. The *Pittsburgh* had received orders to undertake this unusual operation at 1115, but it wasn't until 1400 that the feat was realized. The almost impossible task of leading a 6-inch cable over to the *Franklin* was accomplished with no power or winches. Superhuman strength by the able-bodied crew, especially the African-American messmen, was undeniably a feat to be recognized. A slow buildup of speed was initiated in a southerly direction—away from the combat zone.

Down in the bowels of the ship, EM2 Bob St. Peters and his host of fellow unfortunates had been sustaining themselves by sucking air through the one-inch pipe leading from the bilges. Convinced the ship was sinking, they were determined to extricate themselves from the situation. The bombs exploding in compartments above had not abated, but they just had to find a way.

In the pitch-black darkness, the other men followed Bob with his one-cell flashlight, going from one hatch to another only to find them stubbornly locked down. The hatches were either buckled or dogged down so tightly that even the sledgehammer someone found proved useless. They finally found a compartment hatch that could be opened. By now it was early afternoon, and the traumatic effects of being bombarded from above with constant explosions and the fear of the compartments being flooded or the ship capsizing from its severe list were taking their toll on even the most stable individuals. Finally, a route led them through a passageway near the mess hall, where the decks were slimy with spilled food. They went around a corner and up through the Marine compartment. Things were smoldering there and they could hear men moaning. At the hangar deck, they got their first breath of fresh air. There were many bodies strewn about. It appeared that the ship had been abandoned, but they soon learned that all surviving hands were on the flight deck fighting fires. At least Bob and his small group had saved their own lives.

                                            *   *   *

Except for the low-order explosions of ammunition such as 40mm and 20mm rounds, the major blow-ups had pretty much subsided by early afternoon. At this time the starboard list had also stabilized at 13 degrees, but she was down at the stern by 3 feet. The crews tried to maintain what ship's integrity was left and used flooding countermeasures to correct this discrepancy. By midnight she had come upright, but then rolled over to a port list that finally became steady at 9 degrees by 0400. In the meantime, the *Pittsburgh* got the tow under way so that by midnight it had reached 4 to 5 knots.

During the night, with the safety equipment available, the engineering officer and his crew braved the contaminated elements to inspect the machinery spaces. They discovered a generator that would work and began the process of flushing out the smoke-clogged machinery areas with the workable ventilation system. Working through the night, they were able to make a fireroom habitable and prepared to light off a boiler. Between 0700 and 0800 the next morning, two boilers were fired up, which assisted the *Pittsburgh* to increase speed to 6 knots. By 1000 speed was up to 15 knots.

A muster on the early morning of March 20 showed only 300 of the original ship's company of 603 fit for duty. Navy Air Group 5 no longer existed aboard the *Franklin*. It was during this period that the *Franklin* started burying her dead. But first came the gruesome task of retrieving the bodies from the debris-strewn cracks and crannies of the ship's compartments.

The dead—all heroes—were consigned to the deep. It was a solemn and reverent ritual. Each burial service was brief, but the ceremony was hallowed and spiritual. The two surviving chaplains, O'Callahan and Lt Grimes "Gats" Gatlin, offered the prayers. Don Russell, the two surviving doctors, and a detail of many enlisted men officiated in this solemn undertaking. It took two days for the burial detail to slip the bodies one by one into the sea.

There was not much time for mourning, for every hand was preoccupied with additional duties, duties necessary to keep the ship alive. But deep inside, every man felt the weight and crush of sorrow. From the perspective of the cruiser *Alaska,* the human element came to the fore as well. The scene wrenched his soul as Gunny Smith saw one body after another going over the side from the hangar deck of the *Franklin.* All the crew was bent to the gravity of this terrible tragedy—chastened and humbled by the observation of these last rites.

By 1233 on that second day, the USS *Pittsburgh* cast off her tow, and the *Franklin* withdrew under her own power toward Ulithi Atoll. But there were still more enemy air attacks. Just before 1500 a lone Judy making a kamikaze attack was shot down at the last minute.

By heading south, the *Franklin* was slowly putting herself beyond the danger zone. The *Santa Fe* remained as her escort, but the *Alaska* and the other cruisers returned to their respective task groups.

The fires aboard the *Franklin* had been burning for four days but, finally, by March 22, they had either burned themselves out or been extinguished. The flight deck by this time was virtually demolished. For all practical purposes, this tired old lady would never see battle again.

CHAPTER 22

A Squadron in Limbo

On that morning of March 19, 1945, when my flight and I were returning from the early-morning mission over Honshu, the ominous sight of that black cloud on the horizon stirred our worst fears. Well before we approached our task group, there was an excessive amount of chatter on the air, and even though I was preoccupied with things in the cockpit, the name *Franklin* seemed to prevail through the interference.

Then I saw the explosions and the boiling pall of smoke towering upward, and realized that this was my ship. This was the *Franklin!* It was a devastating sight. Even though I had already received a vector and instructions to land aboard the USS *Hancock*, which had a ready deck, I seemed to be drawn hypnotically toward that cataclysmic scene. A sense of desolation overwhelmed me as I thought of my friends down there. How could they possibly survive that holocaust? But it was happening, and no amount of averring could prevent its crippling effect on the mind. A glance back at wingman Gerry Vetter confirmed the debilitating impact this sight had on us all when I saw him slowly shake his head. But I was alive. I was well. What were these inconceivable forces that picked one but not the other? It was baffling and at the same time heartrending.

I landed aboard the *Hancock* along with the rest of my flight without further incident

* * *

Also on a predawn mission that morning were Lts Dale Oakes, Kenny Bennett, Walt Hurst, and Chuck Hill. After being catapulted off for combat air patrol, they were immediately vectored by Fighter Director Control aboard the *Franklin* to a bogey in the overcast. The overcast was about 1,000 to 1,500 feet thick and it became a cat-and-mouse game trying to make contact. But a gap in communications occurred and, as the dawn skies became brighter, they were patrolling on station by visual means only. But then another carrier took over Fighter Director Control, and it was assumed the *Franklin* had experienced radio difficulty. Then they saw a ship burning in the distance, and the truth began to sink in when they were told to land aboard the USS *Hancock*.

On still another mission that morning, Lt Johnny Cox was assigned to a division of Corsairs that followed Maj Stan Bailey's flight on its predawn mission over the main island of Honshu. Nearing the island he saw the lone Japanese plane being attacked by about twenty-four of our fighters. Once again the frozen-gun syndrome set in. Besides that, Johnny was having trouble siphoning his belly tank and was running short of fuel.

Major Bailey ordered the section leader to escort Johnny back to the carrier. They received a prep-Charlie from a ship they thought to be the *Franklin*. On the downwind leg the escort noticed that this ship, unlike the *Franklin,* was a camouflaged carrier and pulled up. Johnny was indicating about 25 gallons of fuel remaining, so he waved good-bye to the escort and landed aboard. It was the USS *Bunker Hill*. On the bridge the air officer informed Cox that the pall of smoke he had observed prior to landing was the *Franklin*. It had been exploding for hours.

Johnny was invited to have coffee in the wardroom and was thanked over the loudspeaker system for the airplane. In the meantime, the chaplain aboard kept all hands informed of the kamikazes making runs on the fleet. First the 5-inch guns would open up, followed by the 40mm. When the 20mm began firing, it was time to set down coffee cups and start sweating. The announcement that the kamikaze had been shot down meant time for another coffee break. Johnny spent two days aboard. Major Hank Ellis, skipper of VMF-451, tried to get Johnny transferred to his own squadron but was refused.

* * *

Many refugees landed aboard the USS *Hancock* (CV-19). Under ordinary battle circumstances, a certain amount of regimen and direction normally prevailed, but now there was a sense of disorganization and near panic. I came aboard with my flight just before Wally Wethe and his. We were all without a plan, and circumstances would have to dictate the next course of action. It wasn't long in coming.

Many of the *Hancock*'s strike flights were in the air, and their return was imminent. She needed to prepare to recover those planes, but there just wasn't any more space available. A possible solution would be to dump ten planes overboard, and it was considered. A communications blitz ensued among the whole carrier fleet for a quick solution. The USS *Yorktown* (CV-10) and the USS *Intrepid* (CV-11) immediately offered space for five Corsairs each. Once this decision was reached, I took command of ten Corsairs for the brief flight to Task Group Four (TF 58.4). In the murky distance, I could see the other carriers of this task group. The *Enterprise,* the *Langley,* and the *Independence* were also plying a northerly course just off the island of Shokoku. My flight split in the air, and I landed with five aboard the USS *Intrepid;* and Lt Dale Oakes landed with five aboard the USS *Yorktown*.

This was a new twist in events. Blimpo Fletcher, Gerry Vetter, and I would still be involved in further missions on the Japanese mainland as the *Intrepid* steamed in a northerly direction. And by the same token, a few hundred yards away, Dale Oakes, Kenny Bennett, and Walt Hurst would be on forays in the same vicinity. In a way, we were lost souls with an uncertain future, our destiny in the hands of someone else, far removed.

In the meantime, Capt Wally Wethe, along with Emmons Maloney, John Lawrence, and Norry Hanson, hunkered down on the *Hancock* in the same manner as the rest of us on our refugee carriers. The mood and conditions aboard were parallel on each carrier, and the plight the same. It was a ruffled situation any way you looked at it but, considering the circumstances, it certainly was to be expected. The assignment to an officer's stateroom involved the addition of canvas cots set up in the middle of the room. The rooms were small and designed for two people, but now they billeted three or four. At night General Quarters was in effect. For ship integrity we were locked down in the stateroom area the whole night. Considering the ever-present possibility of bombing or kamikazes, it gave one a lot to ponder.

The day after the *Franklin* bombing, our Marine fliers aboard the *Hancock* were assigned combat air patrol over the task force. By this time the *Franklin* had been taken under tow by the *Pittsburgh* and was steaming southerly at about 6 knots; the combat air patrol guarded their route. Lieutenant Maloney noted in his debriefing how they saw two enemy aircraft in the distance, but each time there were four to eight Navy aircraft jockeying for position to shoot them down.

Three days after the *Franklin* bombing, we discovered that there was someone looking out for us after all. The refugee pilots aboard the various carriers in the area were to be transferred by bosun's chair to destroyers. These destroyers were temporarily used to facilitate an eventual transfer of the *Franklin*'s aircraft crews to Guam.

The *Hazelwood* hove to on the *Intrepid*'s port side, and the tackle was rigged between the two. The seas were rough and the two ships rocked back and forth, whipping the breeches buoy up and down as it was being winched to the destroyer. Sometimes the buoy would even touch the water and then pull taut, almost enough to snap the lines. I was first in line with my fellow Marine fliers, awaiting my turn. I watched the crew who manned this operation gauge the tension and slack of lines between the two ships. Suddenly, the tail of the line on the deck looped around the ankle of one of the seamen and, in a flash, he was jerked to the winch 10 feet above. His foot was practically severed, and he fell to the steel deck, severely injured.

Once we were aboard the *Hazelwood,* she turned and headed for a rendezvous with the USS *Bougainville* (CVE-100). Typhoonlike weather laid the destroyer more on its side than upright. At mess we had to lock our legs around a stanchion and hold on to our plates. At least that was the case for those not seasick. It was a long two days of pounding, and then we took the breeches buoy to the *Bougainville,* and the *Hazelwood* returned to station with the task group.

We would learn sometime later that three days after our transfer, the *Hazelwood* was obliterated by an attack of five kamikazes. The ship didn't sink but was left a floating mass of debris. I've often wondered if the person who heisted my Smith & Wesson .38-caliber revolver while I was aboard ever lived to enjoy the pistol. But, considering his possible fate, I felt no ill will toward him.

* * *

Many pilots, both Navy and Marine, had taken refuge aboard the USS *Bougainville.* Even though she was an operational escort aircraft carrier, this new refugee role relegated her to troop transport. The *Bougainville* headed for Guam.

The time for reassessment and regrouping was at hand. This meant a hard look at the cataclysmic event that had just occurred and how its repercussions affected us all. Where did we now stand? What had we accomplished? The whole thing was a ghastly disappointment, and that mood would prevail for a long time. A backward glance at a year of hard work, with all its implications and its intertwining meld of pleasure and sorrow, was impossible to avoid. The pain of the past suddenly weighed heavily against the seemingly hopeless future. Five of our boys had died trying to achieve what was right and proper. We had weathered the rigors of conformity and then had gone on the line to show it could be done. We had gone through all that for what amounted to hardly more than one lousy day in combat. Only one day and—*wham*—it was over. I was greatly disappointed, and any incentive I had for reforming another squadron had completely disappeared. My heart wasn't in it and I was tired.

It was a cruel blow by the hand of fate that smote the crusade of a determined squadron that knew no bounds. We were now cowed to the knees in an unworkable situation. A sense of defeat hung like a shroud over that heretofore ambitious drive to be the best.

My thoughts moved back to our time at NAS Santa Rosa and to the people who were not selected to go aboard the *Franklin.* I wondered how those people might have fared had they been chosen. Each was so zealous in his determination to go. But could there have been some kind of divine intervention—the kind that saves lives? No one will ever know.

I thought about Jack Stack and the disappointment he must have felt about that lost chance at becoming an ace. He needed only one more victory. The vagaries of war were obviously multifaceted and its glories just as elusive.

Aside from our personal resentment of these events, there was the redeeming knowledge that our contemporaries all over the Pacific were carrying the torch right to Tokyo. This was undeniably a morale booster that had to be nourished and supported. It would help us recover from our disappointment and perhaps return us to our former spirit of competition and superiority .

CHAPTER 23

The End Justifies the Means

One can't help wondering about the fate of that Japanese pilot who wreaked so much havoc aboard the *Franklin*. In a way it is ludicrous to make a David-and-Goliath analogy but, in grim reality and retrospect, that's about the way it was. In this case, only his homeland would dignify him as a hero and, in the frenzy of war, it is doubtful that he was ever recognized by name. That Japanese pilot may have had only a minute or two to relish his outstanding accomplishment, for he was dead shortly thereafter.

There was much conjecture at first as to who actually did shoot that Japanese airplane down. For years I assumed it was our carrier air-group commander, E. B. Parker. That's the way the grapevine had it. Also later, Parker's hometown newspaper in San Francisco showed his photo and the blaring headline: "BAY HERO BLASTS NIP BOMBER." Follow-up sources, however, revealed that Cdr Parker could never be reached to either confirm or deny that initial report.

There was also much conjecture as to identification of the Japanese plane used to destroy the *Franklin*. It was generally agreed that it was a twin-engine bomber. At this stage of the war, the Mitsubishi G4M twin-engine bomber, code-named Betty, was almost as recognizable as the Mitsubishi A6M Zero, code-named Zeke. Several sources indicated that it was, indeed, a Betty that dropped the bombs.

Initial credit for engaging and shooting down the subject Japanese airplane went to Lt (jg) Locke Hickman Trigg, flying from the carrier USS *Bataan*. A dispatch from the captain of the *Bataan* to the commander of Task Force 58.2, RAdm Ralph Davison, stated simply, "MYRT SHOT DOWN AFTER DROPPING BOMBS ON FRANKLIN BY LT. (JG) L. H. TRIGG WHO FLEW THROUGH INTENSE FLAK IMMEDIATELY AFTER LAUNCHING TO ENGAGE PLANES."

Also confirming this action was a statement by Capt M. B. Rotner, MC USN (Ret), written in 1988 to *Military* magazine:

> I was a radar man on the USS *Bataan* during that operation. *Franklin* was sailing on our port beam.
> When she was hit, we were launching a strike at that time and at the moment that *Franklin* was hit we launched an F6F flown by Lt (jg)

Locke Trigg. Trigg made a 180-degree turn after launching and chased
the bandit aircraft. He caught up with it and shot it down.

But then other so-called factual elements entered the scene that altered the
theory of the twin-engine bomber. Still later, all this became tempered by other
evidence going back to Cdr Parker and to Lt Kenneth Linder of VMF-214.
They, and Locke Trigg insist that the Japanese plane involved was single-
engine with a rear gunner. Because these three were the most exposed and
closest to the action, the identification of the plane as a Myrt or a Judy was
pretty much agreed upon—with the Judy being the favorite. The Myrt was a
Nakajima C6N Saiun light carrier–based reconnaissance plane. The Judy was
a Yokosuka D4Y Suisei with a single V-12 liquid-cooled engine. They both had
rear gunners.

Commander E. B. Parker was to lead the first strike group of the day on that
morning of March 19. It was to be an attack on the Japanese naval ships and
shipyards at Kobe, Japan, on the Inland Sea. The predawn fighters had taken
off, and Cdr Parker's launch commenced at 0657. Five Corsairs had just
cleared the flight deck when the lone Japanese plane dropped its bombs at
0708. Ken Linder was in the middle of this group of five and had turned downwind to effect a rendezvous well aft of the *Franklin*. He was in a climbing turn
and concentrating on the rendezvous with Cdr Parker's division. At the
moment, he did not even know about the bombs just dropped from the
Japanese plane. He was aware of a radio transmission by some pilot who said
he had just expended all his ammunition. But suddenly he was also aware of a
plane ahead flying level. Ken was almost on his wing when his eyes became
riveted on the red-disk insignias the plane was carrying. Ken moved into position for attack. It was a single-engine airplane with a rear gunner, who
appeared slumped over his gun. In the meantime, Cdr Parker also saw the
Japanese plane and moved in behind Linder for the attack.

In the conflict of battle, when concentrating on an adversary, it's easy to be
oblivious to other elements in the skies. Thus it is believed that Lt (jg) Locke
Trigg got in the first licks that began the demise of the Japanese airplane. But
it is also believed that Cdr Parker and Lt Linder delivered the coup de grâce
that sent the Japanese Judy to the ocean below.

Locke Trigg's involvement and account of events that morning are, to say
the least, "intrigging" (pun intended):

The morning the *Franklin* was hit, our ship—the *Bataan*—was
steaming close to starboard and all carriers were in the process of
launching aircraft for a big strike. I had just been launched (my wheels

and flaps still down) when I saw a plane drop out of the overcast. I picked up my mike and yelled into it something like, "Don't dive on the ship, you nut!" Before I got my message completed, I saw a couple of bombs drop. I guess I saw the bombs hit. I'm not sure. I was hurt and mad to think that some S.O.B. could do this to our great task group. So I took out after him.

Trigg goes on to explain how he made a 180-degree turn immediately after launch. This was strictly against the rules in such a confined airspace, especially in view of the hundreds of aircraft taking off from the various carriers in order to rendezvous for the strikes that morning. But rules and regulation be damned, Locke surged ahead, caught up with the Japanese plane he thought was a Myrt, and positioned himself behind and slightly higher. As he fired all six .50-caliber machine guns at the plane, he could see its rear gunner returning fire. Like Parker and Linder, Trigg also saw the Japanese plane hit the water at an almost 90-degree angle and explode.

Trigg goes on to describe the scene:

My group had long before departed for the attack area and, since no planes had been sent to protect the *Franklin*, I became an air patrol of one and circled the burning ship to help in any way I could. The ship was a mess—fire and smoke over most of it. Two other ships from the task group had been dispatched to render what help and protection they could. After what seemed a long, long time, the *Franklin* went into a tight turn (to wash as much burning fuel off the flight deck and hangar deck as possible). I really believe this move might have saved the ship. It looked like the sea was on fire around the ship. At one point, one of the ships beside the *Franklin* vectored me out to check an aircraft. If it was an aircraft, it took off before I got there.

Shortly thereafter, I was recalled by my ship. Other task group planes arrived, to take up their protective positions. Upon returning to the *Bataan*, our ship's skipper, Capt Heath, had his orderly call the fighter ready room and "invite" me to his stateroom for toast and coffee. He was most interested in the action and asked many questions. Later, our ship's executive officer, Cdr Fred Reeder, shook my hand and told me, "It was the bravest damn thing I'd ever seen." Coming from Cdr Reeder, that was a real ego builder.

Marine Lieutenant Ken Linder's account of events leading to the demise of the Japanese pilot was just as attention-getting as Trigg's. In retrospect, Linder pondered how interesting it is that history is sometimes colored by what angle one sees it. Using Locke Trigg's narrative as a basis of what probably happened, Linder's view is as follows:

> When I opened fire on the Jap (I thought it was a Judy), the rear gunner did not return fire and I assumed I had killed him. Obviously, Trigg must have done so. From there on it gets mysterious, because I was gaining rapidly on the Jap, firing on him, and I could see my tracers hitting around the cockpit. By now I was close to him, and the air group commander slid in for a shot. I believe the Jap pilot was badly shot up as he climbed sharply toward a small cloud. (It was quite overcast.) As I stated before, he pulled through a sort of a loop but never pulled out. I was right above him when he went straight in. Naturally, I thought I had been responsible for the kill. I too flew through a lot of our own flak chasing the Jap, and wonder to this day why I wasn't shot down by our own guns. Lots of different colors. I have no remembrance of seeing an F6F anywhere near. Trigg must have lost him somewhere, as I picked him up after takeoff and behind the fleet. The carrier was hit shortly after my launch.
>
> I have just reread the Air Group 47 air op memo, and I recall an F6F pilot on the radio, saying he had chased a Jap through the whole fleet and shot up all his ammo. This was when I picked the still-attempting-to-escape Jap, fired on him, and watched him crash to his death.

Shortly after that March 19 action, VAdm Marc A. Mitscher wrote a citation in the name of the president of the United States and presented the Distinguished Flying Cross to Lt (jg) Locke Hickman Trigg.

It seems that such a presentation would have called for a grand ceremony of sorts. Not so in this case. There was a war going on, and every bit of time and energy was totally consumed in the hostile encounter. Locke Trigg eventually received his Distinguished Flying Cross, but it was via the U.S. Mail.

Even though this award should have been a share-and-share-alike victory for the three pilots involved, Cdr Parker received recognition only in the San Francisco newspapers. Lieutenant Kenneth Linder received backslaps and congratulations only from his closest buddies in the VMF-214 Blacksheep squadron.

Later on back in the States, however, Lt Ken Linder's hometown newspaper in Arcadia, California, gave him the credit he deserved with headlines that boldly stated, "ARCADIAN AVENGES *FRANKLIN* BY SHOOTING DOWN JAP PLANE."

CHAPTER 24

Truth and Consequences

Ten days had elapsed between the time the *Franklin* dealt the devastating blow and the *Bougainville* left us on Guam. Up until that time, there had been no information whatsoever on the fate of our comrades.

The reunion on Guam was more a search for answers than a meet and greet. Curiosity about the fate of our comrades was foremost in all our minds. The answers came very gradually, and a redundancy of information was necessary in order to confirm the truth. Later we would sort out what was reliable, and then try to deal with the negative impact.

Bit by bit, we learned the sequence of the *Franklin* disaster. There were many, many dead. The news was painful and the stories heartbreaking. In the confined shipboard quarters aboard the *Franklin,* we had developed warm friendships, not only with our Marine squadronmates but our Navy counterparts as well. There were many heroes—some of whom would never be properly recognized, for they were dead. Many of those and the ones who survived had displayed the fortitude of Superman. Many we knew well. The inferno aboard the *Franklin* was unparalleled in the Pacific carrier war.

In Guam we pilots reassessed our state of affairs. The Red Cross provided us with gray dungarees and some personal necessities, as up to this time we had been living in our flight suits. All personal effects were lost aboard the *Franklin*—uniforms, cameras, personal keepsakes, important papers, pay records, and, most important, flight logbooks. Everything was gone. Most of us would never return to the *Franklin* again.

What would be our destiny now? That was a question we all asked. It only stood to reason that the pilots of Air Group 5 would be replacement pilots for squadrons aboard other carriers. The invasion of Okinawa was imminent, and there would be an obvious need there. We pondered our plight.

Commander E. B. Parker, the air-group commander, was as distraught about the loss of the *Franklin* as anyone else. He took it hard but, in the spirit of "never say die," he was ready to consolidate, mobilize the air group again, and go aboard another carrier. Higher commands dissented, however, and Navy Air Group 5, for all practical purposes, became nonfunctional.

As we languished on Guam, we learned more about the complicated details that eventually unified our group once more. Earlier, the cruiser *Santa Fe* and the destroyer *Hickox* had escorted the *Franklin* to Ulithi Atoll, where the wounded were transferred to the hospital ships *Relief* and *Mercy*.

Before landfall at Ulithi, Lt Pete Schaefer enjoyed the cuisine while aboard the *Hickox*. The head cook aboard the destroyer was an older Greek man, who had lied about his age to get in the service. He owned restaurants in the San Francisco area. Pete feasted on some of the best food he had ever eaten— embellished with fresh vegetables and fruit. The ice-cream machine under the tarp on the starboard side was going twenty-four hours a day to feed the new complement of men. It was a pleasant surprise.

After arrival at Ulithi, Pete ended up on the hospital ship *Relief*. When the USS *Franklin* limped into the harbor under its own power, some of the more mobile hospitalized members of Air Group 5 were allowed aboard the *Franklin* in hopes of retrieving personal belongings. They used crowbars to break open safes in the staterooms and were able to get some of the items. The squadron booze, locked down when we embarked at Alameda, was broken into and the full footlocker was salvaged. This included some of the Cheyenne citizens' contributions from the previous summer. For the first time in a long time, there was optimism in the air as Pete surreptitiously took custody of the booze and contemplated a squadron party sometime in the not-too-distant future.

Those pilots placed what gear they could salvage from the *Franklin* into a cargo net to be lowered into a launch for the trip back to the *Relief*. While doing so, Pete saw that a burial detail was still consigning the dead to the deep. More bodies had been found, and the ritual continued right next to the cargo net that was lowering material into the picket boat. As the boat cast off and headed for the *Relief*, Pete turned and took one long last look at the derelict *Franklin*.

When the hospital ship *Relief* slipped its moorings and departed Ulithi Atoll for Guam, so did another transport ship, which accommodated such passengers as Lts Rocky Staples and Joe Warren. Rocky had been one of the many refugees off-loaded from the *Santa Fe;* Joe off-loaded from the destroyer *Marshall*, which had plucked him from the sea at the scene of the *Franklin* disaster. For a week these two had been living aboard a "hotel" ship at Ulithi, more properly described as a "miserable scow." Now with better accommodations, they were on their way to Guam.

The days on Guam were wearing and boring, but they were also relaxing. It was interesting to note how that relaxation came in the form of potato whiskey. Pete Schaefer was one to confirm this. He was still wrapped in bandages but was very mobile. He remembers someone somehow acquiring some potato whiskey, probably purchased from a native.

But what he remembers most is the day after—and what a big head potato whiskey can make.

Things like this deserved a laugh. We also laughed at the plight of the
Marine colonel whose jeep was hijacked with the colonel in it. It may have
been a trick the native potato whiskey played on that young pilot, but it was a
very serious breach of military decorum to the colonel. It was night and the
young ensign simply commandeered the vehicle. As it trailed off into the dust,
the colonel shouted for him to stop the jeep immediately. The jeep went full-
bore ahead. Finally, the colonel drew his gun and fired a bullet through the
floor panel of the jeep. The ensign readjusted his attitude in a hurry and discovered to his chagrin that the person in the jeep was not just an ordinary
Marine.

CHAPTER 25

Golden Gate and Forty-Eight

The next bit of news received sent a shock wave through us all. If there was a disturbance to any semblance of reverie acquired while inactive on Guam, this news wasn't minded at all. It sent all hands scurrying to comply with the orders. We were to embark aboard the USS *Barnes* (CVE-20) for return to the States.

The *Barnes* was a Kaiser-built transport converted to an aircraft carrier. She was a tub in every sense of the word. Once the ship departed Guam, she plowed through heavy seas, and the steel plates buckled with the resounding crash of kettle drums each time she hit a wave. She was now acting as a troop transport, with cots set up on the hangar deck for the enlisted men. The officers stacked up in the staterooms from the deck to the overhead.

On the first night out of Guam, the ship's captain came down to the ward-room for mess. He appeared almost fascinating in his unorthodox dress: The white silk shirt with epaulets didn't seem quite official, and those black trousers seemed more tuxedo than Navy. In fact his whole demeanor seemed more British than American. We sensed that once ship's company, including the captain, found out we were Marine pilots, the quality of food deteriorated rapidly.

Meals were served in shifts aboard the *Barnes*. The ship's company had the first shift and then the air group. Common fare was lots of rice, and orange gelatin that tasted like licorice. It was soon discovered that ship's company was served ice cream for dessert, but the Marines got a lot of orange gelatin. I heard later about a small group of our Marines who broke into the galley one night and served themselves an ample supply of good food. They also took a side of beef and had a tremendous feast. It could only be assumed that Pete Schaefer was the instigator of this foraging activity.

* * *

On that fateful day of March 19, 1945, 798 officers and enlisted men died aboard the *Franklin.* Of those, 65 were Marine aviation personnel, and of that category 33 were members of our own squadron, VMF-452. I personally knew each one of these squadronmates—if not intimately then at least by sight and reputation. Now aboard the *Barnes,* my attention turned to addressing each of the next of kin with an informal account of what happened to each casuality so far as I was able to determine. These letters would follow the terse telegrams sent out by the Washington Marine Headquarters to next of kin. It was a sad duty.

My first attempts at trying to write a satisfactory letter were handicapped by a certain amount of procrastination and a tendency to circumvent the truth. In the first place, there was no such thing as a satisfactory letter under these tragic circumstances, and there was just no way to get around the cold, hard facts. Finally, summoning up the courage to perform this alien duty was the result of an unremitting force that tugged at the heart and soul and demanded that an explanation be offered.

The recipients of these letters responded in various ways over the next two or three years. Sometimes the wife, or the mother, or the folks replied in a pleading, almost desperate sort of way. So many were still hoping: "Was it possible he survived in some way?" "Might he have swum ashore on some deserted island?" "Could he be a prisoner?" "Perhaps his name ended up inadvertently on the wrong list." All their hopes were to no avail.

The following is a copy of the letter written to the widow of TSgt Louis Barrilleaux:

"My Dear Mrs. Barrilleaux,

It is with deep regret that I write you concerning the death of your husband, Louis, who died March 19, 1945, as a result of enemy action. This letter is written with the sincere desire that we may, as much as possible, express the deep sense of loss which we share with you in the tragic news of your husband. Perhaps the knowledge that each and every member of the squadron feels the loss of a fine squadronmate will in some way ease your grief.

Here are the circumstances so far as I am permitted to tell: Our squadron was engaged in strikes against the Japanese mainland. It was at the time when preparations were being made for takeoff on another of these strikes that a Japanese plane dropped a bomb which dealt our carrier a mortal blow. From what little information we have gathered, it is known that Louis was on the flight deck attending to his duties as he always had, and as a result of fire and explosions, gave his life. His body was found and buried at sea, his soul committed to God in a memorial service by our chaplain.

Louis gave his life for his country in this, our battle
to free an oppressed world, and I feel humbled in the light
of his supreme sacrifice. He was a husband of whom to be
proud and a man of great honor in the heat of battle.

If any of his personal effects can be removed, please rest
assured that they will be forwarded to you. If I can be of
help in any way, manner, or form, please don't hesitate to
get in touch with me and I will do my utmost on your behalf.

I know that mere words cannot console you at this time,
but I would like to express my own, as well as the rest of
the squadron's, kindest sympathy in your hour of sorrow.

Sincerely yours,
C. P. Weiland
Major, USMC
Commanding

* * *

The USS *Barnes* docked at Pearl Harbor on April 9, 1945, for a temporary delay. Some of the pilots went ashore and found quarters during the stay. The anxieties of getting home overshadowed the hospitable ambience of this lush, tropical paradise.

One afternoon we watched the crippled USS *Franklin* enter port. She had just returned from Ulithi Atoll under her own power with Capt Leslie Gehres still in command. We studied this disfigured ship with awe. She had a severe list. Her decks were buckled, and the elevators and superstructure were askew. Everything else was at a topsy-turvy angle. She was a sad and pitiful sight. Exactly one month earlier to the day, March 3, she had shipped out from this port with a complement of thirty-three hundred officers and men. Now, on April 3, she was returning with a crew of 706.

Once the USS *Barnes* arrived at Pearl Harbor, LCdr Mac Kilpatrick was transferred ashore and assigned as fighter training officer for ComAirPac at Pearl Harbor. The overall training officer in charge was Capt Tom Hamilton, USN. A squadron on the way out, which was training at Hilo, Hawaii, needed an executive officer so Captain Hamilton asked Mac to get all his experienced lieutenant (jg) officers together to see if a volunteer would take the job. Mac was able to assemble three or four of them and popped the question. Their answer was, "Yes, if you'll go, we'll go." It was a real challenge, and Mac wasn't sure whether they meant it.

He reported this to Hamilton: "They said that, if I'd go as skipper, then they'd go. Otherwise a flat no."

The captain blew his stack. "What's this Navy coming to?"

Right then up the channel came the *Franklin*—looking the color of burned ashes. Mac and his boss could see it from their third-story office building on Ford Island. She still had a list, and there was a straggly line of seamen in blue dungarees manning the rails and only four people playing instruments for the band.

Mac looked at Hamilton and said, "Captain, this is why they don't want to go. Take a look at this."

On this same day, there was another very concerned observer watching the *Franklin* enter port: PFC Jack Eggleston, younger brother of Sgt Bob Eggleston. He had been writing home to find out if the folks had heard from Bob. Of course they hadn't. This wasn't unusual, as mail was often held up and came in bunches. Jack Eggleston gazed upon the seared hulk of the *Franklin*, hoping for the best but certainly fearing the worst. He couldn't write home about what he had just seen. First of all, it would upset the family with no concrete evidence and, second, censorship wouldn't allow it. But Jack suffered with his own dismal thoughts of what the consequences might have been.

While waiting to depart Pearl Harbor for the States, we received a last-minute mail call. One letter from my mother lamented the death of Ernie Pyle, the war correspondent. She was an avid reader of his columns. I was too. I remember vividly Ernie's reference to his wife back home: "She thinks everything I do is wonderful. She even thinks I'm beautiful, which is the only flaw in her judgment."

A few days later, the *Barnes* put out to sea and was homeward bound for San Francisco. After two days out, my roommate, came into the wardroom to announce the death of President Franklin Delano Roosevelt. We sat there dumbfounded. It was like a personal loss. On the following day, the Protestant chaplain held a memorial service on the hangar deck.

* * *

The sight of the Golden Gate Bridge was highly emotional for everyone. "Golden Gate and Forty-Eight!" we yelled as we entered the harbor and docked at Alameda.

The forward echelon of VMF-452 disembarked at Alameda on April 14, 1945. At the same time, orders were received from the commanding officer of Navy Air Group 5, terminating temporary aviation duty beyond the seas. The squadron was then directed to report to the Department of the Pacific (Marines) in San Francisco. This was accomplished that same day, with further instructions to report back the next morning at 1100 for orders.

My first order of personal business was to call home. I made the call to Laguna Beach, and Rosalita Reames answered the phone. She was the wife of Dr. James Reames, our flight surgeon back at Mojave. When I said, "This is Pat," she burst into tears. A rumor had it that I'd been killed in action, and everyone had been trying to keep it quiet from Josie until the bad news came in officially. Like the old sage said, "News of my death had been greatly exaggerated."

That evening we had a much-needed night on the town. Good old San Francisco was a safe haven—for a change. It opened itself to a carousing, frolicking good time. Hotel rooms were scarce, but eventually some were found at the Marine Memorial Club, the Palace Hotel, and others. Captain Wally Wethe and Lt Johnny Cox put up at the Sir Francis Drake, where a newspaper photograph was taken of them. First Lieutenant Pete Schaefer and others eagerly joined up with 1stLt Rocky Staples, whose friend was the assistant manager of the Saint Francis Hotel. Once again a suite of rooms was offered complete with bar and buffet. Lieutenant Joseph C. "Joe" Wilson III, in between drinks, made paper airplanes to sail down from the third floor to the plaza below, inviting anyone interested to come up and join the party.

It was time to celebrate and that we did. The uniforms we wore were still the same Red Cross dungarees, rather than the proper elite green Marine attire that was so emphatically specified. But this was no time to exercise discipline. I caught sight of Lt Norwood Hanson dangling off the end of a cable car, living it up. He was allowed that.

At the Department of the Pacific, further orders stipulated that the squadron report for duty to Marine Fleet Air, West Coast, Miramar, California, then for further assignment to Marine Air Group 42 at MCAS El Centro, California. We were to board a troop train immediately for San Diego.

The troop train (or cattle car) headed for San Diego with the remnants of VMF-452 aboard. The gray painted seats were hard and ran parallel to the windows. Down the middle of the car were gray partitions. The old steam engine coughed smoke, and the journey became a grimy, grueling, sooty experience. With windows open, we soaked in the grime. Yet this was stateside and nothing else seemed to matter. Someone had brought a couple of cases of beer aboard and that helped a little. Many of the cars were loaded with Army troops, including a WAC car. This was separated from us by the dining car, however, to keep them safe and sound.

After a two-day trip, we arrived in San Diego, where there were many debriefings of the pilots. At Fleet Marine Air Headquarters, Maj Stan Bailey and I were interviewed by Col "Sad Sam" Moore and Col Paul Fontana. We answered their questions and gave as much detail as we could about of the *Franklin* disaster. The hurt on their faces was obvious.

All pay records had been lost aboard the *Franklin*, so the paymaster was hesitant to release funds. Finally, we were allowed to withdraw funds on the premise that as soon as records were received from Headquarters Marine Corps, Washington, D.C., our pay would be checked on subsequent paydays. Two of our pilots overdid it and drew out large sums of money. They didn't see a paycheck for months.

Buses picked up the forward echelon of VMF-452 and on April 19 transported us to MCAS El Centro, in the desert east of San Diego.

* * *

One person conspicuously missing from our Marine group was SSgt Ted Gore, who was not among us on Guam. We knew he was safe somewhere but we didn't know where. Eventually, we learned of the distorted route he took to return to the States.

After the wounded Gore dropped from the *Franklin*'s horizontal antenna onto the deck of the cruiser *Santa Fe*, he went to Ulithi, where he was transferred aboard the hospital ship USS *Mercy*. A few days later, he was transferred to another hospital ship, the *Relief*, when the *Mercy* left for Iwo Jima to take on wounded. He was released from the *Relief* at Ulithi and then transferred to a "receiving ship," which was owned by the Navy but manned by the Coast Guard with the Army in charge of personnel.

Shortly after Gore boarded the ship, it was announced that survivors of the *Franklin* should report below in order to draw clothing. He was the only Marine among them and was wearing the Seabee shirt and pants given to him when he'd left the hospital ship earlier. When it was his turn to draw clothing, the Coast Guard ensign told him that the clothing was for Navy personnel only and not for Marines. This turned Gore into a raging bull. In no uncertain terms, he told the ensign what he thought of him and where he could stick the clothing.

The "receiving" ship reached Pearl Harbor, and Gore was still in his Seabee shirt and pants. The stitches were still in his leg. The Navy left him stranded on the dock. He now felt like persona non grata, with no identification whatsoever. Out of desperation he confronted two MPs in a jeep, who agreed to transport him to the brig. The wheels of justice ground slowly as the future of this questionable character was contemplated. Out of sheer coincidence, Gore spotted WO McDowell, who had been quartermaster at Mojave and was now officer of the day in Hawaii. Gore's pessimism turned to optimism, for he knew his friend would vouch for his identity. Even then Gore was kept in isolation for three days awaiting verification. Eventually, he was issued Marine clothing and given a small sum of money for incidentals. McDowell was indeed a friend in time of need. He took Gore to the officers' club for one of the best meals he'd had in a long, long time.

Gore went aboard an escort carrier, *White Plains,* at Pearl Harbor to return to the United States. He said, "The ship was so crowded with personnel, we had to stand to eat our meals." Upon arriving in the States, Gore was sent to Miramar for a short time, and then to El Centro to rejoin what was left of VMF-452.

Another missing man was 1stLt Jimbo Ormond. From Ulithi Atoll, the hospital ship *Relief* returned Jimbo to Guam. He spent several weeks in the hospital before he was airlifted to the Base Eight Hospital at Oahu, Hawaii. They confined him there for a month before he went by ship transport to an auxiliary hospital in San Francisco. He was there another several weeks before being transported by train to the U.S. Norfolk Naval Hospital at Portsmouth, Virginia. Jimbo recounted two experiences at the Norfolk hospital that were momentous. The first involved the doctor who operated and fused his ankle:

> Doctor Arthur Weiland was an uncle of my skipper, Major Pat Weiland. I was fortunate that he was noted as one of the top orthopedic surgeons in the country. He had been stationed in England and had wards filled with men he had treated for similar wounds from mine explosions during the D day invasion.
>
> The other was that one of my physical therapists was Ensign June Turnbaugh from Tulsa, Oklahoma. We were married in Tulsa on April 6, 1946.

*   *   *

In the meantime, back in Kansas City, the Eggleston family was in turmoil. They received a telegram bearing the terse news that "Sergeant Robert Eggleston is missing in action." Monica, Bob's little sister, then eight years old, was most distraught. She comprehended the tragic impact of what the message implied about the brother she loved so much. Fifty years later, the memory of that time was no less harsh as Monica recounted those sad days:

> One of the last letters we got from Bob talked about his memories of growing up. He thanked Mama and Daddy again for the bicycle they got him the Christmas he was fourteen. It meant so much to him. I remembered that Christmas. The boys got bicycles and I got a tricycle. My folks couldn't afford that during the Depression. Bob knew it, and it meant all the more. I remember those years, too, and lying on the

floor with Bob and Jack, listening to Jack Armstrong on the radio while eating oranges and crackers.

Mama looked for Bob in every newsreel for a long time afterward—hoping he'd been picked up and rescued or was even a prisoner of war. Projectionists at movie theatres were always cooperative while we checked over and over; they stopped the reels so we could take a closer look at the boys who were rescued or those who were prisoners.

Then one of Bob's shipmates came by to see us. He told us that the *Franklin* was very close to the Japanese coast and that they had been working day and night for several days. He said that they were taking turns watching out for one another while they grabbed a nap. They would go down and sleep in the hammocks that held the bombs in the bomb room. Bob was asleep there when they were hit. There was no chance. He had been killed instantly.

Now my family was ripping apart. My parents were considering divorce. They argued often and even separated. They sold our house. Bob's wife, Lois, and the baby moved away on their own.

Nothing was ever the same. Mama and Daddy never got divorced, but things were never right again. Jack got married and named his firstborn son Robert Emmett Eggleston. Bobby died at ten of leukemia. Jack never got over either death.

* * *

At the Marine Corps Air Station, El Centro, the officers and enlisted men formed groups to talk about what was first and foremost in our minds. The conversations reflected the somber effect of lost comrades—the questions of why and the miracle of how we survived. Those memories would be forever engraved on our minds. We so-called vagabonds were often surrounded by "green" Marines, eager to hear the stories, hanging on to every word.

Now I was home in South Laguna Beach for a brief respite of rest and relaxation. How simple this life was! No need to worry, no need to be tense and at the ready every minute. The calming effect was saturating and it enveloped both my mind and body. The neighbors welcomed me with open arms. All they knew was that I had just returned from the western Pacific, flying off carriers. The *Franklin* calamity was top-secret—the news had not yet been broken to the public.

When I turned on the radio that Thursday night of May 17, 1945, to listen to Gabriel Heatter, my favorite news broadcaster, I suddenly snapped to rigid attention as I heard him say the following:

This grim piece of news was made public just one minute ago. It was on the aircraft carrier *Franklin*—27,000 tons—operating with the

task forces off Japan, when a Jap dive bomber scored two hits—341
men were killed—more than 300 wounded—341 are missing in
action.

It was on the morning of March 19th—many of the *Franklin*'s
planes were on deck—loaded—prepared to take off—suddenly a Jap
dive-bomber came out of a patch of clouds—he dropped two 500-
pound bombs. He was shot down one minute later but within that
minute tragedy had come to a great ship. The Japs said the carrier was
sunk—they were sure of it—they had every reason to think so for she
seemed mortally wounded. Yet Captain Leslie Gehres and those of his
men who survived fought to save their ship and brought her back
12,000 miles to the Navy yard in Brooklyn.

That ship is gone, said Japan. This ship will live, said her gallant
men. Back she came with her charred and battered hull. This ship had
lost a greater number of men and sustained more battle damage than
any ship which ever came in New York Harbor under her own power.
Yet back she came—her flag high—her story an epic of raw courage.

One bomb struck beneath the flight deck, where the planes, fueled
and loaded, were waiting to take off. Another on the hangar deck,
where other planes, fueled and loaded, were waiting to be taken to the
flight deck.

Tons of bombs and ammunition on board began exploding and the fires
were fed by thousands of gallons of gasoline on board. It was a blazing
Niagara. Every man on board that ship saw the face of war that morning.

Yet there was no panic.

Belowdecks, several hundred men were at breakfast when the ship was
hit. Smoke, flames, and battered bulkheads blocked every exit. In time the
oxygen began running low—there was death closing in—and James E.
Russell, signalman first class of 1913 Denwiddie Avenue, Richmond,
Virginia, told of how the flight surgeon, Lieutenant Commander James L.
Fuelling of Indianapolis calmed everyone—"Sit down," he said, without a
tremor in his voice as he spoke. "We are trapped here—for the time
being—stay calm—be quiet—use as little air as possible—stay close to
the deck—say a prayer." The men were calm and quiet and they prayed—
and waited—and rescue came—deliverance came.

Lieutenant Donald Gary of 320 Millsbara Avenue, Oakland,
California, who was in that room, turned to his men and said "I will be
back." He disappeared into clouds of flame and smoke. But he found
an exit—through the ventilation tubing—he kept his word—he came

back—not once but a dozen times, each time leading others to safety—every man but one trapped in that mess hall was saved.

Lieutenant Commander Joseph O'Callahan of 300 Newberry Street, Boston, Massachusetts, was Catholic chaplain on the ship. Ten times he risked his own life to help save other men. Leading men into leaping flames—carrying out bombs and shells before new explosions could set in—pausing at every turn to administer the last rites to dying men—he was a figure inspired.

Death was robbed of many a life that morning when this man led a group of volunteers into one of the main ammunition magazines and wet everything down in time to prevent even worse explosions. They called him the bravest man we ever saw.

A man completely without fear.

Wallace L. Klimkiewicz of 36 Washburn Street, Jersey City, nineteen years old—a Marine orderly, private first class—he was ordered to abandon ship. He asked for permission to remain—to man an antiaircraft gun. Wave after wave of Jap planes came in—Wallace Klimkiewicz never broke—never moved away from his gun.

He might have moved to safety—he had his chance—he asked only to remain where he was—near the gun—and the great ship so badly hurt and seemingly done for must have known she had to be worthy of that kind of courage, for with the rents in her frame and the fires and explosions, she managed nevertheless to hold fast to her antiaircraft guns and they remained accurate and powerful and the ship Japan said was dead fought back and lived.

James P. Odom, a machinist's mate first class, Route Number 2, Waynesboro, Mississippi, was standing his watch in a fire room when the Jap bomb touched off a terrifying explosion from ammunition magazines—for three hours with a gas mask on his face he fought to keep steam up—and after that, exhausted, limp, almost unable to stand, he dragged himself to a flight deck and manned a hose.

And when that blaze was under control, this same man volunteered to join a rescue party to bring out men who were trapped. In five days of fighting fire on that ship he slept a total of six hours.

Gerald Smith, fireman first class, of 29 Williams Street, Oswego, New York, kept his firehose in operation when it seemed impossible—when it seemed no man could stand where he did and remain alive.

During the most desperate hours when the ship seemed in its greatest peril, the cruiser *Santa Fe* came alongside to remove wounded men—one of the firehoses pumping water was cut in two—Smith volunteered to remove it and bring a new line into play—held by the ankles by two of his shipmates, he dangled head down over the deck edge and unfastened a damaged hose, his life in peril every second.

All that time men fought to keep a blazing ship afloat—fought for time to move out wounded men—two destroyers, the *Hunt* and the *Marshall,* rescued more than six hundred—the *Hickox* and *Miller* saved many others. When the *Santa Fe* came alongside, there was a piece of seamanship men would never forget, for the *Santa Fe* came so close she damaged gun platforms on the carrier.

But with that piece of daring, hundreds of wounded men were saved—as you would rig up a makeshift breeches buoy to carry a mailbag they rigged it up to carry out wounded men who were lowered into the arms of bluejackets on the *Santa Fe*'s deck.

Early that afternoon with the fires under control, the carrier was taken in tow by the heavy cruiser *Pittsburgh.* Before the day was over more boilers were put in operation—the tow line dropped and the proud lady began her fight to come back on her own power—this ship which Tokyo said was gone.

There was no electric power—and little food. A small walkie-talkie powered by batteries was her only radio equipment. Her steering gear was completely wrecked—it was only by varying the speed of her main engines that her course was directed. There were 12,000 miles to go— she prepared—she was determined to make it—to go it alone.

And the high courage of her men pulled her through and robbed Japan of her prize. Night and day a skeleton crew worked to keep her afloat, to keep her moving—night and day men were alert, waiting for new peril.

And the men on board knew a miracle had come to pass when that very ship, battle-scarred and rent in so many places, actually achieved a speed of 23 knots under her own power and turned home.

Into New York Harbor she came with a cruiser escort, this great ship which had only been launched in October 1943 and commissioned in January of last year—now her mainmast leaned at a sharp angle—her foremast was only a jagged stump—her steel plates were buckled and torn, her flight deck was completely destroyed.

But her flag was high and the devotion of her brave and gallant men high enough to reach into the very heavens where her dead were now in the tender embrace of God.

Within 60 miles of Japan's coastline she received what the Jap thought was her mortal wound—as he thought all ships he damaged at Pearl Harbor would never come back to claim their retribution. As he thought his treachery would find us weak and confused only to find us now a little more than 300 miles from his home islands . . .

With the sky over those pagan islands blood red with flames of his war machine disappearing into smoke and rubble and ashes. He miscalculated everything, but more than anything else he never knew these men who would man our ships or fight their way into the beaches of islands leading to Tokyo or make the sky over Japan their very own road to Tokyo.

All those foul little men in Japan or Germany who not being free themselves could never know the passion with which free men would fight back—not believing in peace, how could they know the wrath with which men who wanted peace would fight for it—knowing nothing of mercy or compassion, how would they ever know the heroism it would inspire in men who believed in mercy and compassion and would offer their lives for their comrades—for their country—for the ship which in war becomes a part of man's very own fiber and being—as it was on this ship and countless others.

They miscalculated every time. In Germany Heinrich Himmler organized a school and trained hundreds of men for weeks at a time to masquerade in Allied uniforms—to infiltrate Allied lines—to find an opportunity for sabotage and eventually try to kill leading Allied generals, including General Eisenhower . . .

When the test came it failed miserably—they were trapped by the most innocent questions—in the same way the Jap fails in every trick he employs to stave off defeat on Okinawa.

The bloody campaign on Okinawa will soon be over. The battles of Saipan and Guam brought us outside that home line. One by one the Jap cities will turn to ashes—one by one as in Nagoya, the cities will disappear—one by one—each will feel the wrath and power of a free people.

Until the aircraft plans disappear as Germany's aircraft plants vanished under the hail of fire—until the last of Japan's suicide fanatics has made his last flight—until the airports are gone and the Jap is forced to come in as Germany's pirates came in and lie about his fighting an honorable war but stand revealed before all the world as Germany now stands revealed.

A brute and a barbarian brought to his knees.

And there will be peace on earth and boys will be home again and you and I and millions of Americans will say whether this sacrifice and death and all this heroism is to be lost or won and held fast and honored with the kind of world in which men will never again be asked to suffer all that these men on the great carrier *Franklin* endured—for us.[1]

1. Gabriel Heatter's account of the *Franklin* disaster, broadcast May 17, 1945, copied by MBS News Division.

I reflected upon everything Heatter had to say, then sat back to digest those words and the impact they must have on the public. The next morning the newspaper headlines blazed across the country with the delayed catastrophic news of the *Franklin.* The neighbors took a new look at me and couldn't believe it. But I was back to the mundane way of life and so their cares weren't even considered.

* * *

Josie had acquired a small white collie dog while I was gone. In about three days after I returned home, Bonnie and I had become fast friends. One morning I dressed in casual clothes and walked down the hill with Bonnie to the main throughfare of U.S. 101 through South Laguna, where a post office and corner grocery store was located. I needed spending money and decided to cash a check. Bonnie and I walked into the grocery store and found the proprietor. He studied my $25 check and said, "No, I'm sorry. We don't cash checks for strangers."

I turned to leave and said, "Come on, Bonnie, let's go."

The proprietor interrupted. "Hey, there. Do you know Bonnie?"

"Yes, she's my dog," I said.

He was quick to continue. "Well, then, of course we'll cash your check. We know Bonnie very well!"

Imagine a dog having to vouch for a check to be cashed! In a way it was humiliating. I noted a smile on Bonnie's face as she trotted beside me all the way home.

* * *

Once at El Centro, many of our people were allowed to take thirty days' leave. This meant going to all parts of the country by any means available. The destination for Lts Pete Schaefer and Rocky Staples was the Midwest. They caught a ride in a Lockheed Ventura airplane as far as Grand Island, Nebraska. It had to be by rail from there on, so they went to the Rock Island railroad depot. Pete told the ticket agent that his destination was Chicago and that Rocky's was Kansas City. There were trains going through, but there would be a wait for some time.

The ticket agent recognized that these two were Marine pilots. The conversation soon led to the harrowing events aboard the *Franklin,* and the name of 1stLt Tom Pace came up. They described how he was shot down and lost at sea and were surprised when the ticket agent suddenly asked that they stay right on that spot until he returned. He said Tom Pace's father worked for the railroad and would like to talk to them. Shortly, Tom's father and sister arrived and they hung on every word the boys had to say about the incident.

* * *

When what was left of the squadron reassembled at El Centro, transfer orders came in for most of the personnel of VMF-452. I was transferred to the Marine Corps Air Station at El Toro, California, and joined the Marine Air Group as operations officer. Most of the pilots were transferred to MCAS Mojave to re-form VMF-225 under the command of Maj Dave Marshall. They would be flying F6F Hellcats.

Lieutenants Pete Schaefer and Bill Rogalski remained behind as squadron commanding officer and executive officer, respectively. They had a complement of 144 enlisted men, four Corsairs, two SB2C Curtiss Helldivers, four jeeps, and two command cars. It wasn't long before the Corsairs were sent elsewhere.

The two SB2C aircraft saw double duty in flying hours. Pete and Bill were able to do much ferrying, picking up anyone who had just returned from overseas and flying them to destinations within an 800-mile radius.

On Memorial Day 1945, Pete flew to Sacramento to be entertained at a party by friends. He was enjoying the spaghetti and red wine when he got a phone call from El Centro to report back immediately because some enlisted people had gotten in trouble. At 9 P.M. Pete went to the airport. It was late when he took off and climbed to 8,000 feet. He set a course on automatic pilot and dozed off. Much later he awoke and discovered it was almost dawn and all he could see below was water. With a little dead reckoning, he set a southeasterly course and made landfall at San Pedro. Shortly thereafter he landed safely at El Centro. At the end of the roll-out, the engine quit. Pete called the tower to tow him in, as he had just run out of gas.

Later that morning he was confronted by a colonel about the trouble the enlisted men were in. Many of them had been out on seventy-two-hour passes, as duties aboard the base were not demanding. Pete had to shut down a bar/gambling parlor and girly joint outside of town that had been set up in a defunct gas station. He also curtailed a black market operation in which some of his boys were selling goods in San Diego. Pete was becoming familiar with some of the more unusual woes of a commanding officer.

Pete and Bill received a call from Col Frank Shiltz of MarFairWest in San Diego, who was interested in knowing what had happened aboard the *Franklin*. They flew the SB2C to see him and accomplished the mission. At lunch that day, the colonel asked what duty they would like next. Both Pete and Bill asked to be transferred to Patuxent River, Maryland, for test-pilot duty. This evoked a chuckle from the colonel.

"You and every other naval aviator. What's your second choice?"

The conversation ended, and Pete and Bill flew back to El Centro.

In July 1945, higher echelons sent down orders to decommission VMF-452. Staff Sergeant Ted Gore had done most of the paperwork, and Pete signed the documents. It was the end of an era, short as it had been.

Pete and Bill received orders to MCAS Cherry Point, North Carolina, with a recommendation to be included with the next billet of ten pilots ordered to Patuxent River, Maryland.

*   *   *

With the war in the Far East still going on, one had to rekindle his spirits in order to maintain the fight. The war in Europe had ended and now full mobilization for Operation Olympic was in effect. Operation Olympic was so top-secret that at lower echelons no one had even heard of it. This was to be the invasion of Japan with the mightiest force the world had ever known.

At El Toro I was reassigned as commanding officer of Marine Carrier Air Group 12. It was composed of a Corsair fighter squadron and a Grumman torpedo-bomber squadron. Long-range plans envisioned assignment to the new escout carrier USS *Palau* (CVE-122), with eventual participation in Operation Olympic. But these plans never materialized.

*   *   *

In August 1945, bombs were dropped on Hiroshima and Nagasaki, and the war was finally over.

With the war over and demobilization in effect, Marine Carrier Air Group 12 was decommissioned, and I reverted back to squadron commander of VMF-461. I would eventually make the first landing aboard the USS *Palau* and operate aboard her for the next three years. It would be an action-packed tour with one particular episode having a link with the past. Perhaps it was more a brief side excursion of sorts, insignificant to anyone else, but very heartfelt for me.

By 1947 the USS *Palau* had been homeported in Norfolk, Virginia, and we had seen numerous cruises at sea with maneuvers in the Caribbean. In late June the ship received some exciting orders; we would be making a goodwill tour to Liberia, Africa, to help them celebrate their centennial. Presidents, kings, native paramount chiefs, and representatives from every country in the world would be present for this grand occasion.

America's contribution to this celebration would be the presence of the USS *Palau* and its dignitaries. We would also stage a flight demonstration with live ordnance and cap it all off with an air show for the whole country—and its celebrants—to see. President William Tubman of Liberia and his staff were aboard the *Palau* when we put out to sea for the flight demonstration, and he was duly impressed. Later, at the grand opening of the ten days of ceremonies, President Tubman would knight me with the Liberian Order of Distinguished Service. But that's another story . . .

To return to my original narrative, I must go back to the beginning of this voyage to Liberia. We had departed Norfolk and steamed up to New York Harbor to anchor and pick up certain State Department people and ambassadors-at-large. One of these notables was BriGen Benjamin O. Davis, U.S. Army, Retired. Benjamin Davis was the very first black general to be commissioned in the U. S. Army. It happened at San Juan Hill, where Teddy Roosevelt made his famous charge during the Spanish-American War in 1898. Another ambassador-at-large was Col Benjamin O. Davis, Jr., son of the general. Colonel Davis was the first black graduate of West Point. He distinguished himself during World War II, when he commanded the 332d Air Group, which fought in North Africa and later in Italy as part of the XII and XV Fighter commands. He later became the first African-American general in the U.S. Air Force.

The layover in New York Harbor lasted five or six days, and I seized the opportunity to take the launch to Manhattan to see some Broadway shows and other sights. But there was another, more important mission I had to make. It would be a sentimental journey to see the USS *Franklin* for the last time.

The *Franklin* was now fully repaired and lay at a berth in the Navy yard at Bayonne, New Jersey. I caught a ferry to Bayonne, and from a distance, the *Franklin* again seemed a proud ship, awaiting action. But she lay alongside an abandoned wharf, now part of the "mothball fleet."

There were very few people about her at the wharf, and they represented the maintenance personnel tending her. I was allowed to go aboard, up the ladder on the port side, and I entered by the hangar deck access. I scanned that wide sweep of hangar deck, fore and aft. The steel deck exhibited a distinct warp—an undulating wave, the result of the hot fires on that infamous day two years earlier.

I stood there gazing at what had once been a blur of activity of men and machines. My gaze was stoic and unfathomable—and then it was with a different kind of blur. I moved slowly, pausing at certain junctions to recollect those incidents that came to me of people so close but now gone. Then it was time to leave. It was as much a final visit to that grand old lady as it was a symbolic farewell to that Marine squadron dear to my heart—VMF-452.

I approached the quarterdeck to leave the ship by the port gangway. I patted the bulkhead and then instinctively faced aft to salute the U.S. ensign. But this vessel was no longer in commission, and the colors did not appear. Out of deference and respect, I saluted anyway and then strode smartly down the gangway. I didn't look back. The mission was accomplished.

CHAPTER 26

Life After VMF-452

The direction life took for each member of VMF-452 once the squadron was disbanded is a fascinating story in itself. The following are minibiographies of all those worthy souls who went aboard the *Franklin* with the forward echelon as well as those who were denied the privilege. The latter category, which, in a sense, was an unforgiving twist in the scheme of things, included almost half of the original squadron members. The twists and turns in the lives of all these members of VMF-452—and a few who were closely associated with us—follow.

STANLEY R. "STAN" BAILEY: Stan became a Regular in the Marine Corps after the war and eventually ended up in Hawaii in a night-fighter squadron flying twin-engine Grumman F7F Tigercats. In February 1948 Stan became squadron commander of VMT(N)-533 at Kaneohe. It was less than a week later, on a night-fighter practice intercept mission, that Stan was killed in a midair collision. The blip on the radarscope disappeared and Stan was never seen again. It was ironic that the accident should happen off the southern coast of Hawaii, exactly three years to the month after the *Franklin* was plying those same waters on a shakedown. Two of Stan's pilots lost their lives in a midair collision in the same area at that time.

ROYAL A. "BERRY" BARKER: Berry did not go aboard the *Franklin*, but from Mojave he was eventually transferred to the Admiralty Islands and thence to Leyte, Philippines, to join VMF-218. Other VMF-452 pilots who joined him there were A. J. Beretzky, David M. Cheeseman, Lanman T. Holmes, and Sturgis L. Cashon. They eventually made the landing on Mindanao and then flew Corsair missions from the new landing strip there. The squadron lost six pilots in combat. In September it was a stint in Peiping, China, flying Grumman torpedo bombers.

Berry came back to the States in February 1946 and was released from active duty in June. He attended the University of Wichita and graduated in 1949. He then received his M.D. degree in 1953 from the University of Kansas Medical School. After a three-year internship and a practice in Peabody

Hospital, he became chief of staff of the hospital at Council Grove, Kansas, where he practiced general medicine, surgery, and obstetrics.

His wife, Claire, also with a medical degree, managed a hospital and raised five children; she died of cancer at age fifty. Berry then married Betty, a schoolteacher. Between them, they have seven children and six grandchildren.

KENNETH "KENNY" BENNETT: After the *Franklin* disaster, Kenny ended up in a fighter pool at MCAS Santa Barbara. He elected to be released from active duty and was then accepted at Stanford University as a student. He joined the Reserves and kept up his flying for a few years. After college he spent most of his working life in the resort hotel business.

In 1980 Kenny started a real estate brokerage appraisal business at Pogosa Springs, Colorado. During that nine-year period, he was also appointed municipal judge. In early 1991 he received an appointment from the governor to the State Board of Assessment Appeals.

Kenny and his wife, Barbara, now live primarily in Denver but maintain their home in Pagosa Springs. They had nine children and several grandchildren. Kenny died of encephalitis on May 21, 1996.

A. J. BERETZKY: No information available.

ARTHUR D. "DON" BOYD: Don was killed in a Corsair crash at MCAS Mojave on March 23, 1944.

ROBERT L. "BULGY" BRYSON: The turn of events prevented Bulgy from going aboard the *Franklin*, even though he was more than qualified. He ended up at MCAS Santa Barbara, where he helped form a Marine carrier air group. He later became the commanding officer of VMF-472 in the air group. He remained in that position until released from active duty in January 1946.

The second child of Bulgy and Naomi was born deaf, necessitating a move to Chicago for the child's special education. Bulgy eventually joined the Reserve squadron at NAS Glenview and was made commanding officer of the squadron there. During the Korean War, he was CO of VMF-212. Subsequently, he commanded a squadron at Opa Locka, Florida, and then one at MCAS Cherry Point, North Carolina.

In 1955 he was assigned to the Reserve staff at NAS Glenview, Illinois, and remained with the Reserves for the rest of his active duty in addition to a couple of overseas tours. He spent a year as chief of staff, Marine Air Reserve Training Command, and then two years as deputy director of the Marine Corps

Reserves at Headquarters, Washington, D.C. Col Bryson retired fully in October 1967.

Bryson and Naomi have raised seven children and now have a number of grandchildren and great-grandchildren. They live on the western slopes of Colorado near a town called Paonia, where they enjoy raising horses and working the cherry tree orchard.

STURGIS L. CASHON: No information available. (He did not go aboard the *Franklin.*)

DAVID M. CHEESEMAN: Deceased. (He did not go aboard the *Franklin.*)

RUDOLF J. "RUDY" COLLETT: No information available.

STANFORD E. "STAN" COOLEY: Stan did not go aboard the *Franklin,* but in January 1945 joined VMF-331 on the Marshall Islands and staged through Ulithi for the invasion of Okinawa. The squadron downed sixty-seven Japanese planes in ten weeks. Stan received two Distinguished Flying Crosses and many Air Medals. After the war Stan received a discharge and returned to his home at Yreka, California. He attended the College of the Pacific in Stockton and married the campus queen while there.

In 1953 Stan was recalled during the Korean War and opted for helicopters, becoming the 1,185th naval pilot to be certified. His squadron was sent to Japan and, after completing that tour, he resigned and returned to Yreka. He had two children, who run each of his two businesses.

JOHN F. "JOHNNY" COX: Before joining VMF-452, Johnny had attended two years of college and then, after naval cadet training, received a commission in August 1943. After the *Franklin* disaster, he was assigned squadrons at Mojave and Santa Barbara, including one operating off the CVE *Mindoro* at Norfolk, Virginia. He also received a regular commission at this time. Duties took him to Corpus Christi, Texas, and Pensacola, Florida, in the Training Command and then to Cherry Point, North Carolina, in Station Operations.

He married Navy nurse Anne Lowe in September 1950, and they eventually had two sons. Subsequently, Johnny joined two Corsair squadrons, including one in Korea under the command of Bulgy Bryson. After a stint with the 1st Marine Division in Korea, he was transferred to Cherry Point and assigned to VMR-252, flying R4Qs. After another tour in Japan, he returned to the States and earned a degree at the University of Omaha.

Johnny retired from the Marine Corps on June 30, 1964, but went right to work with United Airlines in Denver, Colorado. He became a technical specialist and earned many awards of merit for his work. His wife, Anne, died of cancer in 1986. He has since retired to the Denver area.

PHILLIP L. "PHIL" CRAWFORD: Phil left the squadron in August 1944. No other information is available.

DONALD L. DECELLES: Donald was killed, along with his instructor pilot, in an "under the hood" instrument flight at Mojave in 1944.

ALEX DUTKIN: Deceased.

ROBERT EMMETT "BOB" EGGLESTON: Bob was killed on March 19, 1945, aboard the USS *Franklin*. The memory of Sgt Bob Eggleston was made vivid before me during a reunion fifty years later, in 1995, in Charleston, South Carolina, aboard the USS *Yorktown*. The reunion was also attended by Bob's widow, Lois; his daughter, Corliss; and his sister, Monica. I was able to exchange confidentialities concerning the tragedy so many years ago and learned much of the tender relationships and love those three had for Bob. Their pilgrimage to the reunion was a sentimental journey and a culmination of the grief they had suffered all those years. The feelings were summed up thusly: "I believe that, in some way, healing of very old wounds occurred there for both the living and the dead."

JOHN E. FARLEY: John did not go aboard the *Franklin*, but joined a squadron aboard an escort carrier out in the Pacific. After the war he married Jean, settled in San Diego, and raised several children. John spent most of his working years with Consolidated Aircraft. At the time of his retirement, he was in sales of the L-1011. John died September 3, 1988.

RALEIGH E. "BLIMPO" FLETCHER: After the *Franklin* disaster, Blimpo went back to Mojave with VMF-225, then to Hawaii and aboard the CVEs *Makassar Strait*, *Corregidor*, and *Prince William* for both day and night operations. Once again back in the States in 1946, he married Garnett Wells from Ellenburg, Washington. He was discharged on June 7, 1946, and lived in Seattle, where he worked for five years as an Oldsmobile mechanic. He was recalled for active duty during the Korean War to fly F7F night fighters in VMF (N)-542. In Korea he flew with VMF-312 aboard *Bataan* and *Sicily*. Back in the States, he flew the F3D night fighter and had a series of duties at the School of Justice, the All Weather Flight School at Corpus Christi, and then helicopter school at Pensacola.

A second tour in Korea and Japan ended in January 1956. In May he was released from active duty and joined Humble Oil Company as a helicopter pilot, flying crews to oil rigs off Louisiana. It was then a job with smoke jumpers in Idaho, followed by Humble again, then with Hughes Tool Company. Hughes made him manager of flight operations at Culver City, and he tested hundreds of Army and commercial helicopters each month. He retired from Hughes in 1979 and returned to his ranch in Idaho.

Blimpo built up a phenomenal flying record of 4,100 hours in experimental test flying and 3,700 in production flight testing. He made the first flight in the Army's Cayuse helicopter in 1963 and the AH-64 Apache in September 1975. Raleigh and Garnett have a son, two daughters, and four grandchildren.

D. W. "DOUGLAS" FREDRICK: Douglas was born and raised in Gillette, Wyoming. His father was a World War I veteran and had gone to Wyoming to homestead. Douglas was never ordered aboard the USS *Franklin*, but remained in the rear echelon at Mojave. After the war he was discharged with the rank of corporal on March 27, 1946, at Camp Pendleton, California. He now lives in Superior, Nebraska.

HORACE H. FRITZ III: Horace was another fine pilot who did not accompany the forward echelon aboard the *Franklin*. Well after the war, in civilian life, he was killed when run down by a vehicle in Las Vegas, Nevada.

THEODORE K. "TED" GORE: After recuperating from wounds received aboard the *Franklin*, Ted rejoined the squadron at El Centro, California. He helped process the paperwork to decommission VMF-452. He was then sent to the Great Lakes Naval Training Center for discharge on November 21, 1945.

After his discharge Ted attended Evansville College and in 1952 earned a degree from Blackstone School of Law in Chicago. He retired in 1985 after involvement with commercial real-estate developments and the oil business. Ted and his wife have a son and two grandchildren. Ted retired from the Marine Corps as staff sergeant with military classification of first sergeant.

BRUCE A. "THE OX" GUETZLOE: The Ox finished his career as a Marine aviator in 1953, and the subsequent pursuits of livelihood became phenomenal. The lure of the sea prompted him to obtain an education as a mariner.

For ten years he captained vessels from Coastwise Strategic Air Command at Tampa, Florida, to Standard Dredging Company tugboats, and finally to captaincy of the yacht of Anheuser Busch, Inc.

In 1965 The Ox received his B.A. degree from the University of South Florida, and in 1969 an M.Ed. degree from the University of Florida. His excellence in education and teaching seems to have covered the whole scientific spectrum: meteorology, chemistry, geology, astronomy, and earth and space science. Over the years this excellence has been rewarded with many honors.

In 1962 Bruce married Eleanor Garden, who also has an outstanding educational record. They have two boys and one girl, who are now working in the consulting, printing, and computer fields. They all live in the Clearwater, Florida, area.

NORWOOD R. "NORRY" HANSON: We have it on pretty good authority that Norwood's was the last plane off the *Franklin* prior to the ship's holocaust on March 19, 1945. After the war, he chose separation from the Marine Corps in order to pursue higher education, and then became a widely recognized scholar. He was considered a genius in his field of abstract mathematics and mathematical thinking. In England he served with preeminence on the Oxford University faculty. He was brought to Indiana University as a brilliant young professor in the new and demanding field of "history and philosophy of science." Later, at Yale, he remained one of the most important figures in that field and was appointed a fellow—a real achievement in the arts and sciences. He and his wife were allowed to "live on campus." At Yale, a friendship developed with another *Franklin* shipmate, who was going to Yale Law School at the time—Macgregor Kilpatrick, who was skipper of VF-5, the Navy fighter squadron aboard the *Franklin.*

Norwood Hanson was killed in 1976 in a Grumman F8F Bearcat fighter plane that he had acquired long after World War II. He was flying into Ithaca, New York, to give a lecture at Cornell when the accident happened. He was making an instrument approach at night during a snowstorm, crashed, and was killed. The memorial service at Yale was a session of chamber music by a string quartet in the commons (dining room) of the college, with students, faculty, and friends wandering in, sitting for a few minutes, and then going on their way. Hanson's life was cut short by that plane crash, but he'll be long remembered by all his squadronmates.

ROBERT L. "BOB" HARRINGTON: Instead of boarding the *Franklin,* Bob underwent training in Tiny Tim firing practice at El Centro. Then it was carrier qualification off Santa Barbara. At the time the war ended, he was sent to Hawaii and then aboard various escort carriers for transport to Guam and Saipan. By November he was back in the States and, a month later, married Cleo at Long Beach, California. He was eventually discharged and returned home to Kansas. Bob and Cleo spent most of their lives in Kansas. Bob owned an office-supply business for twenty years, with intermittent trips to the Orient, Greece, Spain, and the West Indies. They have one son and four grandchildren. Bob retired in 1984. He died June 4, 1993.

CHARLES E. "CHUCK" HILL: What little information that is available is provided by Baxter "Bo" Little, who was with Chuck aboard the escort carrier *Mindoro* when he was killed. Bo relates that just prior to a flight operation, he went to Chuck's stateroom to awaken him. Chuck's response was, "I want to rest and enjoy this day as it is Marsha's and my wedding anniversary." Chuck did meet the flight schedule, however, and was killed when the wings of his Corsair folded on takeoff.

LANMAN T. "LANNY" HOLMES: Lanny never went aboard the *Franklin,* but in late 1944, along with thirty other pilots, he left San Diego for the Solomon Islands. Shortly, he qualified off carriers while based at Ewa in the Hawaiian Islands. He later was among a cadre of about three thousand pilots at Saipan, awaiting assignment. This translated into flying off the CVE *Admiralty Islands,* which ferried and supplied new aircraft to Task Force 58. On D plus one, he began ferrying Corsairs into Okinawa. On that first night, the Japanese landed seven kamikaze troop planes on the airfield. After the war ended in Europe, the cadre operated out of Zamboanga, Philippines. Lanny finally came home via jeep carrier and was released from active duty.

In early 1946 Lanny resumed his old job with an insurance company in New York City. Things didn't work out as expected, and he pursued other sales adventures with negative results. This developed into a drinking problem. Some kindly people guided him in recovery, and he once again became employable in a form that was spiritually and emotionally fulfilling.

Lanny's most enjoyable avocation was playing amateur hockey before and after the war in the old Madison Square Garden. During the war Lanny married Anne, who had four children. They then had three sons of their own. Lanny died on January 31, 1993.

WALTER B. "WALT" HURST: After returning to the States after the *Franklin* disaster, Walt became involved with a group of pilots ferrying aircraft out of MCAS Mojave. The war had ended and Walt found himself one of the last two pilots on the base. In deference to his family, Walt decided to be discharged from the Marine Corps and take up residence at his home in North Dakota. Health problems set in, which bothered him for most of his life. In between bouts of multiple sclerosis, he worked for Standard Oil, and then later in the construction business.

Walt and Ruth have nine children, fourteen grandchildren, and some great-grandchildren. Walt is a wood carver and writer of local history in North Dakota.

JOHN E. LAWRENCE: Deceased.

BAXTER R. "BO" LITTLE: After the *Franklin,* Bo joined VMF-112 at Mojave. He also served aboard the escort carriers *Mindoro* and *Siboney* for a time. Then it was the Navy Supply School at Quantico, until a tour of Tsingtao, China, came up. There he met our old squadronmate Paul Piana, who insisted that Bo change his mind about a discharge from the Marine Corps. Bo received his discharge in November 1948.

Bo was unsuccessful at applying for the Berlin airlift, and even tried to become active during the Korean conflict, but the doctors grounded him for his chronic leg disability. He worked for twenty-eight years for the U.S. Postal Service before retiring at age fifty-five. Bo is married to Maria.

PAUL MAGINNIS: Deceased.

EMMONS S. "MAL" MALONEY: Mal was born in Green Bay, Wisconsin, on December 8, 1922. He went to parochial school, public high school, and St. Norbert's College in Green Bay. After cadet training at Pensacola, he was commissioned second lieutenant USMC, on August 17, 1943. After the *Franklin* disaster, he joined VMF-225 at Mojave. Mal integrated into the Regulars after the war ended. He attended the Corps professional schools appropriate for the different command and staff assignments to come. In addition, he became expert in certain aircraft, weapons delivery, military justice and supply, and electronics systems.

Mal stayed in the Corps for thirty years, retiring August 1, 1972. His tours took him through three wars with billets of notable distinction. His awards include two Distinguished Flying Crosses, seven Air Medals, a Bronze Star, two Meritorious Service Medals, and many other theater and unit citations.

Mal and Eloise were married in 1945, and they have six children and a number of grandchildren. After the Corps, Mal worked for the Tucson Power and Light Company for many years. They now live in Fallbrook, California.

WALLACE "WALLY" MATTSFIELD: Deceased. Wally was killed aboard the USS *Franklin* on March 19, 1945.

WILLIAM D. McDOWELL: Deceased.

FRANK T. MORRISON: Once back in the States after the *Franklin* disaster, it was first things first for Frank. In May 1945 he married Jean Sterling. Shortly after the war ended, Frank was discharged from the Marine Corps and returned to college. He received a combination engineering (industrial and commercial) and business degree. He found his niche in commercial auditing and in 1959 started an auditing company that grew into a statewide firm in California. It's been a great marriage for Frank and Jean. They had four sons and daughters, which they parlayed into eleven grandchildren. In 1967 they moved to the Los Altos hills, just ahead of the Silicon Valley boom. The whole family enjoys another home at Lake Almanor in the mountains.

Vacation trips in the RV or their luxurious motor home, as well as travels all over the world, have made them very much aware of just how good the old USA is.

EARNEST D. "DALE" OAKES: Dale was discharged right after World War II and has lived in Cheyenne, Wyoming, ever since. No further information is available.

CARL OMASTA: It was only by a fluke that Carl became part of the forward echelon aboard the *Franklin*. The compromise of which ordnance officer to conscript went to VMF-214. However, that particular officer seemed to have all kinds of personal excuses for not wanting to go. Carl Omasta was thus the right man for the right job to take his place.

Carl retired from the Marine Corps at the Sandia Base in Albuquerque, New Mexico, in 1959. Past experience as a liaison officer between MCAS El Toro and Orange County in California helped him to find employment in law enforcement. He became assistant marshal and, sixteen years later in May 1976, he retired and has since lived in Santa Ana, California.

Carl Omasta suffered from a heart problem in May 1993. In fact, he "died" of a heart attack while driving his pickup truck in downtown Santa Ana. The paramedics team gave up trying to revive him at one point, until a young woman on the team insisted they try "just one more time." For two years, it was a lingering, slow recuperation. But eventually he came out of it. In essence, he won another battle.

JAMES F. "JIMBO" ORMOND: Following release from the Norfolk Naval Hospital on May 1, 1946, Jimbo was assigned as quartermaster for the Marine detachment at the Norfolk Navy Yard. By September he had enrolled at the University of Tulsa in the Petroleum Engineering School and, a month later, separated from active service. After receiving his degree in 1950, he went to work for Sunray Oil Company of Odessa, Texas. An incident during which he saved the life of a fellow worker who had touched a high-voltage line, by using the Schafer Prone Pressure Resuscitation method, earned him the President's Gold Medal from the National Safety Council.

Jimbo's livelihood centered around his expertise in the "oil boom" business from Snyder to Odessa. Over the years he was involved with the oil well service business, specializing in acidizing, a process of pumping hydrochloric acid and other chemicals into wells to dissolve calcium formations. The last eleven years he worked in a partnership. It was a successful operation, which they sold in June 1981, just before the bottom fell out of the oil business.

Jim and June reared two children: Anita was born in October 1948, and Neil in April 1952. In 1964 Jimbo's lifestyle was interrupted by a bad fall, which tore up his right knee. The result was two operations and nine months out of commission.

The Ormonds moved to Midland, Texas, in 1958 and have lived in the area since. Playing golf, refurbishing old trunks, and pursuing genealogy make for a great retirement.

THOMAS D. "TOM" PACE: Deceased. Tom was shot down by one of our own destroyers March 19, 1945, off Kyushu, Japan.

DONALD R. "DON" PHILLIPS: Deceased.

PAUL PIANA: Deceased. Paul was killed in action during the Korean War.

JOHN W. "BILL" ROGALSKI: Bill was executive officer of VMF-452 at its closing days in the summer of 1945. He, like Pete Schaefer, was transferred to Cherry Point, North Carolina. As a test pilot at Patuxent River Test Center, he was assigned to the F2G project, the super Corsair. He also flew the FH-1 Phantom, the Lockheed TV-2, and the FJ-2 Fury.

Bill was recalled during the Korean War and was attached to Photo Squadron VMJ-1, flying the McDonnell F2H-2P Banshee.

Bill married Joan in 1948 and they had two children. She died in 1985. Bill was employed by the Hager Hinge Company in Cleveland, Ohio, for thirty-two years, then retired in December 1992. Bill maintains a farm in northern Michigan and works the cherry trees.

DONALD H. "DON" RUSSELL: Don received the Silver Star for his heroic deeds aboard the *Franklin*. Because he was a civilian, he could not be given the coveted Navy Cross.

In the late 1960s, Don flew down to Beaufort, South Carolina, from Norfolk, Virginia, to see me. It was a great reunion. In conversation I lamented losing my factory model Corsair. A week later I received a brand-new one in the mail from Don. Don died in 1982 from a brain tumor.

PETER L. "PETE" SCHAEFER: After signing the decommissioning papers of VMF-452 at MCAS El Centro, Pete was transferred to MCAS Cherry Point, North Carolina, then to Patuxent River, Maryland, as a test pilot. He was assigned to test the "Fox Two George," the super Corsair. It was equipped with a Pratt & Whitney R4360 engine developing 3,650 horsepower. At the end of the ninety-day tour at Patuxent, Pete picked up his discharge papers and returned to his home at Wilmette, Illinois.

For two years he flew Corsairs with the Reserves, but his father's illness prevented further participation and the planned college education. He became entrenched in his father's haberdashery, dry-cleaning, and tailoring business.

Pete married Shirley in 1948 and they had six children. Shirley died in 1976. A year later he married Alice, who had four children. He sold the business to her son in 1983. In January 1986 Pete lost Alice to cancer. The following July, he married Ginger. The combined family now represents fourteen children and seventeen grandchildren.

Pete and Ginger now live in Pauma Valley, California—it's a fine retirement life.

WALTER M. SHIRLEY: No information is available.

CLAYTON W. "SMITTY" SMITH: Smitty went to the hospital of his choice to recuperate from the shattered ankles suffered aboard the *Franklin*. At Providence, Rhode Island, his former home, he married a neighbor's child, who had grown into a beautiful sixteen-year-old girl. Smitty, then in his forties, resumed limited duty at El Toro, California. In 1946 Smitty and his new wife visited me in my home at South Laguna. His new wife wouldn't allow him to partake of liquor unless he paid her 50 cents per drink. Out in the kitchen, I would slip him doubles and no one ever knew the difference. Four years later things had changed radically. Smitty was baby-sitting while his wife was out on the town. In the end, Smitty gave his wife the baby, the house, and the car and just left town.

After he had been living for thirteen years by himself in a little house on the beach in Puerto Rico, I made contact with Smitty and he came up to see me. His warm personality spilled over to the grandchildren and we had a great reunion. When Smitty went back to Puerto Rico, it was the last I ever saw of him. Years later I learned of his death but was never able to determine the date or the cause.

JOHN RUMBOLD "JACK" STACK: Jack began an illustrious career at Guadalcanal when he shot down two Japanese Zeros. He was in VMF-112, commanded at that time by Paul Fontana. That squadron had left the States earlier, when they departed San Diego on October 15, 1942, aboard the *Lurline.* The ship sailed directly to New Caledonia with four squadrons aboard; two were Grumman Wildcat fighter squadrons and two flew Douglas Dauntless dive-bombers. They were airlifted to Guadalcanal in early November via Espiritu Santo.

Just before Christmas many of the pilots were pulled out of Guadalcanal and sent to Sydney, Australia, until New Year's Day. That's where Jack met Joan. On his second trip to Sydney, Jack and Joan were engaged; on the third trip, over the Fourth of July 1943, they were married. Upon returning to the States, Jack was assigned as an instructor in the fighter training unit at El Toro, California, then later joined up with me in VMF-452 at Mojave.

After twenty years in the Marine Corps, Jack retired, and he and Joan returned to her native land. Much later, Jack died in Australia.

EUGENE S. "ROCKY" STAPLES: After the war Rocky returned to the University of Missouri for a year and then went to the University of the Americas in Mexico City, where he graduated with a degree in Spanish language and literature. He then became a correspondent for United Press International in Mexico and Central America.

In 1951 Rocky joined the Foreign Service and, as an information officer, spent six years in Uruguay and Chile. Back in Washington in 1957, he found himself serving as Vice President Nixon's press officer on the Latin American tour during which that worthy gentleman was the target of rocks and spit.

In 1959 Rocky was the deputy general manager of the first U.S. National Exhibition in Moscow, where the kitchen debate took place between Nixon and Khrushchev. After intensive Russian-language training, Rocky became cultural counselor of the U.S. Embassy between 1961 and 1964. Rocky joined the Ford Foundation in 1964 and was later asked to take over the foundation's Asia programs. In 1973 he went to Bangkok as the foundation's representative for Southeast Asia. In 1976 he moved to New Delhi as the foundation's representative for India, Nepal, Sri Lanka, and Bangladesh. He was back with the Foreign Service in 1981 in the capacity of senior Foreign Service officer, International Development. In 1985 he went to Pakistan as director of the U.S. Aid Mission. Rocky's first wife, Charlotte, was mother of his two children. She died while they were living in India. Rocky later married Suzanne Fisher, a foreign correspondent for UPI.

Rocky retired in 1988 but keeps busy teaching occasionally at Columbia University and writing a book about Asia.

The awards Rocky received included the Presidential Meritorious Service Award, the International Development's Distinguished Honor Award, and the Sitars Qadi-Azan award given by the president of Pakistan for distinguished service to the people of Pakistan.

WILLIAM R. SWENSON: Deceased.

FRANCIS I. TAYLOR: Deceased.

GERALD J. "GERRY" VETTER: After leaving VMF-452 and the Marine Corps at the end of World War II, Gerry entered the University of California at Berkeley and graduated with a B.S. degree in 1948. His first job was with a San Francisco insurance firm for a year, then a job in San Jose with a small insurance brokerage firm. That was a fateful decision, as Gerry met his future wife, Enid, there. Enid worked out but the job didn't. Gerry's folks needed help running the ranch in Reedley, California, so he took a job with an insurance firm in Fresno and helped out on the ranch. To make it even busier, Gerry and Enid had seven children.

In 1969 the company demanded a move to Oakland, but Gerry took up with a junior partnership in Bakersfield, California, instead. That was a mistake, so he quit in 1974. His luck changed dramatically when he joined the Marsh & McLennan organization. He opened a branch office in Bakersfield and developed a successful business. He retired in 1987.

Gerry and Enid now enjoy nine grandchildren. They spend much of their time both winter and summer happily in their mountain cabin, where the fly fishing and skiing are terrific.

JOSEPH R. "JOE" WARREN: After the *Franklin* disaster, Joe received the Purple Heart and, by December 1945, was separated from the service. Joe's return home to Greenville, South Carolina, coincided with that of his twin brother, who was also a Marine pilot. He went to Wofford College in July 1946.

In August 1947, Joe married Jennille Lee of Spartanburg, South Carolina, and then moved to Charleston to work with the Civil Aeronautics Administration in the Charleston tower. He flew SNJs on weekends with the Navy's Reserve unit.

A transfer back to Greenville in 1949 did not prevent Joe from fulfilling Reserve duty. Annual tours to Atlanta and Jacksonville allowed him to fly Corsairs and Hellcats. He joined a Marine Early Warning Unit at NAS Atlanta. By 1964 Joe was elected chief of Macon Tower/Robins RAPCON. At this time he took the option of retiring from the Reserves with sixteen good years instead of twenty.

Joe retired from the FAA in 1976 and settled in Greenville. When President Reagan fired the air-traffic controllers in 1981, Joe spent seven months at the FAA Academy in Oklahoma, teaching newly hired controllers.

Joe and Jennille had twins—a boy and a girl—and another son. Jennille died in 1990. Joe is now married to Sara.

CARL L. WEBBER: No information is available.

CHARLES P. "PAT" WEILAND: In 1946 Pat transitioned to the Regular Marine Corps. His tenure as squadron commander of several squadrons finally ended in the fall of 1948. Early in the Korea War, Pat was air officer for the 1st Cavalry Division and then the Army X Corps, where he wrote the air plan for the Seoul–Inchon Operation.

There was a three-year stint at the Pentagon and then a tour at Iwakuni, Japan, before his final billet at the brand-new Auxiliary Air Station at Beaufort, South Carolina, in 1957. Pat was executive officer of MAG-32, and then executive officer of the Beaufort Marine Corps Air Station before retiring in June 1962. He was awarded three Distinguished Flying Crosses and ten Air Medals during his career in the Marine Corps.

Pat acquired an old plantation home facing the Broad River just outside of Beaufort. He named it CAVU. It was a diamond in the rough. He married Moran in 1965, and she came out and put the facets on it. He works the ten acres surrounded by gargantuan live oak trees amid Deep South ambience. He retired in 1981 as manager of a wholesale distributor business, which he brought to Beaufort from Charleston.

Pat Weiland is a sculptor and craftsman. His larger-than-life-size concrete sculpture *Buck Schott, Retired Marine*, took him twelve years to complete. He had a 28-foot sailboat built in Japan, which was launched June 27, 1957. This is probably the reason why he is a charter member of the Beaufort Power Squadron and a life member of the U. S. Power Squadrons. Life has been very good to Pat Weiland.

CHARLES W. WEITZEL, JR.: No information is available

WALLACE S. "WALLY" WETHE: Deceased.

JOSEPH C. "JOE" WILSON III: Deceased (?). Notice the question mark. This information cannot be verified; it is based on word sent to me by Jimbo Ormond in September 1993. Kenny Bennett had mentioned that Joe had attended the University of California, so Jimbo wrote the Alumni Association with a self-addressed card, asking for the address. He received a reply that said, "Mr. Joseph Wilson was reported deceased 1/8/87 by his wife, sorry." The Social Security index shows a Joseph Wilson who died in January 1987, and the death residence was Baltimore, Maryland.

It has not been verified that this is the Joe we knew.

To Set the
Record Straight

Colonel Stan Carpenter, USMC (Ret), was a secretary of the Marine Corps Aviation Association. He had read my preliminary manuscript and in his review described my involvement in VMF-452 as a "womb to the tomb" story. The demise of the squadron occurred in July 1945 (we thought), when orders were received from higher Marine Corps echelons to work up the heap of paperwork and documents in order to effect the decommissioning of the squadron. I had already been transferred to El Toro, California. First Lieutenant Pete Schaefer, now commanding officer, and SSgt Ted Gore, in administration, were then the last two remaining members of the squadron. In order to meet the deadline date, these two worked until 2200 or 2300 every night. Sandwiches were brought in from the mess hall for the evening meal. Ted did most of the work, and Pete signed the decommissioning papers. The documents were turned in to Marine Air Group 42, El Centro, California, for forwarding to higher echelons. With this last act of administrative paperwork accomplished, the squadron door was closed and locked and Pete and Ted went their separate ways. Pete was to carry out his transfer orders to Cherry Point, North Carolina, and Ted was to transfer to Great Lakes Naval Training Center, Illinois, for discharge. The demise of VMF-452 had been effected. For fifty years this fact was firm in the minds of all the original squadron members.

Suddenly, irrefutable evidence was received from PFC Harold Wallenburg, who had joined VMF-452 as an administrative man and performed duties as a payroll clerk. He related how he served in the squadron until it was finally disbanded (or decommissioned) in 1949. I received a rolled-up photo in a mailing tube sent by him. I spread out the photo on my desk in front of me. I couldn't believe what I saw. It showed a group of officers and enlisted men in dress blues in front of a Corsair. The placard in front of the group read:

VMF-452
Lt. Col. R. M. Huizenga
Commanding
Major R. H. George
Executive Officer
26 March 1949

When I received the belated news of the squadron being alive and well long after July 1945, I had to make a hasty retreat. It was fifty years now after the so-called fact (July 1995). The first thing I did was to phone Pete Schaefer in California and Ted Gore in Indiana to make a feeble attempt at refuting this photographic evidence. We were not only trapped as a result of this new knowledge, but much surprised at this revelation. Perhaps we owed those people who composed the squadron then an apology for the recognition they did not receive from us, the previous tenants. Or perhaps just a simple salutation of "Semper Fi" would be appropriate. I'm sure in their hearts they would know the mutual loyalty and respect we all had for that great squadron.